## By Kathryn Casey

*Non-Fiction*
DELIVER US
DEADLY LITTLE SECRETS
SHATTERED
EVIL BESIDE HER
A DESCENT INTO HELL
DIE, MY LOVE
SHE WANTED IT ALL
A WARRANT TO KILL

*Fiction*
SINGULARITY
BLOOD LINES
THE KILLING STORM

# KATHRYN CASEY

## DELIVER US

**THREE DECADES OF MURDER AND REDEMPTION
IN THE INFAMOUS I–45/TEXAS KILLING FIELDS**

## HARPER

*An Imprint of* HarperCollins*Publishers*

DELIVER US is a journalistic account of the murders of young women around the I–45 corridor that runs south from Houston into Galveston between 1970 and 2000. The events recounted in this book are true. The personalities, events, actions, and conversations in this book have been constructed using court documents, including trial transcripts, extensive interviews, letters, personal papers, research, and press accounts. Quoted testimony has been taken from court transcripts and other sworn statements.

## HARPER

*An Imprint of* HarperCollins*Publishers*
195 Broadway
New York, New York 10007

Copyright © 2015 by Kathryn Casey
Map by forensic artist Suzanne Lowe Birdwell (www.dovelyart.com)
ISBN 978-1-62953-361-2

Printed in the United States of America

*This book is dedicated
to all the lost boys and girls.*

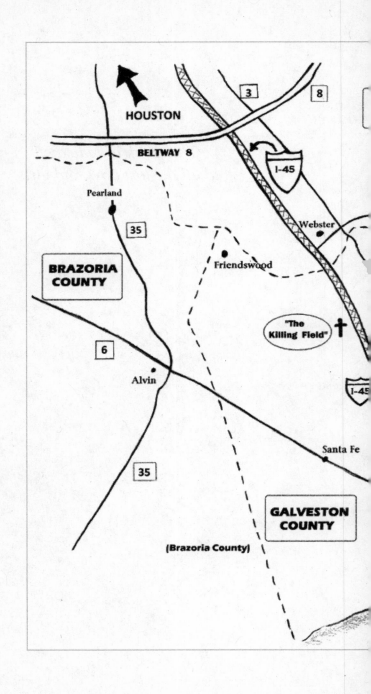

# Contents

# DELIVER US

# Prologue

It's only natural to want to believe we are in control, that when we wake each morning, *we* decide what we do, that our lives don't rest in the hands of others or, even worse, of that unseen yet eternal influence commonly referred to as destiny. We humans crave the ability to plan. We set goals, bargaining off today in exchange for where we want to be tomorrow, even what we hope to be doing a decade in the future. Much of the time, that's a wise decision, one that brings prosperity and happiness. Yet doing so is a risk, for fate is always a factor, and fate can be capricious.

In 2006, a few months after my mother died, I was preoccupied and missed my freeway exit. Instead, I took another. A mile down the road at a traffic light, a young man texting behind the wheel plowed into the rear end of my small SUV. The result: a back problem that's plagued me ever since that day. How many times when I push myself out of bed in the morning have I lamented missing that exit, wondered if the pain I endure could have been avoided by simply paying more attention and getting off the interstate sooner. A fleeting moment, I was distracted, and chance claimed control.

Yet, I've been lucky. I have few complaints.

Thirty years writing true crime, first for magazines, then books, and I understand what can happen when chaos truly takes over. Others may debate if evil exists in this world; I've looked it in the eye. In courtrooms, in prison interviews, killers describe how lives were taken. Sometimes there's sadness, the belated realization that wrong has been done, yet more often, years later, there's no empathy for the victim. Instead, even when a murder is admitted, I've witnessed an indignant righteousness, an entitled anger, a scowl as a killer describes a victim, one that implies the dead bear the blame. The victim was flawed, she caused the events that led to her death, or she was simply too accessible, not careful enough, and that led to her murder.

Since 1985, I've often written about sensational Texas murders. But my journey didn't begin on the Gulf Coast. In the fifties and sixties, I lived in Milwaukee, Wisconsin. My father was a factory foreman, my mother a school secretary who loved to read. I have three brothers, and we lived in a small house on an abbreviated street where maples and elms shaded the homes in summers, and in winters we shoveled snow into banks that we recycled into stiff, twig-limbed snowmen with clichéd carrot noses and button eyes.

My parents cautioned me when I was very young that there were dangers hidden in the shadows. I heard tales about the ubiquitous boogeymen, the frightening Rumpelstiltskin-like figures that waited for imprudent children, especially little girls who strayed from the safety of their homes. The outcome was always described in obscure manners, perhaps nothing more than the raising of eyebrows or tight-lipped frowns that implied unlucky children suffered tragic ends. Yet the message was clear: There were forces to be wary of, people to fear.

Sometime in the sixties, a segment aired on the local news reporting that a girl had disappeared from a nearby park. Then a teenager, I'd walked a dirt path that led from my home to the community swimming pool for years, a trail that bordered the verdant banks of the meandering Menomonee River. I'd grown up playing on the riverbank, among the trees. It was where I smoked my first and last cigarette while reclining on a sturdy yet graceful branch of a massive oak.

When my parents handed me a newspaper account of the kidnapping to read, I was ordered to stay out of the park. From that day forward, I was to walk not on the trail but across the street, on a sidewalk that ran in front of the homes facing the parkway. I argued against it, but they were steadfast. A young girl had mysteriously vanished, a warning that wasn't to be ignored. All girls were in danger. But it was the sixties, a time when the hubris of youth made news across the country, a stormy era when danger seemed in the very air as neighborhood boys headed off to war. Vietnam dominated the evening news. Flags burned and life felt electric. With so much to consider, the disappearance of one girl carried little impact. I was coming of age, and the world was opening up for me. I felt strong and invulnerable.

So I ignored my parents' entreaties and continued walking the footpath until the day the lost girl was found. I honestly can't recall where her body was or how long she'd been missing. Yet I'll never forget the fear in my mother's eyes as she repeated her warning to be vigilant because there were wicked people in the world.

I can't say that I never entered the park again or walked leisurely yet defiantly along the peaceful pathway, where I tore off the tips of evergreen branches. I rubbed the weblike needles between my fingers, releasing a near-intoxicating fragrance of pine. But there were times, when a car slowed or I sensed movement in the dense shadows of the trees, that I darted across the street to the perceived safety of the sidewalk, within shouting distance of front doors. Was I safer there? I don't know.

In truth, Milwaukee even then was a fairly big city, home to many young girls, the vast majority of whom grew up playing safely in their front yards, skipping to their friends' homes, walking to and from school. The movement in the bushes? Undoubtedly a soft breeze. For the most part, we were safe. Yet a girl had been murdered.

It was disquieting.

Then something happened in July 1966, an event that

made an even bigger impression. Again the news came in headlines, this time describing a scene of horrific carnage. In a Chicago flat a little more than an hour from my home, Richard Speck had raped, tortured, and murdered eight student nurses. How was such evil possible?

It would be another decade, the late seventies, before I first heard the term *serial killer*. It was in conjunction with the unfathomable darkness that was Ted Bundy. Like many across the globe, I read and watched legions of news accounts on the handsome, charismatic young man with the piercing eyes, mesmerized by the former law student who'd left a trail of blood extending from Washington State to a sorority house in Florida.

Just before his execution, Bundy admitted committing thirty murders, but authorities speculated that he'd killed many more. His name became synonymous with wanton slaughter, and he forever changed the image of the dangerous stranger. No longer could we tell ourselves that we would recognize the face of evil. Now it could be lurking behind the eager smile of a neighborhood boy or the pleading face of a handsome stranger asking for help in a parking lot. For the first time, America wondered what lingered in the hearts of the solitary figures jogging our streets, the drivers of the big rigs that passed us on the interstates, the good Samaritans who stopped to help us change flat tires along the sides of deserted roads. Good deeds were not to be taken at face value. Bundy tricked his victims, and they paid with their lives.

In 1981, my husband and I settled in Houston. I can't remember the first time I encountered an article in the *Houston Chronicle* that detailed a strange phenomenon along Interstate 45, beginning south of the city and extending onto Galveston Island. It was most likely around the time fourteen-year-old Sondra Ramber ambled out her front door in Santa Fe, a small, mostly rural community not far from the interstate corridor. In October 1983, Sondra was last seen walking to a store. When her father returned home that evening, the house was unlocked and empty. He reported her missing the following morning. Who took her? Why? Did she simply walk away? If so, she left with biscuits baking in the oven and without her coat and purse.

Frightening? Yes. It would have been more so had I known that over the previous decade nearly a dozen other girls had disappeared in and around that same slice of the metropolitan area. Some bodies were eventually found. Others were never recovered.

The first reference I read to the plot of land dubbed *The Texas Killing Field* was around September 1991. A body had been discovered in an oil field off Calder Drive, not far from I-45. Janet Doe was the fourth victim found in that same location over a period of seven years. It was then that the *Houston Chronicle* ran a full-page article documenting the history of unsolved murders of young women along the southern I-45 corridor, two decades of murder: sixteen young women, sixteen grieving families.

It seemed that there was no end to the horror.

Five years later, in March 1996, thirteen-year-old Krystal Jean Baker, by family legend a great-niece of screen-icon Marilyn Monroe, walked a few blocks from her grandmother's house and called her mother from a tire-store phone. Moments later, fuming over not getting her way, Krystal huffed off toward a friend's house. Her bloodied, bruised, strangled body was discovered in a neighboring county under a freeway overpass.

The next murder sent waves of anger throughout all of Houston, when in April 1997, Laura Kate Smither, a bubbly twelve-year-old ballerina with curly brown hair and playful eyes, went for a jog on the rural roads surrounding her home. Laura was only supposed to be gone for twenty minutes, but seventeen days later her corpse was recovered from a retention pond. Thousands of volunteers had scoured the fields surrounding her home, and law enforcement, including the FBI, searched for clues, all to no avail.

That hot Texas summer, the tally grew when, four months later, Jessica Cain, a young actress and soon-to-be college freshman, disappeared within a few miles of her home. Her pickup was found on I-45's shoulder, heading south. Did someone force her off the road? Jessica left her purse inside the truck, as if only planning to step away for a moment, but she never returned.

Houston-area newspapers published the first illustrations of the terror, charts depicting the abductions and murders, in the late nineties under headlines that read variously MYS-TERIES ALONG I-45, and UNSOLVED. With her disappearance, Jessica Cain joined so many others whose faces stared out from grainy newspaper photos, a black-and-white gallery of smiling girls and young women, school pictures, snapshots, family photos, the last images of the dead. Below each ran a name, dates, and brief descriptions of their disappearances. At times, the heartbreaking list changed when crimes were solved. Serial killer Anthony Allen Shore, for instance, was arrested in 2004 and the photos of three of his alleged victims, Dana Sanchez, sixteen, Maria Carmen del Estrada, twenty-one, and Diana Rebollar, nine, were deleted from the list.

Sadly, more often than the deletions came additions, new photos appearing as more girls and young women died along I-45 at the hands of unknown killers. Through it all, grief spread from family to family. Unimaginable pain. Unforgettable horror. No closure. Rarely justice.

I don't know when I first realized that I would write about these tragedies just down the highway from my Houston home. Perhaps I always knew. As I went from reporting on sensational murders in magazines to books, I cut out and kept articles on the I-45 murders. The young girls in the newspaper pictures troubled me, seemed to ask for help, wanting their stories to be told. Whenever I saw their faces, I considered how quickly and unexpectedly life turns. I knew it could have been my photo or that of someone I loved, and I wondered how so many cases remained unresolved. I had to do something because the victims were real, they mattered, and they deserved not to be forgotten.

One version of the chart documenting the unsolved I-45 cases.
*(Courtesy of the* Galveston County Daily News*)*

As I began writing this book, my goal was simple: to tell not all but some of the victims' stories along with those of the people who toiled to bring their killers to justice. I hoped to share the trials of the families, those who never overcame their grief and others who used it to build a better world. For even in the deepest despair, there were those who found inspiration and redemption.

At the same time, I wanted to give a voice to those suspected of the crimes, for they, too, had important stories to tell.

In many ways, recounting these murders transported me on a journey through my own life, back to the seventies, when I was young, through the eighties and nineties. The world changed drastically throughout those years. Wars began and ended. Science made great strides. Presidents came and went. Our cities and our towns were redesigned, along with our styles and our habits.

What remained the same was that despite our best intentions, despite all we wish for our world, for our families, in 2014 we have little better grasp of the true nature of evil than we had when the first victim discussed in this book died in 1971. We were no more adept at recognizing its face. And we still didn't know how to stop it.

This book is divided into three sections organized by decades: the seventies, eighties, and nineties. For the most part, the first two, the seventies and eighties, are organized chronologically. In contrast, the nineties unfold in two distinct parts. The first set of chapters explores the 1996 murder of Krystal Jean Baker, the investigation into her death, and the trial of her killer. The final chapters examine one of the Gulf Coast's most infamous cases, the 1997 abduction and killing of little Laura Kate Smither.

What binds these cases? They all center on a fifty-mile section of Interstate 45, running south of Houston, the nation's fourth largest city, onto Galveston Island.

The dead as well share a common bond—all were young women, the majority teenagers, and victims of chance. If they'd taken another road, refused to accept an offer of a ride, or called in sick to work on the days they died, they would likely still be alive. Most if not all would have gone on with their lives, unaware that one choice could have brought them face-to-face with stark terror. By now, they could be mothers with children, some even with grandchildren. Instead, their faces and their stories haunt the Texas Gulf Coast.

*Deliver Us* is an account of the slaughter, the brutal murders of young women around the corridor that runs south of Houston into Galveston, an area loosely dubbed by the press as the I-45/Texas Killing Fields. Three decades of loss and redemption along a busy highway, in our midst, where more than a hundred thousand commuters drive each workday.

"Deliver us from evil," believers plead in an ancient prayer. Deliver us from the evil among us, the hunters, the killers concealed in the shadows. For they exist.

# THE 1970s

- Colette Wilson: 13, taken from beside the road on June 17, 1971, while waiting for her mother after a school band competition.
- Brenda Jones: 14, disappeared after a hospital visit with her aunt, on July 11, 1971.
- Sharon Shaw: 14, vanished with her best friend, Renee Johnson, on August 4, 1971.
- Rhonda "Renee" Johnson: 14. Shaw and Johnson were last seen by a friend on Galveston's Seawall Boulevard.
- Gloria Ann Gonzales: 19, a grocery-store bookkeeper, left on a vacation in October 1971. She was never seen again.
- Maria Johnson: 15, got into a white van on November 15, 1971, with Debbie Ackerman
- Debbie Ackerman: 15, hitchhiked, with her best friend, Maria Johnson.
- Kimberly Rae Pitchford: 16, walked out of a driver's education class on January 3, 1973, and never called her parents for a ride home.
- Brooks Bracewell: 12, allegedly skipped school on September 6, 1974, with her friend Georgia Geer.
- Georgia Geer: 14. Last reported sighting was at a convenience store with her friend Brooks Bracewell.
- Suzanne Bowers: 12, left her grandparents' Galveston house on May 21, 1977, intending to walk home and get a swimsuit. She never arrived.

# Chapter 1

## A Serial Killer on the Island

**Galveston, Texas
1971**

**M**an is drawn to water. It is part of us. It comprises more than half of our bodies, and we require a supply each day to live. Scientists say the sea is where our species began. Perhaps that's true, for certainly it calls to us. Rarely do we feel as invigorated, as cleansed as when we stand on a beach, the sun warming our skin, watching light dance on waves, as we breathe salted breezes

Maria Johnson, like so many of the girls, worshipped the sun and the beach.

and absorb the rhythm of the surf. The tides come and go, the water climbs and recedes, and we stare entranced, engaged in a primitive ritual. Even if we never venture into the white-foam waves, for most of us simply being near a vast expanse of water has the power to clear our minds and relax our bodies. At the end of the day, as the sun sets, we leave refreshed.

In hindsight, water would play a part in many of the I-45 cases, if not in the girls' lives, in the aftermaths of their murders. Nearly all the bodies were found in or near water. Yet it was obviously not for its healing qualities. Why? "Water washes away evidence. It makes it harder to solve the crimes," an aging investigator told me. "They know that."

"They?" I asked.

"The killers." After a long pause, he concluded, "They know."

Despite its name, Interstate 45 is an intrastate highway, linking the Lone Star State's two largest, and two of the nation's biggest cities. From I-45's northern point, Dallas, it slices through the countryside, traveling two hundred miles south to Houston, an immense, sprawling metropolis fueled by the oil industry and the businesses that feed off it. But 45 doesn't end in the mirrored and granite skyscrapers at H-town's bustling center.

Instead, the interstate continues its arrow path. South of Houston, I-45 becomes the Gulf Freeway. It skirts the University of Houston's split-obelisk-guarded campus, then continues on, surrounded by commercial and retail businesses, clusters of stores, car dealerships, businesses, and shopping malls, typical metropolitan spread. Half an hour from the city, the economic forces switch from what's found within the earth to the skies above it, as the Clear Lake exit leads to the Johnson Space Center, NASA's mission control, where engineers and scientists monitored the men who walked upon the moon and shuttle traffic to the space station.

Past Clear Lake, the landscape is wooded but not particularly interesting, flat coastal plain. Flash back to the seventies, when the killing began, and much of this southern I-45 corridor remained undeveloped land dotted by small towns. During the three decades the murders in this book took place, the population mushroomed, as Houston grew from the sixth to the fourth largest city in the nation. In its shadow, the population of Galveston County, including the majority of the I-45 towns, expanded from less than 170,000 to more than 217,000.

Jobs brought many of those who settled here. Residents commuted to work by joining the flow of traffic on I-45 north into downtown Houston, west to the I-10 energy corridor, or east to the pipe jungles of chemical plants and refineries that proliferate along Galveston Bay's winding coastline, immense facilities operated by goliaths Exxon, British Petroleum, Dow Chemical and others. From towering steel stacks, torchlike flares burn off excess hydrocarbons. At night, the flames and refinery lights shimmer against the darkness.

Their names give the towns and small cities separate identities: Alvin, Santa Fe, Hitchcock, Friendswood, La Marque, Kemah, Bacliff, Dickinson, La Porte, San Leon, League City, Texas City, Seabrook, and Webster. Yet as the region developed, many absorbed any vacant land between them, until it became common to leave one burg and enter another without notice.

The official boundaries, however, have importance, including a substantial effect on law enforcement. The towns and cities where the killings took place fall into three counties: to the north, toward Houston, Harris County; to the south Galveston County; and to the west Brazoria County. Each employed a separate sheriff's department, and each municipality its own police department. The result: The investigations, as the murders unfolded, fell under the jurisdiction of eleven different law-enforcement agencies.

What is consistent? Water.

Fingerlike bayous weave through cities and towns, neighborhoods, alongside roads and past oil-collection tanks housed on vast empty acres. These usually shallow waterways flood during downpours, eventually washing discarded rubble into Galveston Bay. At times the debris isn't only fast-food containers or empty beer cans, however, but something far more sinister: human bodies, used and discarded.

In Galveston, I-45 comes to an abrupt end.

A barrier island, 28.9 miles long and 3.2 miles at its widest point, Galveston lies 50 miles southeast of Houston. Attached to the mainland by a mile-and-a-half causeway, the city has an aura all its own, a presence, the feel of a notorious past, a seedy sophistication—think New Orleans or Venice—places haunted by history.

On September 8, 1900, Galveston ranked among Texas' five largest metropolises, a wealthy, thriving commercial center with a busy harbor and a bright future. Then came the hurricane. Standing on the beach staring out into the Gulf of Mexico's pewter surf, it's easy to visualize what it must have been like on that awful day. Decades before television and storm-tracking radar, when horse-drawn carriages provided the primary means of transportation, a blue sky with scattered clouds darkened by midmorning into what at first appeared to be merely a particularly tumultuous tropical storm. But the waves swelled, and the water rose. By the time the island's residents realized a massive hurricane approached, they had no opportunity to flee. The Great Storm, as it's still called, remains the deadliest natural disaster in U.S. history, killing at least six thousand and perhaps as many as twelve thousand. At St. Mary's Orphans' Asylum alone, ten nuns and ninety children perished.

In the decades that followed, Galvestonians built a seawall, a ten-mile, seventeen-foot-high buttress designed to hold back Gulf waters. Based on lessons learned, they trucked in earth and raised the land and more often built homes on stilts. Some of the grand Victorian mansions survived, yet the island was forever changed. Houston dug its own port and flourished, dominating southeast Texas, and Galveston became a beloved appendage, a playground. Prohibition brought bootleggers and The Balinese Room, a casino that attracted A-list celebrities: Frank Sinatra, Bob

Hope, the Marx Brothers, and Texas billionaire Howard Hughes.

This brush with celebrity ended quickly. The Texas Rangers moved in, staking the nightclub out to prevent gambling. The glitter moved to Las Vegas, then to Atlantic City, and from that point on, Galveston's light faded. As time passed, the island drew mainly tourists, college students celebrating spring break, summer-vacationing families, and wealthy Texans who wanted second homes with a beach view.

By 1970, except for the summer months, when tourists elbowed onto the beaches and the population could top 250,000, the island was a sleepy place with approximately 61,000 full-time residents. Along with tourism, the main employers were American National Insurance, founded by the Moodys, one of the island's wealthiest families, and UTMB, the University of Texas Medical Branch, with its teaching hospital and research center.

Off and on, more hurricanes battered Galveston, some dealing devastating blows. Always there was the threat of the next big storm. Perhaps that's part of the city's appeal, the expectation of impermanence, the knowledge that any summer could bring a direct hit from a category five, and much of the island—like the mythical Atlantis—might disappear under the sea.

The killing began in 1971, at a time when the United States experienced a transformation.

Danger and turbulence seemed to permeate the country. In the prior decade, assassination had become not history but reality as a president, his brother, and the nation's most prominent civil rights leader all fell. Despite President Richard Nixon's pledge to end the bloodshed, the Vietnam War still raged, and the draft forced neighborhood boys to risk their lives a world away. Meanwhile, at home, discord invaded living rooms, spawning what became known as the generation gap. "Don't trust anyone over thirty!" the young were advised. "Turn on! Tune in! Drop out!" Drugs invaded popular culture, and intimacy moved out of marital bedrooms, reemerging as a call to casual sex. America's disillusioned youth worshipped freedom, the call of the open road, and the pull of sunshine and water. Teenage girls grew up playing with Barbie dolls, and beauty became redefined as slender, spirited and independent, the tanned and lithe *California Girls* celebrated by the Beach Boys.

Athletic and tan, Maria Johnson didn't understand the dangers.

This milieu surrounded Maria Andrews Johnson, the pretty, chestnut-haired fifteen-year-old pictured here and in the bikini under this chapter's heading. As it would for so many, the world changed around Maria, appearing to offer a limitless future, one without the bonds that tethered women to family and home. Yet for Maria and the other young victims in this book, such freedom was an illusion, one that would end all too quickly in horrific deaths.

Maria Johnson was one of eleven girls, ages twelve to nineteen, murdered south of Houston along I-45 during the 1970s. When the I-45 Unsolved Mysteries charts first appeared decades later, their pictures formed the first two lines of black-and-whites. Many who investigated these vicious crimes believed that during those years a monster roamed Galveston Island and the surrounding area, a serial killer hunting for prey.

Some of the dead put themselves in peril by buying into the belief that they could be footloose and free, unconfined, without worry. Although they weren't to blame, their choices put them in jeopardy. Others were less adventurous, teenagers who did as they were told and never strayed from their parents' example. Yet they, too, died. For all, chance intersected their lives with danger; they could never have anticipated the terrors that awaited.

"Cruising the seawall really was our life," said a woman who grew up on the island and came of age in the early seventies. Her Galveston was one where teenagers in their parents' cars or their first hot rods revved their engines on Seawall Boulevard, surrounded by hotels, condominiums, restaurants and shops, bedrooms for rent with Gulf views. Tourists pedaled surreys topped by awnings on the sidewalk bordering the seawall, while vacationers and locals in swimsuits played volleyball on the sand or perched on gray boulders along the shoreline. Palm trees lined streets, and breezes filled with the invigorating scent of salt water. Summers, the sun beat down resolutely on its worshippers scattered across the beaches. Tropical-afternoon storms cleared the air, and at night the coastline disappeared into darkness that never muffled the cadence of the waves.

The first incident may have been on Galveston's East Beach.
*(Courtesy of Kathryn Casey)*

"The island felt safe. It was this quiet place when the tourists weren't around. And during the summers, it was a never-ending party," she said. "There were different beaches for different groups, the party kids and the banditos, the druggies, the families who brought their kids. But everyone got along, and no one worried . . . not until the killing started."

An unusual event occurred at 4:45 in the afternoon on April 27, 1971.

On that day, a sixteen-year-old girl sunbathed on East Beach, on the island's far eastern tip. It was a Tuesday during the school year, before the crush of summer, and the shoreline was deserted. Later, the teenager would tell police that a white man approached her and forced her into his car, then drove her to the south jetty, a secluded area near the red and green beacons that mark the narrow entrance from the Gulf into Galveston Bay. The girl, unnamed in news accounts, was beaten but somehow managed to escape. When a small article ran about the assault in the *Galveston County Daily News,* it's probable that few on the island paid much attention. After all, what was one such incident? Locals undoubtedly assumed it was someone who'd had too much to drink, a tourist from the mainland. What were the odds that it would happen again? How could anyone have predicted that it would later appear that the crime was an omen of so much more to come?

COLETTE WILSON

In the blink of an eye, Colette Wilson vanished.

On Thursday June 17, 1971, at 12:30 P.M., thirteen-year-old Colette Anise Wilson stood in Alvin, Texas, at the intersection of Highway Six and County Road 99, northwest of Galveston on the mainland. The eighth-grader wore a Mickey Mouse T-shirt and purple shorts.

Her hair long and dark, she carried a black clarinet case and a file of sheet music. Surrounded by cattle pastures bordered by trees, the intersection was a lonely place, the crossing of two sparsely traveled country roads. Yet there was no reason for the girl to be wary. The woods stretched out around her, but the location was familiar, only two and a half miles from her home.

In that day's headlines, President Richard Nixon asked Congress for $371 million to fight America's growing dependence on drugs, and sources unmasked military analyst Daniel Ellsberg as the informant of the leaked Pentagon Papers, a trove of top secret government documents that theorized the U.S. couldn't win the Vietnam War.

On that country road, such concerns must have seemed inconsequential to the teenager. It's far more likely that music drifted through Colette's mind, snatches of selections she'd played with her classmates. She'd just left a multischool band camp, and her instructor dropped her off, then quickly drove away with a car full of other students to deliver. "This was a different time," said Colette's mom, Claire Wilson. "People wouldn't do that today, but back in the seventies, it seemed safe."

At the Wilson house, Claire tended to her other nine children. It was summer, and the house hummed with young voices as she called out asking which of the children would like to drive with her the short distance to pick up Colette, the second oldest. Two of the boys responded, and one of the youngest children, a daughter named Alice. Minutes later, Claire pulled out of the driveway.

Meanwhile Colette presumably stood alone at the corner, expecting her mother to arrive at any moment. A sweet, happy girl, she was unusually eager to get home. There were big doings at the Wilson house. The entire family was preparing for a wedding. Their neighbor was getting married the following day. Close friends of Claire and her husband, Tom, a dentist, the bride and groom were honoring the Wilsons by holding the ceremony on their anniversary. At home,

Colette had a half-sewn dress that needed to be finished, one she wanted to wear to the wedding.

*Peace On Earth*
GOOD WILL TOWARD MEN

**The Wilsons**

When this Christmas photo was taken in 1969, the Wilsons had nine children (Colette is in the back row, second from the right).

With so many children, the Wilson household could be a bit hectic. That meant things didn't always happen on schedule. If her mother was late, Colette had standing instructions to walk to her best friend's house, hidden in the trees just a short distance down the road from the intersection. Did Colette follow those orders that day, or did she wait on the corner? Perhaps she stood in the hot Texas sun for a minute or more, shading her iridescent blue eyes as she looked off to the distance, to where the intense heat radiated off the pavement, melting into a shimmering mirage pool.

Six minutes. Just six quick minutes elapsed between the time Colette exited her instructor's car and Claire Wilson arrived at the designated corner, where she expected to see Colette patiently waiting. But when Claire drove up, Colette wasn't there. Someone else was, someone pulled off the road in an old car. Claire sat for a few moments, looking at the car. A man was behind the wheel. Wondering why he was parked along the road, Claire surmised that the car must have broken down. With little hesitation, she drove off toward Colette's friend's house to collect her daughter.

Colette, however, wasn't at the friend's house. The friend hadn't seen her. On the drive home, anxiety overcame Claire. Where was her daughter? This time when Claire passed the intersection, it was empty. No Colette. And the stranger in the car—the one she'd assumed had mechanical problems? He was gone.

At the house, Claire called Tom at his dental office. "Something's wrong," she said. "Colette's missing."

Authorities were called. Years later, Claire would try to explain how the disappearance of a thirteen-year-old initially caused little official concern. "There weren't any Amber Alerts. The police weren't worried. They said she was probably taking drugs or something, that she'd run away. We knew Colette. We knew that wasn't true. But they wouldn't listen to us."

Frustrated, it was the Wilsons who investigated that afternoon.

One after another, Claire contacted Colette's friends, but no one had seen her. None of her daughter's friends or their families knew where Colette could have gone. Meanwhile, Tom and the older children combed the site where Colette was dropped off. They searched the surrounding woods, hoping to find someone or something that would lead them to Colette. As word spread, their neighbors helped, organizing

search parties, doing the things authorities weren't, looking
frantically for any sign of Colette. Frustration welled, especially when someone found an unemployment check stub
near the site and gave it to the police. To the Wilsons' amaze-
ment, the officer threw it away. "Our neighbors were wonderful, and I'll be forever grateful for all they did. But the police
didn't take any of it seriously," said Claire. "If it weren't for
our neighbors, no one would have been looking for Colette."

Meanwhile, Claire thought back to the car on the side of
the road. Could that have been a stranger taking away her
daughter?

Finally, on Saturday, two days after the disappearance,
police admitted that it appeared Colette Wilson had been
kidnapped. It was only then that they issued a statewide alert
and brought in helicopters. But it was too late. Whoever had
taken Colette had an insurmountable lead. Even when authorities admitted they had a missing teenager, it seemed to
Claire that local officers did little but congregate at the intersection where Colette was last seen and talk to reporters.
"I don't think they knew what to do," she said.

Not dissuaded by the lack of effort on the part of police,
the neighbors continued their searches, extending their efforts westward, into Brazoria County. Despite their hard
work, they uncovered no solid clues. Frantic to find his
daughter, Tom Wilson raised $10,000 for a reward. Eager
to do everything possible, still thinking about the lone car
that day on the road, Claire agreed to be hypnotized. Sadly,
nothing developed from the experiment; she recalled no description or license-plate number to help with the search.

Before long, Texas Rangers and state troopers joined the
efforts, but again to no avail. Disheartened, when Tom heard
that his daughter might have been seen in Louisiana, he
didn't rely on authorities but went himself, following what
turned out to be one of many false leads. As the investigation faltered, Claire and Tom hired a private investigator, but
he, too, failed to uncover any solid evidence.

As time passed without word of Colette, the Wilsons, a deeply religious family, adopted a ritual, every evening kneeling around their missing daughter's bed and praying for her return. Where was Colette? How could she simply disappear? "We prayed that the Archangel Michael would lead us in our battle," said Claire. "We prayed that God would bring our daughter home."

Less than a month after Colette Wilson's disappearance, on Monday, July 12, 1971, a crew on scaffolding painted the Pelican Island Bridge, a steel-and-cement structure extending north from Fifty-first Street, not far from the Galveston Harbor Channel, an industrial zone near the shipyards. They worked and talked, as the water around them glistened, sunlight dazzling on the surf. Around ten that morning, one worker noticed something floating in the distance. Before long, they were all staring at it, calling out ideas, guessing what it might be. A slight chop in the water lapped against the bridge as they worked, an echoing *thunk, thunk, thunk.* Slowly, the object floated closer, growing in size. It was then that they realized they were staring at a dead body.

The call came into the Galveston Police Department at 10:30 A.M., a report of what appeared to be a woman's corpse in the water. When officers arrived, they pulled a lifeless figure from the bay, a young, light-skinned African-American woman. She was nude, her wrists and ankles bound with long, plastic laces. With no identification to tell them otherwise, police estimated that the dead girl appeared to be approximately twenty.

At the scene, however, an officer arrived who recognized the girl. Brenda Jones was only fourteen years old. Entering eighth grade in the fall, Brenda attended the island's Holy Rosary School, the first African-American Catholic school in the state. She was a good student, and she was responsible, so when Brenda didn't arrive home on time the previous afternoon, her family quickly grew worried. "I called and reported Brenda missing that same evening," said Phyllis Southern, one of Brenda's three sisters, describing how everyone in her family impatiently awaited news, wondering where Brenda had gone.

Outspoken and always ready with a wide smile, Brenda loved children and planned to one day be a teacher. The

baby of the family, she tended to be a bit of a tomboy, whipping the neighborhood boys at marbles. Around the house she was a joyous presence, practicing her clarinet for the school band and singing her favorite Rhythm and Blues songs. Her mom, Evelyn, was a widow, and just the year before moved the family into the Cedar Terrace Projects, housing for economically strapped families on the island. "We'd led pretty sheltered lives," said Phyllis. "Mom didn't want to move us there, but she couldn't afford anything else."

Brenda Jones had a personality that could light a room. *(Courtesy of her family)*

Hoping to uncover clues to what led to Brenda's disappearance, her family reconstructed what they could about the afternoon she vanished. It began like any other Sunday. They attended mass at Holy Rosary, then Brenda stayed to teach Sunday school. They gathered and ate dinner, and Brenda told her mother that she wanted to go to the University of Texas Medical Branch's John Sealy Hospital to visit an aunt who'd fallen and broken a leg. Evelyn agreed and gave Brenda bus fare. Brenda kissed her family good-bye and left. "We didn't have a car. Our mom couldn't afford one," said Phyllis. "Brenda took the bus to the hospital. She saw my aunt, and left. Later, the bus driver told us Brenda got on the bus at the hospital and got off at the stop just a few blocks from the house, on the corner of Avenue I (later renamed Sealy Avenue) and Thirty-first Street."

Phyllis Southern and Pearl Smith, two of Brenda Jones's sisters, holding her school photo. *(Courtesy of Kathryn Casey)*

Brenda was in a hurry to get home. Phyllis had just given birth to a son four days earlier, and the infant had entranced his young aunt. "Brenda wanted to come home to hold him," said Phyllis. "She loved babies."

On the corner where she disembarked from the bus stood the school Brenda was scheduled to attend in the fall, Central Middle School. The bus driver saw her walking toward home as he drove off.

So close to the safety of her front door, but Brenda never arrived.

Police wouldn't take a missing person report on the phone from Phyllis that night, saying it was too soon. If Brenda didn't return home the following day, the officer suggested the family could come to the station to file paperwork. That never happened. Instead, early that Monday afternoon, an officer knocked on their front door. Once inside, he asked to see a photo of Brenda. One glance, and he asked Evelyn to accompany him to the morgue. A body had been found floating in the water. There on a slab, Evelyn identified her youngest child. When she'd disappeared, Brenda had worn a satiny white blouse, a blue skirt, and Roman-type sandals that laced up to her knees. When found, her body was nude. Her sandals' long laces had been torn off the soles and used to bind her wrists and ankles.

"Our mother was shattered," said Phyllis. "She couldn't believe anyone would do that to her baby." When police asked if anyone was angry with Brenda, if anyone in the family knew anyone with a reason to kill Brenda, no one had a name to give them. "Everyone loved Brenda. Why would anyone want to hurt her?"

The following day, at the Galveston County Morgue, a medical examiner conducted an autopsy, looking for any visible signs of trauma. Quickly, he noticed something jammed inside the teenager's mouth. Carefully, he pulled at thin fabric, removing the item from between her teeth. Once unfolded, he realized it was a pair of women's underwear. It seemed such an odd thing for the killer to do. Was it to prevent Brenda from screaming? That couldn't have been the case. From the condition of the tissue, the physician speculated that the panties had been forced in Brenda's mouth after she was dead. Why then?

The medical examiner made notes, then continued the autopsy. Based on a lack of bruising, scratches, and cuts, he theorized that the most likely scenario was that Brenda's corpse had been thrown into the water from a boat or pier. As to time of death, a lack of rigor mortis led to the determination that she'd died at most a few hours before being found. That suggested that someone had abducted the girl the afternoon before and kept her alive all night, before killing her around sunrise.

How had Brenda died? The medical examiner documented bruising across Brenda's neck. Under cause of death, he wrote: manual strangulation.

In Alvin, Tom and Claire Wilson continued their search for Colette, following leads that quickly turned cold. On Galveston Island, Brenda Jones's family waited for police to find her killer. They saw little being done. "My mother and I went to the police station, we tried to get them to do something, to find out who did this," said Phyllis. "I had the feeling that they didn't care. Brenda was a black child from the projects. My impression was that they thought her murder wasn't worthy of any real investigation."

Two dead teenage girls in two months, and no answers.

What no one would speculate about until later was that the two cases could be connected. Was it a coincidence that both girls played musical instruments? No one knew. "Brenda was black, and Colette white," said a woman who knew Brenda. "Why would anyone think that the same person could be responsible?"

The Wix Ski School on Offatts Bayou. *(Courtesy of Johnnie Wix)*

"The police came asking questions, I remember that," said Johnnie Wix, her voice heavy with sadness.

In her nineties, Johnnie was a diminutive figure seated on a couch in her daughter's living room, a frail bump under a pile of blankets. I'd arrived unannounced and entered when she yelled at me to come inside. She thought I was a nurse, there to help her dress for the day. On her schedule, a doctor's appointment was inked in for the afternoon. When I identified myself as a writer and explained that I'd come to talk about the girls who died in Galveston in the 1970s, the old woman with her white hair in loose curls cast her eyes down at her gnarled hands on her lap and sighed. "I don't like to think about that. It is more than forty years ago now. I never forgot about the girls, but I got to the point, I didn't like to remember."

Back in those days, Johnnie and her deceased husband, Sam, a marine engineer who'd served in the navy during World War II, ran Galveston's Wix Ski School, on Offatts Bayou, just blocks off I-45. A favorite spot for bird-watching, the estuary between Galveston and West Bays was named after steamboat captain Horatio J. Offutt, who in 1847 bought the surrounding two hundred acres. Urban legends erroneously touted other theories for the source of its name, the most popular that it stemmed from the bayou's location as the first exit past the causeway onto the island. In that version, "off at the bayou" morphed into Offatts Bayou.

The ski school, located on a boat dock attached to the back of the Wixes' small frame house, was a hangout for teenagers who congregated to ski and buy dime cans of pop out of the old, red, soft-drink box Johnnie kept well stocked. Gas was nineteen cents a gallon, and Johnnie charged a dollar to pull a skier on a turn around the wide bayou. When the teens were short of money, she let them earn rides by helping with tasks around the school, cleaning the old boat Sam labored to keep running or working on the ski lines. Sometimes professional skiers from Sea-Arama Marine World, a theme park that had opened on the island in the midsixties, dropped in. "All those who came around, they were nice kids," Johnnie said. "I liked them. And people loved coming to the ski school. Rich people, just regular people. Lots of different kinds of people. It was our sport, and we loved it."

The first two girls the police questioned Johnnie and Sam Wix about were fourteen-year-old friends Sharon Shaw and Rhonda "Renee" Johnson. They disappeared on August 4, 1971. That afternoon, they'd dropped in at the Wix Ski School. Sam told police that Shaw and Johnson stayed only briefly, leaving when he told them that the ski boat wasn't going out because of choppy waters. The Wixes' neighbors later said that they saw the girls leave the ski school and walk east toward Sixty-first Street, a main thoroughfare that led to Seawall Boulevard and the beach.

The girls must have been disappointed that day. Shaw and Johnson worshipped the water, skied, and belonged to a local surfing club. They'd been looking forward to the afternoon at Wix. "They weren't regulars, but they'd show up sometimes. They came maybe once or twice before that day," Johnnie said, her face taut with a troubled frown. "They weren't local. They were rounders."

When I asked what she meant by that, Wix shook her head. "They were attractive girls, and street-smart."

Shaw and Johnson lived in Webster, a small town half an hour north of Galveston on the mainland, just off I-45. When they didn't return home, their parents began searching. One friend speculated that they might have run away. The girls had been talking about following friends to California, to ride the grand waves—so much bigger than Galveston's meager surf—in Malibu. "I don't think at first anyone thought it was anything but that those first two girls had taken off," said Johnnie.

A brief two months after the Webster girls disappeared, there was again little notice when a nineteen-year-old bookkeeper working at a Houston Kroger store, Gloria Ann

Gonzales, was reported missing by her roommate in late October. Gonzales had last been seen at their apartment on Jacquelyn Street in Houston. Brenda Jones's body had been found quickly, but like Colette Wilson, and Shaw and Johnson, Gonzales appeared to have inexplicably vanished.

"If people were really worried, well, I didn't hear anything," said Johnnie Wix, her parchment-thin eyelids fluttering down, then resolutely closing, as if shutting out the memories. "Then we heard about Maria and Debbie. And then we all knew something really bad was happening."

Best friends Debbie Ackerman and Maria Andrews Johnson.

"Debbie was a good kid," said her sister-in-law, Denise. "She loved the water, surfed, and skied. All summer, she was tan, and the sun streaked her hair blond. She and Maria were best friends, together constantly. Debbie was the apple of her daddy's eye. The only girl. And no one in the family ever got over it."

Coming from very different backgrounds, Debbie and Maria weren't an obvious pairing. Debbie had two older brothers, Glenn and Wayne, and lived with her parents, German immigrants, in a small house on the island. Her dad, Joseph, was a janitor, and her mother, Deomeria, called Dee, worked as a supply clerk. They were a close family, and since she was the little sister, they all doted on Debbie. At Ball High School, Debbie was a popular fifteen-year-old, elected to student council, and friends who grew up with her remembered an outgoing girl with an athletic build. She danced on the school football field as a member of the Tornettes, the drill team, alongside the mascot, a menacing-looking yellow tornado.

While the Ackermans were well-known in Galveston and Debbie was BOI (born on the island), Maria, her long dark hair parted down the middle, had just moved to Galveston the previous year. Her father a gynecologist, her parents' marriage ended in a divorce that split her family. At fifteen, Maria moved often in the aftermath, ultimately following her stepfather's work to Galveston. One of Maria's great loves was collecting antique glass bottles that she displayed in her bedroom window.

What Debbie and Maria had in common was a love of the water. They wore bikinis on the beach, surfed with friends, and frequented the two surf shops on the island and Wix Ski School.

That summer, Debbie competed in surfing contests and won her first trophy. "They'd come in and hang out with the other kids," said Doug Pruns, the owner of Doug's Surf Shop. "They were nice girls. They were dating a couple of the guys who came to the shop."

On that fateful fall Saturday in 1971, there was a disagreement at the Ackerman house, when Debbie wanted to spend the weekend at Maria's rather than stay home to help her mother clean. The coming Monday was a school holiday. "Dee was angry about Debbie's leaving. She didn't like Debbie's hanging out with Maria," said Johnnie Wix. "She thought Maria had been around more and was too advanced for Debbie."

As teenagers often do, Debbie divided and conquered by asking her father, who gave his permission. Her parents argued, but Debbie left. After two days at Maria's, on Monday morning, Debbie called and talked to her father again, this time explaining that she wanted to spend the school holiday with Maria as well. Joseph gave his daughter permission but with strict orders to be home by 3:15 that afternoon. The date was November 15, 1971.

That afternoon would be an eventful one in U.S. history, one on which the U.S. government announced plans to concentrate bombing on Laos and Cambodia during the dry season, to cut off supplies to North Vietnam. Meanwhile at the Globe discount store in Galveston, bedspreads sold for $10.88 and women's bellbottoms for $2.97. Once Debbie had her father's consent, she and Maria took off for the day.

A couple of hours later, at approximately 11:15 that morning, two teenage girls working at the Baskin-Robbins ice-cream parlor at Galveston's Port Holiday Mall saw Debbie and Maria on the street and called them over. Debbie had her small suitcase with her from her sleepover at the Johnsons' house. Asked what they were doing, the girls gave the usual teenage reply: "Nothing."

When they parted, one of the girls in the shop looked out and saw Debbie and Maria hitchhiking. Moments later, a white man in a white van with a peace sticker on the back window pulled over. The driver lowered his window and talked to Maria, and both girls scrambled into the van on the passenger side. As the van pulled away, the girls in the ice-cream shop noticed curtains behind the van's back window, blocking the view inside.

The appointed time, 3:15, came and went, and Debbie failed to return home as she'd promised.

At about four, Dee Ackerman contacted Maria's mother, looking for Debbie. The calls continued into the evening, but the Johnsons insisted that they had nothing to tell her. They hadn't seen Maria either. In fact, the last time they'd seen the girls was that morning just after 9 A.M., when the Johnsons said good-bye and left for work. They had no idea where their daughter and her best friend could be.

The following morning, Tuesday, the girls were still missing, and their parents were growing increasingly apprehensive. Maria's father notified the Texas Rangers, and the Ackermans called their sons home from college to help search for their sister. That afternoon, the family canvassed Maria's and Debbie's usual haunts, including the beach, where they stopped passersby and asked if they'd been there the day before and if they'd seen the girls. No one had. The Ackermans went to the mall and the surf and ski shops, but returned home with nothing to help in their quest. Meanwhile, the police put out a BOLO, a be-on-the-lookout, for the two teenagers.

The road leading to Turner Bayou, a remote field with an oil-collection tank. *(Courtesy of Kathryn Casey)*

The call came in the following afternoon, Wednesday, November 17, two days after the girls' disappearances. While fishing, an elderly man happened upon a body in Turner Bayou, on the mainland, near Texas City, a short drive north on I-45 from Galveston.

Police quickly flooded the area, driving down country roads surrounded by cattle pastures, then through a gate onto a gravel-and-dirt one-lane road, onto vacant land where Humble Oil had a collection site. The corpse was partially submerged, near a small wooden bridge that extended across the narrow bayou. Ropes were used to reel it in. The dead girl had long, dark, reddish brown hair. She wore only a pink bra under a shirred maroon blouse, pierced earrings, and rings. From the waist down, she was nude. The first officers on the scene noted what appeared to be bullet wounds, especially one on the right side and center of the neck. Like Brenda Jones's corpse when pulled from the water at the Pelican Island Bridge, this dead girl's hands and ankles were bound.

That evening, Maria's frantic mother and stepfather were called to the Texas City police station. The girl's corpse had been taken to the morgue, but her jewelry was at the police station waiting to be inspected. As soon as they saw it, the Johnsons verified it was Maria's.

ISLE GIRL'S BODY FOUND, Texas's oldest newspaper, the *Galveston County Daily News*, reported the following morning. The coroner estimated that Maria's remains had been in the water for approximately thirty-six hours, suggesting that she was murdered sometime late Monday or early Tuesday morning, ten to eighteen hours after she and Debbie disappeared. Someone in the area of the Humble Oil field reported hearing gunshots that Monday evening. But the search wasn't over. By the time newspapers slapped down on front porches that drizzling, overcast morning, every available officer from Galveston County and Texas City was at the Turner Bayou Bridge searching for a second body.

"Once they had Maria, we all pretty much knew that this wasn't going to turn out well," said Denise. "We knew the likelihood was that Debbie was dead."

"I see something!" a Texas City fireman shouted, when he spotted skin protruding from the water 150 feet downstream from the small wooden bridge where Maria Johnson had been found. There in the tall grass around the bayou's marshy edge, all that was visible was the naked buttocks of a young girl facedown in the water. The corpse, again, was nude from the waist down. And like both of the previously recovered victims, Maria Johnson and Brenda Jones, the girl's wrists and ankles were bound, this time with long black cords that looked like shoestrings. The most recently discovered corpse wore only a bra and a dark purple Banlon-type shirt with a zipper up the front. Robbery obviously hadn't been a motive, as this body, too, wore jewelry. Officers noticed gunshot wounds to the upper back and the right of the spine.

That evening, Debbie's father and one of her brothers went to the morgue to identify the body. "When they got home, they pretty much collapsed," said Denise. "It was over, but it wasn't. The whole family wanted to know who'd done this."

The next day, the *Daily News* banner headline read BODY OF 2ND GIRL FOUND: LEADS SLIM, POLICE SAY. Along with photos of the girls, the newspaper ran one of the fields surrounding Turner Bayou, with a large oil-collection tank in the background and a group of cowboy-hatted men carrying Debbie Ackerman's body covered by a sheet on a stretcher. "That was the first time any of the murders got our attention," said a woman who went to school with the dead girls. "I don't remember being aware of the killings until then."

Word circulated that the last time Debbie and Maria were seen they were hitchhiking. After a hesitation, their schoolmate continued: "We told ourselves that Maria and Debbie were a little wild. We told ourselves we wouldn't do that, hitchhike, so it could never happen to us. But everybody was freaked out. No one wanted to be out at night. Our parents kept us home. We were all afraid."

The next day, the Galveston police chief told not only local press but reporters from big-city newspapers that converged on the island that he believed the motive for the girls' killings was sexual. Noting Brenda Jones's death, he added that Debbie and Maria weren't the first girls to die on Galveston that summer and be found with their hands and wrists tied. The medical examiner, too, granted interviews, detailing a theory that Debbie had been killed first, perhaps shot from above as she tried to shield Maria.

While news of the girls' murders rocked Galveston, investigators tried to nail down Debbie and Maria's activities on their final days. As reports came together, police drew up a timeline. What they discovered was that the day before they disappeared, Maria and Debbie had been seen at a shopping mall on the mainland near Texas City, the closest town to where their bodies were found. They were looking for a birthday gift for Debbie's boyfriend. That afternoon, they returned to Galveston in a taxi but forgot Debbie's purse in the backseat and ended up at a cab stand at eight that evening retrieving it. They slept at Maria's house. The last time they were seen was the following morning, entering the white van in front of the ice-cream parlor.

The investigation continued, but while the police attempted to find the killer or killers, the girls' families turned their attention to the pressing business at hand, burying the dead.

That same week, Maria's body was shipped to a family plot in Plainview, Texas. But Debbie had strong island roots. She'd been born in Galveston, and she'd be buried there. The church overflowed with mourners on the day the Ackermans memorialized their daughter. "People were standing everywhere. Kids, parents, teachers, neighbors, folks that knew the family," said a school friend. "There was a lot of sadness, and a lot of fear. Everyone felt on edge. We couldn't understand what was happening."

As bad as things seemed, they were about to get much worse.

At eight in the morning on the same day Debbie Ackerman was laid to rest, November 23, a man wielding a metal detector walked thro… a heavily wooded area near the Addicks Reservoir, wes… Houston and just north of I-10. A bird sanctuary, the l… s man-made, a dammed-up area used for flood contro… help prevent low-lying downtown Houston from flood… uring hurricanes and the Gulf Coast's sometimes to… al rains. Rather than buried trea-sure, what the man f… was a decapitated, decomposing body.

In this era long be… advent of cell phones, the man drove to the nearest n… r's. A call went out, and police responded, bringing… to comb the area, in search of clues. One of the firs… eries was a skull a short distance away in the und… Based on items found on the corpse—a white knit… and striped slacks, and a ring that read LOVE—it wa… assumed that the decompos-ing body belonged to… Ann Gonzales, the nineteen-year-old Kroger book… ho'd been missing for nearly a month.

That same day, th… s were transported to the morgue for autopsy. C… inless-steel table, the physician in charge noted… d on pressure-point marks, it appeared the remain… down in the woods for an extended period of tim… capitation, the ME specu-lated, hadn't been done… es's killer but animals that ravaged the corpse.

Yet there was an c… stance, a puzzling one. While the body remain… with decomposing flesh, the skull was nearly ske… would the skull be nearly cleaned off and not the… animals have devoured all the tissue off the sk… but he saw no signs of such animal activity. A… s the cause, why hadn't they attacked the body a…

When it came to the… th, the medical exam-iner focused on the sku… y surface, he noted a series of fractures, inclu… that appeared to have been administered by a… w. Could Gloria have been bludgeoned to deat…

Events tumbled one after another, twisting and turning. It would later seem that the mur[ders] were piling up so quickly that it was difficult to keep evidence straight. Perhaps this was never more apparent during the Gonzales autopsy, when suddenly the physician in charge faced a second perplexing find.

Gonzales's mandible remained [on] her body, and he inspected it carefully. Decades before mapping in criminal cases, dental records played th[e] important role in identification. Along with the jaw, the doctor examined teeth found on the scene. S[ome w]ere still attached. The others, found near the body, [f]ully inserted into the bone, [... used] to reconstruct the lower [jaw, ... ]aid in matching it to Gonzales's dental X-rays. Wh[en he che]cked up a molar, however, he suddenly had a prob[lem: t]he tooth didn't fit the jaw.

Perplexed, the medical examin[er took a]nother look, lined up the tooth a second time, trie[d] it, only to again pull the tooth away when it wa[sn']t that it wasn't a match. With that, the physician [a]nd considered the possibilities. Eventually he cam[e to o]nly possible conclusion, writing on the Gonzal[es report]: "It was evident that the molar came from anoth[er individu]al."

"Another individual." Anoth[er ...

Three days later, deputies re[turned to t]he site in the Addicks Reservoir where Gonzale[s ha]d been found, this time with dogs and equipment[ to do a] wider inspection of the area. They were looking[ for a secon]d dead body.

Among those walking thro[ugh the ]grass, picking his way through the thick under[brush was t]he Harris County Sheriff, C. V. Buster Kern, a[ big], heavily jawed man with horn-rimmed glass[es and thinni]ng hair. He was a political man, put in office b[y and it was a good public-relations move to be p[art ... a]iding in the hunt for evidence. But that wasn't[ the only reas]on he'd shown up to help. "The cases of the n[ight ... ate away at him," said someone who knew Ker[n ... ]answers."

Ironically, the sheriff would be the one to find an important piece of the puzzle. Around 10:30 that morning, after fighting off bugs and wading through knee-high grass watching for venomous snakes, Kerns spotted a pile of bones on a bed of decaying leaves fifty yards from the flags that marked the spot where searchers had recovered Gonzales.

The horror of that day would stay with many of those in attendance in the reservoir throughout their lives. First the discovery of Gonzales's decomposing body, a skull, and now a human skeleton. As they compared notes, someone noticed a clue to the second victim's identity, a ring that spelled out the word PEACE on a fragile finger bone. Colette Wilson's parents had described just such a ring when they told police what their daughter wore on the day she disappeared.

No skull was found with the skeleton, but the medical examiner honed in on a mandible with some teeth, a way to find out if their suspicions were true. That afternoon, a call went out to the Wilson household, asking to have Colette's father report to the scene. As Tom Wilson drove to the reservoir to join the search party, his wife had mixed emotions. "We'd been praying and praying that Colette would be found," said Claire. "All we cared about was that we'd find her. We'd hoped to find her alive. Yet if she was dead, we wanted to bring her body home. The worst case was not knowing."

Once he'd joined the others at the Addicks Reservoir, the middle-aged dentist was shown the recovered peace ring. Immediately, he began crying, nodding that it had belonged to his daughter. Yet his obligations weren't finished. In addition to being Colette's father, Tom Wilson was her dentist, and the next thing he did must have been one of the most difficult tasks of his life. Wilson was handed the skeleton's jawbone for identification. "I recognize my work," he said later, after examining the jaw and teeth, some of which contained fillings, sad remnants of a young life. "It's Colette."

Remembering that day, Claire Wilson would attempt to

describe the emotions that overwhelmed the family. "It was terrible, and in another way, we were so grateful," she recalled. "Colette was dead, but we could bury her. We could bring her home. It was so awful, but at the same time, we were happy."

More than five months after Colette had disappeared, the Wilson family's search was over. It had ended in a nightmare.

"There's no doubt about it. That's my daughter," Wilson told reporters as he left the scene, his eyes welling with tears. "Colette was very happy, and God, she was beautiful. I guess we knew that it would probably end this way. We've been looking for Colette since she disappeared, and we won't stop now. We don't have any clues as to who did this, but he'll be found."

While no doubt remained, during his examination of the bones, the Harris County medical examiner found further evidence confirming that the skeleton belonged to Colette. The bones were consistent with coming from a young girl, thirteen to fifteen years of age. And this particular girl, he noted, had a congenital defect in her right hip. Colette's parents had already told police that their daughter had been born with a malformed hip and had spent the first two years of her life with her lower body in a cast.

The following morning, newspapers across Texas reported the findings, and something else, that there were now five unsolved murders of young girls since the beginning of the year in the area around I-45 extending south from Houston into Galveston: the only African-American victim, Brenda Jones; best friends Debbie Ackerman and Maria Johnson; the Kroger bookkeeper, Gloria Gonzales; and the dentist's daughter, Colette Wilson. AUTHORITIES SEEK LINK IN HOUSTON, ISLE GIRLS' DEATHS, Galveston's *Daily News* reported. The *Odessa American* ran the headline: UNSOLVED MURDERS MOUNT IN HOUSTON.

In the days that followed, the searches in the reservoir

continued. Colette Wilson's body had been found without a skull, and there remained the possibility of unearthing more evidence. What searchers weren't prepared for was the finding of a decomposing head on November 30, hidden in the brush twenty-five feet from where Gonzales's body had been located.

The ME now had a decomposing body, a decapitated head, one skeleton, and one skull.

From the beginning, the condition of the original skull, the one found with the body, must have bewildered the physician. Why was it devoid of nearly all tissue when the body was still covered in flesh? When he examined it, he determined that the skull did come from a young woman. Yet the features that identified race, including the thin nasal aperture and rounded shape of the forehead, suggested that the skull found near Gonzales's body was from a Caucasian. Gloria was Hispanic. He then tried to fit that skull to the mandible found with the skeleton, the one Tom Wilson had identified as belonging to his daughter. They fit.

Meanwhile, the decomposing head, still bearing flesh and curly dark hair anchored in a silver barrette, could have come from Gonzales. Its features were consistent with those of a Latin-American woman. The physician placed the head onto the mandible attached to the body and found he had a second match.

Once he had all the remains identified, the ME revisited the question of causes of death for the two girls. Based on the fractures in the skull, the one he now knew belonged to Colette Wilson, he was able to determine how the thirteen-year-old had died: "It is our opinion," he wrote, "that the decedent, Colette Anise Wilson, came to her death as a result of a fractured skull, blunt trauma—homicide."

He then turned his attention to Gonzales's cadaver. Here cause of death was less certain. Yet he had obvious suggestive evidence. When her body was recovered, it was found with a two-foot cotton cord attached to a four-inch piece of wood cinched around her neck. Based on the noose, the physician wrote: "it was probable that Gloria Gonzales was killed by strangulation with the cotton rope ligature."

The headlines were terrifying. Parents across the Houston area held their daughters close, refusing to let them leave the house except to go to school, and a sense of near hysteria invaded living rooms. Politicians called for action, and a meeting was quickly set for all the law-enforcement agencies involved in downtown Houston, at the Harris County Criminal Courthouse. By then, factions were developing, those who saw no connection between any of the killings and others like Kern who leaned toward believing otherwise, describing the killer responsible for Gloria Gonzales's and Colette Wilson's murders as "a homicidal maniac who may or may not be the same person or persons that killed the two Galveston girls [Debbie Ackerman and Maria Johnson]."

Hours after the meeting, which ended with the debate still raging over possible links between the killings, the Houston/Galveston cases were featured on the *CBS Evening News*. The realization that young women's bodies were piling up in Texas was beginning to draw national attention. A somber tone in his voice, Kern told Walter Cronkite that law enforcement had a suspect, one who'd told a woman, "He wanted the law to catch him because he was crazy."

That lead would turn out to be futile, the ravings of a man who'd confessed simply to gain attention. Days later, Kern released a composite drawing of another man he said could have been a homicidal "sex maniac." Kern never explained but later described that, too, as a false lead. Polygraphers were kept busy in Texas that fall, running examinations on suspects. One after another, investigations and lie-detector exams cleared each one.

The beginning of a new year is a time for reflection, and when the months before have been difficult, it's only natural to hope that the change will bring relief from pain, happiness, and in the case of 1971 Galveston, an end to the terror. It wasn't to be. Quickly, 1972 took up where 1971 had ended.

In January, the remains of two more girls were found, again near water, on the banks of an overflow ditch running off Taylor Bayou, east of I-45 and thirty miles north of Galveston near the affluent waterfront community of Shoreacres. This time the dead were quickly bestowed with names: Sharon Shaw and Rhonda Renee Johnson, the fourteen-year-olds who five months earlier friends believed had run away to surf in Malibu.

That meant that the number of young girls murdered in the Galveston/South I-45 area in the previous eight months stood at seven.

The dead girls' parents were frantic, begging for answers. They went before the press, pleading with anyone with information to come forward, hoping to find the man or men who'd murdered their daughters. They demanded law enforcement take action, but the small police agencies along the Gulf Coast had never experienced such carnage, and looking back, many would surmise that they simply didn't know what to do, how to proceed to solve the crimes.

"My sister's death crushed my family," said Renee Johnson's brother. "I don't think people understand how devastating it is for parents to lose a child this way. My father was never the same. It just tore everything apart."

That very year, the Behavioral Science Unit at the FBI would be formed, and profilers would begin studying such cases, yet it would be decades before the practice would move into mainstream law enforcement. For his part, Chief Deputy Sheriff Lloyd Frazier told the *Houston Chronicle* that he suspected the girls' deaths were linked. "I believe that a killer of young girls is lurking in the area," he said, but then admitted that suspicion was all he had. The investigations were stalled. By then, fifteen suspects had been given lie-detector tests, but no arrests had been made.

When questioned further about the cases, Frazier said, "Our problem in each case is that the bodies were found . . .

long after any footprints or tire tracks had disappeared . . . We don't have anything concrete to link these cases except that they were all young girls, but we don't have anything that would lead us to believe they were separate cases. I believe we have one killer."

It wasn't that investigators didn't try. In the months that followed, reports filtered off and on into newspapers of even more suspects brought in for questioning, some of whom confessed to the killings. Yet each led to disappointment when none seemed to be genuine possibilities.

"At school, everyone was talking about it," said a woman who was a girl on the island at the time. "We were calling him the Purple Passion Killer, because there were rumors that every girl who'd died had something purple on." In fact, Maria Johnson and Debbie Ackerman had both been wearing maroon blouses and Colette Wilson purple shorts. "Our parents wouldn't let us leave the house alone, and they'd stop us at the door and make us change our clothes if we started to walk out wearing anything purple. We were all afraid."

Off and on in the newspapers, authorities speculated that they were nearing a break in the cases. In the first months following the discovery of Shaw's and Johnson's skeletons, there were serious suspects. In fact, at one point in March, the Harris County sheriff announced that he had yet another theory about who'd murdered all the girls. This time the man was a former mental patient, one who'd tried to abduct a woman after stalking her. She said the man mentioned the killings, suggesting he could be responsible. That lead faded away, and no arrest was ever made.

Another possibility was a young hippie with a VW bus and California license plates pulled over on a traffic stop. He raised suspicion by asking the officer about the girls' deaths. Police searched the man's vehicle and discovered a rifle. Again, however, a promising possibility ended in frustration when police verified that the man had only recently arrived. He'd come because he'd heard news of the murders on television and had driven all the way to Texas, intending to solve the crimes and collect the thousands of dollars being offered as reward money.

The investigations continued, and off and on men who in a later day's vernacular would be called persons of interest cropped up only to later be ruled out. Perhaps the most viable suspect was a twenty-four-year-old Houston wrecker driver named Harry Lanham. He and a friend, a Vietnam vet named Anthony Knoppa, Jr., were arrested in April 1972 for the murder of Linda Fay Sutherlin in Pearland, a suburb just south of Houston. Her body had been found the previous November, around the time of the Ackerman and Johnson killings, lying in the weeds under a bridge along County Road 89.

In hindsight, Linda Faye's killing didn't bear a lot of resemblance to the other murders beyond that the twenty-one-year-old barmaid's body was found in a ditch. Unlike the others, Sutherlin was fully dressed, still wearing brown go-go boots and a short pink dress, even her sweater. A leg from her panty hose was tied around her hands, and the second leg had been cinched around her neck. She'd been beaten, and shotgun-pellet holes covered her shoulder. The break in the case came when witnesses remembered seeing Sutherlin in a convenience-store parking lot, her car apparently not working, talking to two men in a red tow truck. Police tied the truck to Lanham, who had a long history of violence. Once Lanham, a husky six-footer who weighed 240 pounds, was brought in for questioning, he fingered Knoppa for the killings. Knoppa returned the favor, claiming Lanham pulled the trigger, delivering the fatal injuries.

One of the most chilling admissions was in Knoppa's statement, when he said that after they picked up Sutherlin, they drove around with her in the wrecker for hours. "Harry and I both knew what was going to happen, but we didn't talk about it. We both knew that we were going to kill the girl."

That October, Lanham and Knoppa were convicted of murder with malice aforethought, Knoppa getting fifty years and Lanham twenty-five.

It was while he was in jail awaiting transport to prison in the fall of 1972 that Lanham made claims that he'd murdered the Galveston-area girls. Police from all the towns where killings had taken place descended on the jail to interview him. Whatever Lanham said during those interviews, no additional charges were ever filed.

Not reported in the press was that Lanham had another visitor while in jail, one who had a very personal interest in getting at the truth; Tom Wilson, the dentist who'd identified his own daughter's remains, had heard about Lanham's confession and made arrangements to talk to the man who claimed to have murdered Colette. That day, whatever the convicted killer said, Wilson didn't believe him. When he returned home, Tom told his wife that Lanham's confession didn't ring true. "Tom said that man wasn't the one who killed Colette," said Claire, a painful catch in her throat, the sadness still palpable. After a pause, she whispered, "He wasn't the one."

Speculation about Lanham's possible involvement in the killings would continue, but hope of interviewing him further and confirming or disposing of his claims faded months later, in December, when the convicted killer was shot and killed while wielding a knife during a botched jail escape.

So many unanswered questions; so many false leads.

The victims' families prayed for answers that never came, and their misfortunes seemed to multiply. Many found no peace, as they anguished over a lack of even modest closure, not knowing who'd murdered their daughters. In Galveston, the Ackermans could never forget what happened to Debbie, going to the media on the anniversaries of their daughter's death, pleading for help in finding her killer. Every year when November approached, Dee Ackerman walked resolutely into the Texas City police station demanding assurance that the police hadn't stopped looking for Debbie's murderer. Her heart remained broken, and many would say that it would never mend.

"We're still wanting to know who did it," Dee told reporters. "We're still grieving. The hurt is still there. No, no, never will I get over it. It will be in my mind forever."

Tears spilling from her eyes, Brenda Jones's mother, Evelyn, talked of her lost daughter often, considering how the future would have been different if Brenda hadn't died. "I wonder what she would have done, if she would have become a teacher," Evelyn said. The loss seemed to envelop her at times, a sadness that would never leave her. "I wonder if Brenda would have had children, and what she'd look like all grown."

In the Wilson household in Alvin, Colette's family, too, grieved.

"I believe what happened to our daughter killed my husband," said Claire Wilson, painfully considering all the killer had taken from her. Four years after their daughter's murder, Tom Wilson died at the young age of forty-two. He'd never stopped looking for Colette's killer, and he'd never been able to move past the grief. "By then we had two more children, but he never got over what happened to Colette. I have no doubt that grief over Colette's death caused the heart attack."

The one ray of hope, one promise of closure for any of the cases, centered on an arrest in June 1972, charges tied to the murders of the two Webster girls, Sharon Shaw and Rhonda "Renee" Johnson. So many cases unsolved, so many questions, but for Shaw and Johnson, perhaps, there would be answers. Yet later many wondered if such tattered justice yielded yet another tragic turn.

# Chapter 2

## All That Remains
## The Murders of Sharon Shaw and
## Rhonda "Renee" Johnson

**Webster, Texas**

"It was a different time. We were young, and we felt like nothing could hurt us," said Glenda Willis. "Looking back, of course, it was foolish. I mean, we weren't afraid of anything. We never thought anyone was truly evil. I guess that wasn't a good thing, but we just didn't know."

I'd contacted Willis the week before, asking for an interview. She'd been close to Sharon Shaw and Rhonda "Renee" Johnson throughout the summer of 1971, the final months of their lives.

The Taylor Bayou Ditch, best friends Sharon Shaw and Rhonda "Renee" Johnson, and Renee's grave.
*(Collage courtesy of Kathryn Casey)*

many teenagers, Shaw and Johnson felt invincible, and their worldviews centered firmly on their own wants and needs. "Our big deal was whether there was going to be sunshine, because we wanted to go to the beach," Willis said. "That's all we cared about. Having fun. Then, Sharon and Renee disappeared, and it all unraveled . . . Nothing was ever the same."

"I was the conservative one," said Willis.

Sharon Shaw, an outspoken, stunning young girl with a feisty temperament, long dark hair parted down the middle, and thick straight eyebrows, was something of a tomboy. All the girls were athletic, but especially Shaw, who lived for the beach. In the group of friends, her nickname was "Wild S." Highly competitive, she seemed older than her years and intent on having her way. "We didn't want to wear bikinis around Sharon and Renee, because they were so in shape. Really toned. There wasn't anything, any sport that Sharon couldn't do. Once she learned to water-ski, she outskied everyone. A couple of weeks, and she was doing jumps and flips like the Sea Arama performers."

Of the two girls, Renee, her dark blond hair swept over her forehead and trailing down her shoulders, was the more reserved. "But if Sharon did it, Renee was going to do it," said Willis.

In Webster, Shaw and Johnson were neighbors. And in the rural town surrounded by cattle and rice fields, the Johnson family was well situated. Renee's grandfather, Roy Johnson, was a councilman who later became mayor, and her father was a local businessman. "Renee was the one the boys were all crazy about. She was petite and a flirt. She was a magnet for boys, always laughing, never took anything seriously," said Willis. "She knew how to talk to boys."

Much of that summer was spent twenty-two miles south of Glenda Willis's house on the island. They hung out with friends, including two Galveston girls named Deb and Peachy. "That was how we started going. We went to their houses, then to the beach," said Glenda. If they didn't take her car, they rode bikes. But for Johnson and Shaw, no method of transportation held as much allure as sticking out a thumb to attract a ride. "They loved it. Sometimes I'd offer them a lift, and they'd turn it down, preferring to find someone to pick them up along the road," said Willis.

Galveston was a natural destination for their daily treks. They felt the pull of the water, the beaches, and the venues where teenagers congregated, a triangle made up of the Wix Ski School and the island's two surf shops, Jericho's and Doug's. Rather than splinter off, the teens circulated in groups, whiling away lazy afternoons on the beach, listening to music, slathering up with baby oil and perfecting their tans. When the hot Texas sun burned, they retreated to the water. While far from the spectacular surf in California or Hawaii, on days when Gulf waves built enough to give them a modest ride, they grabbed their boards and rode on a crest of white foam.

As evening approached, the friends habitually returned to Glenda's house. "Everybody would come here. And on Saturday nights, this house rocked," said Willis. "It was the seventies. Back then it was drugs, free love, the hippie era. We listened to Alice Cooper, Chicago, the Rolling Stones, the Beach Boys, and the Beatles. We all went to hear Rod Stewart in the old Coliseum in downtown Houston."

When Willie Nelson hosted an open-air concert in an Austin field, the friends packed Willis's car and went, claiming a patch of land to camp out. "There were probably a hundred kids from this area, thousands from all over Texas," she said. "It was a blast."

Rock and roll scored their lives that summer. Liberty Hall had recently opened in a shabby section of downtown Houston, and there the girls danced and sang along to ZZ Top. "You could smell the pot, and everyone was drinking." Although the legal age was twenty-one, that never presented a problem. Older guys in their twenties escorted the girls into bars and clubs where the rock and roll blared, including one on the island where they danced on the sand. "It was a dump, but it had music, so we didn't care."

Rather than drive back to Willis's house in the early hours of the morning, they often stayed on the beach, sleeping in tents, on the sand, or on the bed of a friend's pickup truck. "One weekend, there must have been a hundred kids camped on the beach," said Willis. "We were up partying most of the night."

Like many of their friends, Renee and Sharon sometimes smoked pot, one night getting so high they danced naked on the roof of the Willis house in the rain. A neighbor woman called the League City police, who responded but rather than immediately end the show, took their time and watched. "They let them dance for fifteen minutes before they made them get off the roof," Willis said, laughing at the memory. "Sharon and Renee weren't hippies or flower children. They were just themselves. They wore their bikini tops, blue jeans, and cutoffs, hip huggers, halter tops, and no bras. We were all young and free."

What seemed unimportant was the future. They never discussed what they wanted to accomplish when they became adults, what they hoped the world held in reserve for them. "Our big thing was to get out of school and get out on our own," said Willis. "We were living in the moment. All we cared about was where the party was the next day."

Then something changed. In mid-July, Sharon complained that her mother talked about shopping for school clothes. Sharon and Renee were scheduled to start high school. Neither of them wanted to go. "I don't know why they were upset about high school," said Willis. "And Sharon didn't want to go shopping with her mother. She didn't want to have to wear the clothes her mother picked out. Both the girls said they didn't want anything to do with high school."

As the days of summer ticked off, Shaw and Johnson became increasingly distraught. Before long, conversations on the beach and in Willis's living room dissected ways to leave the Houston area, how and when to run away, and where they could find a parent-free refuge. They talked longingly about the hippie movement and the throngs of teenagers descending on San Francisco's Haight-Ashbury district, the media-christened center of the hippie subculture. The site was so storied that it was held in special reverence. Four years earlier, The Mamas & the Papas hit single commanded those who went to arrive adorned with flowers in their hair.

Yet Shaw and Johnson, for all their pluck, were leery of going alone. After a chance meeting, it appeared that they wouldn't have to. "Sharon and Renee met these older guys," said Willis. "The guys talked about going to California, and Sharon and Renee started saying that they were going with them. They were dreading high school. Their plan was to be gone."

August 4, 1971, a Wednesday, Sharon Shaw and Renee Johnson woke up at the Johnson house. They were so close, they rarely spent a night apart. That morning, they grabbed breakfast and, since the sky was blue and the sun shining, cajoled a neighbor into providing a ride to Galveston for a morning on the beach. Their only instruction was to be sure to return to the Johnsons' home by one for lunch, when Renee's parents would call to make sure they'd followed orders.

A little more than half an hour later, the neighbor dropped Sharon and Renee off at the Wix Ski School, on Offatts Bayou. Despite the sunshine, the chop was substantial that morning. Sam Wix would later tell police that the two girls were there only briefly. Once he explained that the water was too rough for skiing, they left, swimsuits in hand, heading toward the beach.

In League City that morning, Glenda Willis slept in. When she awoke, she packed her car and drove to the island, picking up a couple of boys who were friends along the way. Then late that morning, she crossed paths with Shaw and

Johnson at their usual meeting place, Thirty-ninth and Sea-wall Boulevard, across the street from a Galveston land-mark, Gaido's, a low-slung seafood restaurant with a giant, blue-clawed crab sculpture perched menacingly on its roof.

The front occupied by Willis and the two boys, Sharon and Renee scrambled into the convertible's backseat, and the teens drove along the seawall. By then, Shaw and John-son were contemplating how to get home. Glenda offered to drive them but not until later, not before three. She and the boys were meeting other friends on Stewart Beach. Shrug-ging it off, Sharon and Renee explained that they needed to be at the Johnsons' at one for the phone call. Rather than wait for Glenda, they said they'd hitchhike home to Webster, check in at the house, then find a ride back to Galveston.

"Okay. If you want a ride home later, I'll be around," Glenda said. She drove a few miles down Seawall Boule-vard before dropping the girls at the sidewalk in front of the Flagship Hotel, a boxy structure built over the water. Sharon and Renee scurried from the car.

"I'll be heading back to the house about five thirty. I can meet you here," Glenda called out as they rushed off. The two girls waved, shouting that they'd see her then. With that, Glenda drove away. "They looked really happy. They were both laughing, walking along the seawall."

Moments passed, and Willis, recounting that day, said nothing but closed her eyes as if reliving that painful instant out of her past. Her voice broke with aching emotion, as she whispered, "I never saw them again."

At five thirty, after her day on the beach, Glenda drove back to the spot where she'd dropped Sharon and Renee. Glenda assumed her friends would be waiting, that they'd wave at her and run to the car, eager for a ride home, banter-ing about the evening's plans. But that didn't happen. Sharon and Renee weren't there.

Presuming that they'd arrive at any moment, Glenda pulled the Cougar over in front of the hotel and parked. She watched sunbathers on the shore and occasionally scanned the seawall. Time passed, and Johnson and Shaw didn't come. "I had to be home by six. About then, my dad drove by each day to check on me," Glenda said with a shrug. "So I left. When Renee and Sharon didn't show up at my house that night, all of us didn't think anything of it because it wasn't unusual for them to stay overnight in Galveston. For all we knew, they were sleeping on the beach."

When the girls' parents called, Glenda covered for her friends, making up excuses, telling them that Renee and Sharon had just stepped out. When it went on for days, Glenda became worried. "I talked about it with the other kids, about how Sharon and Renee better get their asses home. You can only tell parents so many times that the girls are sleeping. The next thing I remember is Sharon's mother knocking on the door. She said they hadn't been home. I admitted I hadn't seen them, and that's when she filed a missing persons report."

Yet Glenda and the girls' other beach friends still weren't worried. They never considered that Shaw and Johnson could have been in danger, instead agreeing that the two girls had undoubtedly carried out their plan and run away, maybe to California. By then they could have been in San Francisco, or surfing in Malibu.

In the weeks that followed the girls' disappearances, police officers descended on the Willis home asking questions. When they stopped, Sharon's mother arrived, demanding answers. Presumably desperate and disconsolate about her daughter's disappearance, Sharon's mother, like so many of the other victims' parents and siblings, undoubtedly struggled with the uncertainty and the insurmountable fear. Where was her daughter?

As she remembered those grim times, Glenda spent long hours with Sharon's mother, traveling the streets of Galveston, pointing out places the girls hung out and helping Sharon's mother in her frantic search. "We drove from place to place, but no one had seen them. I didn't think anything of it. I knew they'd just taken off and that they'd be back at some point," said Willis. The weeks passed, and Sharon's mother stopped coming. Glenda continued searching on her own. "I wanted to find someone who'd had contact with them, to tell them to call their parents."

School started in September, and the freshman class arrived at Clear Creek High School. Sharon Shaw and Renee Johnson weren't among them. By then, Glenda's father had heard about the girls' disappearances. Not wanting her involved, he packed her up and moved her back to the Baptist boarding school in San Marcos, south of Austin.

At school, Glenda Willis didn't hear the news a month later, in November, when Debbie Ackerman and Maria Johnson disappeared, their decomposing bodies found days later in Turner Bayou, their wrists and ankles tied. If Willis had, perhaps she wouldn't have been as certain that Sharon and Renee had willingly absconded in search of freedom. The holidays came and went, and still Glenda refused to consider any possibility other than that Sharon and Renee had left voluntarily to enjoy life on the road.

Five months almost to the day after Sharon Shaw's and Renee Johnson's disappearances, on January 3, 1972, two teenage boys in small boats rowed down a drainage ditch attached to Taylor Bayou. Situated near State Highway 146 and the upscale community of Shoreacres, a coastal town across the bay from Galveston, Taylor Bayou resembled the site where Maria Johnson's and Debbie Ackerman's bodies had been found nearly two months earlier. The land surrounding the ditch was covered in brush and trees. It was a lonely patch of ground, one with few visitors.

On that afternoon, the boys saw what they at first thought could have been a volleyball bobbing in the water. Yet when they ventured closer, they realized it was something very different. Marking the spot with a broken oar plunged into the mud, they rushed home to bring one of their fathers to investigate. It was late, and the man suggested they wait until the next morning.

At first light, the tide rolled lazily in, while the two boys and the man in a boat searched the shoreline. When the man saw something glistening under the water near the broken oar, he reached deep into the muck and brought the object up. He put it in the boat, and they hurriedly rowed home. When police arrived, the boy's father directed them to the garage. There he unwrapped a blanket, revealing the object pulled from the Taylor Bayou ditch: a human skull.

At any time, such a grisly discovery would have required further investigation, but in the context of so many murdered girls, law enforcement moved in quickly. In the days that followed, divers explored the water for clues, while deputies searched the land surrounding the ditch where the skull had been found. Once the skull was in the hands of the medical examiner, he inspected its delicate features and determined that it came from a girl. After he measured her thin nasal aperture, he wrote on the autopsy report that the skull was from a Caucasian. Finally, he examined the skull's suture lines, areas that fuse as humans age. When he assessed the degree of ossification, rigidity caused by the growth of bone, he judged the age at between thirteen and seventeen.

Another dead teenage girl.

Even with such a small piece of a skeleton, there was hope that the dead could be identified. In a lucky twist, the skull included a jaw segment and five teeth, some with fillings and one with a crown. A list of missing girls in the Houston/Galveston area was compiled, and investigators fanned out, beginning the grim task of notifying parents and tracking down dentists, bringing pictures and written descriptions of the skull's dental work to interviews.

At the same time, on the banks of the Taylor Bayou ditch, others congregated, and the search continued, in hopes of finding more of the girl's skeleton. That the ditch was a popular place to dump garbage made the task tedious. A substantial complication was that floods had come and gone during the previous year's back-to-back hurricanes, leaving behind a thick layer of silt. Heavy equipment and dogs were brought in, and mechanical sieves were employed to sift through the sludge. Slowly, more teeth were recovered and sent off to assist in identification. Then a handful of bones were found. Some turned out to be from animals, but a singular delicate left-arm bone was spied in the woods. Not long after, a human sacrum, the large triangular bone at the base of the spine, the one that forms the back of the pelvic cavity, was found under a pile of dead leaves.

On the surface, it all appeared to fit. The medical examiner pegged the sacrum, too, as being from a young female. Yet did all the bones come from the same girl? Although they had no way to conclusively tie the bits of recovered skeleton to the skull, the coroner tentatively linked the findings based on their proximity.

While the search of the recovery site continued, investigators compared dental records. Finally, nine days after the skull's discovery, its owner had a name: Rhonda "Renee" Johnson. The young, blond teenager with the flirty personality was dead. The day her skull was found would become Johnson's official death date on state records, but it was obvious to all who saw her sun-and-water-bleached bones that the teenager had died months earlier, probably not long after her disappearance.

Johnson's identification, of course, raised the question: Where was Sharon Shaw? The obvious answer was that there was a strong possibility that she'd met a similar fate.

The quest continued, this time searching the ditch and surrounding area not only for additional pieces of Johnson's skeleton but also for any signs of Sharon Shaw. "We were out there all day, day in and day out for what seemed like forever," said an officer who helped look for the bodies. "We had sieves, and we went through the mud looking for bones, anything we could find. We found some pieces of jewelry, things a young girl would wear. We fanned out, walking the bayou, poking into the high grass, watching out for nests of snakes."

Eventually, the hunt was abandoned. While it was presumed that Sharon Shaw was dead, blaming the hurricanes that flooded the Gulf Coast the previous September and the animals that roamed the area, including coyotes, authorities reasoned that the second teenager's bones were most likely scattered and would never be found.

That wasn't what fate intended, however, for on February 17, six weeks after the discovery of Johnson's skull, at just after 5 P.M., a twenty-year-old man walked the banks of the bayou. Why? Decades later that would be unclear. Perhaps he'd heard about the search and wanted to help. Or maybe he was simply a local taking a stroll along the bayou just as dusk fell. As he made his way along the bank, he noticed something hidden in high grass. Bending down to investigate, he identified the curious objects as a pile of human bones. The man marked the spot, then ran quickly up the banks. He drove to a chemical plant, one of the many under construction on the nearby coastline, and rushed in and asked to use a telephone.

Sharon Shaw's remains lay a mere half a mile from where Johnson's skull had been found.

Recovered along with nearly a full skeleton was a skull, like the first, detached from the body, but not necessarily by a killer. Instead, it was thought that both skulls might have become dislodged through decomposition. Five days later, the newly discovered jawbone and yet another set of dental records led a medical examiner to officially rule what everyone involved in the case already assumed—the pile of bones found on the edge of the Taylor Bayou ditch belonged to Sharon Shaw.

One coincidence—or was it—caught investigators' attention. The previous September, just a month after Shaw and Johnson vanished, a decomposing, headless, handless, footless torso wearing a shirt from one of Galveston's two surf shops, Jericho's, had been found in that same area along Taylor Bayou's shores. At the time, the torso was misidentified as belonging to a missing teenage boy, but years later he reappeared alive and well, explaining that he'd changed his name and served in the armed services.

In hindsight, pondering the discovery of the two girls' remains and the lack of Johnson's full skeleton, many wondered if that unidentified torso could have been hers. Yet based on the structure of the pelvis—one of the two bones along with the skull used to determine sex—the assistant medical examiner who conducted the autopsy of the torso in the fall of 1971 pegged the body not as female but that of a teenage boy, sandy-haired and standing about five-foot-seven.

Over the decades, many would come to wonder if the assistant medical examiner was wrong and that the Jericho Surf Shop T-shirt torso was Renee Johnson's body, found months before her skull and her friend Sharon Shaw's skeleton. That led to theories about why Johnson's body might have been beheaded, and why its hands and feet were removed. Did that shed any light on the murders?

To unravel the mystery, decades later the Harris County Medical Examiner's Office would attempt to locate the torso's remains to run DNA, to determine sex and answer the questions surrounding the unidentified body. In the end, the ME's office would issue a statement saying that no remains were found from which to obtain DNA. In the four decades since the torso's discovery, everything had been lost.

The identity of the Jericho Surf Shop torso remained like so much else about the cases, an unanswered question.

In the weeks following the discovery of Shaw's and Johnson's bones, investigators considered their deaths, comparing the evidence to the murders of the other dead teenage girls, especially the two Galveston girls whose bodies were found just two months earlier, Debbie Ackerman and Maria Johnson; Sharon and Renee, too, were best friends who'd disappeared together, apparently been murdered together, and their bodies dumped together into a water-filled ditch, where the killer could count on the water and wildlife to consume their flesh and destroy physical evidence. Keys were found on the site, but police failed to determine who they belonged to. And on a later search, some clothing discovered in among the trees matched the description of what the Shaw and Johnson girls wore on the day they disappeared. The searchers also collected thick black string they theorized might have been used to tie Shaw and Johnson, reminiscent of the bindings found on not only Ackerman and Johnson but Brenda Jones, whose body had been found months earlier floating near the Pelican Island Bridge.

So little remained to glean information from, the medical examiner ruled Johnson's and Shaw's causes of death as undetermined. On the cover of both girls' autopsies, he wrote: "There was no evidence of trauma. However, in view of the known circumstances of this case, it is our opinion that the manner of death was homicidal."

That February, Glenda Willis was at home in League City for a few days when police knocked on her front door. They told her that Sharon's and Renee's remains had been discovered, and they wanted her to identify the jewelry found near the scene. "I was the last one to see them alive, so they wanted me to verify that I remembered what they'd found," she said. On the trip to the police station, she felt noncommittal about even participating. "I didn't believe it was them. I told the police that they were wasting their time. I kept telling them that the girls weren't dead; they were in California."

At the Webster police station, however, she was shown photos of the skeletons and jewelry found nearby, including ankle bracelets. One piece she knew instantly, a thick, rustic-looking surfer's cross on a chain. "That's Renee's," she confirmed. Although she'd been told of their fate, Willis remained unable to comprehend what she'd just learned, so much so that she asked, "Where are the girls?"

"Your friends are dead," the officer said, his voice firm yet quiet. "Like I said, this was found near their skeletons."

"Even then, I didn't believe it," Glenda would admit years later. "It was a long time before I could accept that Sharon and Renee weren't ever coming back. From that point on, my parents went into serious protection mode and shipped me off."

Her friends' deaths had left Willis traumatized. She suffered nightmares and thought back often to that summer. "I had dreams where we were in my car, and Sharon and Renee wanted to hitchhike, and I'd tell them no," she recalled. "I'd tell them no, but they'd go anyway. Then I'd wake up, and they'd be dead."

The next painful event would leave Glenda Willis with still more to regret. "I wish I'd known about Mike Self," she said, accompanied by a sad shake of the head. "I would have told them that he didn't do it. He didn't murder Sharon and Renee."

# Chapter 3

## A Case of Russian Roulette
## The Prosecution of Michael Lloyd Self

### Webster, Texas

One of Michael Lloyd Self's mug shots. *(Courtesy of the Harris County Sheriff's Office)*

"If you put what happened to Mike Self in the context of the law and what we do today, you're never going to be able to reconcile it," said Dewey Meadows, the former prosecutor turned defense attorney who in 1972 was assigned by a judge to represent Michael Lloyd Self against charges that he'd murdered Sharon Shaw and Renee Johnson. We were in a windowed conference room inside the modern Houston high-rise where Meadows's firm was located, a building that didn't exist at the time the drama we gathered to discuss unfolded. "Back then, things were different. We defense attorneys used to carry guns to the courthouse, then sit in the coffee room, talk about the judges, and show the guns off, sometimes trading them. Things were wilder then, not so controlled. And the police got away with more."

In 1972, when Renee Johnson's and Sharon Shaw's bodies
were found, Michael Lloyd Self worked at a gas station on
Nassau Bay Road in Webster, close to the Johnson Space
Center, then in full throttle with the burgeoning space program. A slender man with soft dark hair and a longish,
slightly crooked jaw, Self had grown up in the area. Glenda
Willis had crossed paths with him over the years. "My
family knew his family," she said. "It was such a small town
back then, everyone knew everyone around here. We always
referred to him as Slow Mike. We joked about it. There was
something not quite right with Mike Self."

Adopted as a young child, Self lost his father when he
was only ten. His mother, a second-grade schoolteacher,
became a single parent, and friends described Self as a shy
momma's boy. He never did well in school, frequently on
the verge of failing, and a doctor who examined him in
fourth grade pegged the cause on what he called "minimal
brain injury." From a young age, Mike Self talked haltingly
and sometimes appeared to have difficulty comprehending.
Family friends and his mother would say he was "vulnerable" and "easily led." They used words like *passive, nonag-
gressive*, and *insecure.*

Out of high school, Self signed on at the gas station
back in the days when full-service attendants filled tanks
and checked oil. But his true love was volunteering at Webster's fire department, housed next door to the police station. Those who knew him described Self as something of a
law-enforcement hanger-on, making friends with the police
chief and frequenting the station. Mike Self liked to banter
about cases in the news although there weren't a lot of serious ones in the small town, at least not until Sharon Shaw
and Renee Johnson turned up dead. At that point, what Self
wanted to talk about were the two girls' murders.

In those first few months after Shaw's and Johnson's remains were found, there wasn't a lot to discuss. Like the
investigations into the murders of the other five girls who'd
perished in the area in the previous year, 1971—the dentist's

daughter, Colette Wilson; the schoolgirl whose body was found floating near the Pelican Island Bridge, Brenda Jones; the grocery-store bookkeeper, Gloria Gonzales; and the two best friends whose bodies were found near the Turner Bayou Bridge, Debbie Ackerman and Maria Johnson—the inquiry into Shaw's and Johnson's deaths quickly stalled. After the discovery of their bones, months went by without a solid lead. Until attention turned to Mike Self.

Glenda Willis would be perplexed at the idea that Self would have even been considered: "Mike wasn't a part of that group. He didn't even know the girls. And he just wasn't the kind of guy who would have hurt anyone." Those are the things she'd later wish she'd been able to tell the police, but that opportunity wasn't there. "My mom told the police that I was away at school. She never told me they wanted to talk to me. I didn't find out until later."

How did the case against Self come together?

Decades later, the story those involved told was that Renee Johnson's grandfather, the Webster City councilman, pulled strings. The loss of his granddaughter was understandably devastating to the entire family, and Roy Johnson took it particularly hard. Infuriated that the murders remained unsolved, the politician and his political allies jettisoned much of the city's police force, including the chief.

At the time, Donald Ray Morris was a Texas Department of Public Safety trooper, a traffic officer assigned to the Webster area. On May 20, Morris hired on as Webster P.D.'s new chief. He brought with him his DPS partner, Tommy Lee Deal, as assistant chief. Their prime duties, of course, included solving—in all hopes quickly—the double murder case, thereby bringing Renee's family justice.

How did Mike Self become a target? Days after Morris took the job, the gas-station attendant attracted the new chief's attention.

In the beginning, Morris's interest in Self revolved around a completely different matter: whether Self had stolen gas from the fire chief's station wagon. It would later seem that brief investigation set the tone for their future encounters. "I leaned on Mike real hard about it," Morris later testified, describing the first time he interrogated Self. "He respected me as far as what I could do to him."

"Was Mike Self afraid of you?" a lawyer asked.

"That's a fair statement. Yes," he responded. At other times, Morris said much the same in even stronger terms, admitting that Mike Self was "scared to death of me."

When it came to the question of where the bad blood originated, some said that Morris resented Self because he was a friend of the former police chief, whom Morris made it clear he couldn't abide. Weeks before he was even questioned about the two murders, Self, who'd had psychiatric treatment after he'd been accused of being a Peeping Tom, told a Webster police officer that Morris had "threatened to get him."

It was around daybreak less than a month after Morris took over as Webster's police chief, when Tommy Deal and another officer were dispatched to the Texaco station where Self worked to talk to him about the girls' murders. Finishing up after working the night shift, Self agreed to report to the police station when he punched out. By seven thirty, he was in an interrogation room where Deal read Self his Miranda rights. Half an hour later, Don Morris arrived at the police station. At approximately nine thirty, Self allegedly confessed.

What happened would later be recounted in depositions by other officers who ventured in and out of the interrogation room that day. They heard Morris shout at Self, who cowered, handcuffed, in a chair. At one point, witnesses said Morris held a billy club in his hand, hitting his palm with it while he cursed at Self, demanding the confession. Mike Self would later contend that Morris rammed the stick into his abdomen and hit him across the back, telling him that he wouldn't get out of the interrogation room until he admitted killing the girls.

It would later appear that the tactics worked. One officer reported that he saw Mike Self looking to Morris to tell him what to write in the confession. The officer, who initially heard Self adamantly claim his innocence, described Self as terrified.

Looking back, Dewey Meadows believed Self could have been an innocent man. *(Courtesy of Kathryn Casey)*

That same June 1972 morning, Michael Lloyd Self was arrested by Webster police for Shaw's and Johnson's murders. Using a common tactic, a Harris County assistant DA charged the gas station attendant with murdering both girls, but proceeded toward trial only with the murder of Sharon Shaw. The plan was to try him on the Shaw case and hold the Renee Johnson murder in reserve. If they failed to get a conviction on the first murder, prosecutors had the option of trying Self on the second. Soon after, a judge contacted Dewey Meadows and appointed him to represent the defendant.

Once assigned to the case, Meadows, who'd just left a

slot as a Galveston County prosecutor, picked up his office phone and called the Webster Police Department, asking to talk to his client.

"He can't talk to you right now," someone told him. "He's being interrogated."

"Well, I'm his lawyer," Meadows said. "You need to stop talking to him right now. Tell Mr. Self that his lawyer told him not to talk until we've had the opportunity to consult, and I can be there with him."

That, however, didn't happen. Instead, Self was questioned for hours. By the time Meadows met with him, Self had signed a confession, describing in detail how he murdered the two girls. Yet when Meadows talked to Self, he insisted that he wasn't guilty, that he'd never even met the girls.

"I asked him, 'Why'd you sign that?'" said Meadows. "Mike told me he was afraid the police chief was going to kill him."

In that first meeting with his lawyer, Self rolled up his shirt to display a reddened area on his abdomen where he said Chief Morris had jabbed him with a nightstick. "Then Mike described how Morris pulled out a gun," said Meadows. "Mike demonstrated how Morris took bullets out of the chamber but said that he left one in. Morris spun the barrel and put it to Mike's head. What Mike said was that Morris played Russian roulette, pulling the trigger."

"I think that man's crazy," Self told Meadows. "I'm afraid of him."

The following morning, news articles announced Mike Self's arrest, reporting that he'd voluntarily confessed. It seemed an open-and-shut case. Chief Morris crowed to the media about his success, boasting that his hard work could pay off for other police departments in the area. In Morris's assessment, Self looked like a viable suspect in the other girls' killings.

Time passed and, eager to explore the possibility, Galveston County deputies and Texas Rangers dropped in at the jail and interviewed Self about their three unsolved murders of young girls: the girl found floating near the Pelican Island Bridge, Brenda Jones, and the two best friends from Galveston, Debbie Ackerman and Maria Johnson. The deputies and Rangers left, however, without connecting Self to any of the crimes. Harris County detectives showed up as well, asking Self about the murders of the Kroger bookkeeper Gloria Gonzales and the dentist's daughter Colette Wilson, whose remains were both found in the Addicks Reservoir, their turf. Yet they also never pursued any charges.

Despite Morris's contention that he'd caged a heinous double murderer, the case against Mike Self had problems. The first: Two days after his arrest, Self was given a polygraph. He failed. The examiner judged that the confession of the man under arrest was not truthful.

Adding to the muddle it quickly became apparent that much of what Mike Self had written in his confession didn't match the physical evidence.

The contradictions were glaring. In the confession, Self wrote that he threw the girls' bodies into not Taylor Bayou or the ditch where they were found but nearby Taylor Lake. Another inconsistency was that he said he picked up one girl at her house. That wasn't possible since it supposedly occurred hours after her parents were home and had reported her missing.

One of the most obvious examples of the discrepancies between the confession and the physical evidence, however, involved his description of how he murdered the girls. Self wrote that he beat the girls on the head with a Coke bottle, knocking them out. The problem was that neither Shaw's nor Johnson's skulls were fractured, which seemed unlikely if he'd pummeled them hard enough to render them unconscious. Finally, Self claimed he removed the girls' clothing from the scene, driving miles away before disposing of it. Yet Renee's and Sharon's clothes were found not far from their bodies.

Such inaccuracies were potential land mines in a trial. In response, Self was again interrogated by Webster police. Before they finished, the agency's prime suspect had signed confession number two. This time Self's account of the murders more closely resembled the case facts.

Meanwhile, Self's defense attorney, Dewey Meadows, felt exasperated. He'd never been notified by police that his client was again being interrogated. "The police questioned Mike even though I said they couldn't. He signed confessions, then told me and his mother that he didn't kill the girls." At their meetings, Meadows noticed how Mike Self appeared unable to defend himself, instead looking to his mother for guidance. The man seemed weak but not necessarily guilty. "But what about the confessions, Mike?" Meadows prodded.

"They told me what to put on the paper and told me to sign it. They said it would make me feel better," Self answered. "They said if I did, I'd be able to see my mother."

"Why did you sign it if you didn't do it?" Meadows asked.

"I was scared," Self answered yet again.

Later, it would be alleged that Mike Self led police to the site where the girls' bodies were found. In pictures snapped that day, Self could be seen gesturing, as if indicating where he'd dumped Renee's and Sharon's bodies in the Taylor Bayou ditch. Did he really know the details, or was someone instructing him to act out the scene for the camera? "I don't know," said Meadows. "But Mike said they told him what to do, and he did it."

There seemed little question that Morris and Deal enjoyed the publicity heaped upon them for being the first to make an arrest in any of the notorious cases. Even before Mike Self's trial began, the chief and his assistant granted interviews to detective magazines. Praise was abundant, as Deal was described as "an outstanding officer" with "a sterling record."

The title of one of the articles read TWO PASSENGERS TO ETERNITY, accompanied by suggestive photos of young girls

on a beach. Another was called: "Sex Slayings of Two Pretty
Teenage Surfers." "Within a few minutes of questioning and
having been shown pictures of the girls, Self allegedly admitted that he knew both girls and had killed both of them,"
the latter article stated. In the depiction of events in the
piece, Mike Self voluntarily waived all of his rights, signed
a confession, and then led the investigators to the scene of
the crimes.

If Self had any luck at all, it came not from Texas but
Washington, D.C. Shortly before his trial, in a case entitled
Furman v. Georgia, the United States Supreme Court ruled
the death penalty unconstitutional due to the "arbitrary and
capricious" manner in which it was applied. It was a ruling
that would stand until 1976, when modifications were made
to the laws. The result: When Mike Self walked into the
courtroom on May 7, 1973, his life didn't hang in the balance, but his freedom did.

The first day of Self's trial, before the jurors were seated,
attention focused on the all-important subject of Mike Self's
confessions. "They were the ballgame," said Meadows.
"Nothing else tied Mike to the murders. Not one piece of
evidence."

A motion brought by Meadows contended that the confessions had been coerced. If successful, both would have
been ruled inadmissible. The case rested on the outcome of
the hearing, and each side argued hard. For the prosecution,
Assistant Police Chief Tommy Deal testified that Self freely
and voluntarily confessed. Meadows countered by putting
Self on the stand, who repeated his account, that he'd signed
the confessions only after being threatened, intimidated,
and terrorized by the Webster police. Before the judge, Self
recounted Chief Morris's alleged game of Russian roulette.
Bolstering his friend's claims, Self's roommate took the
stand and relayed his experiences with Morris, including
that the police chief appeared out to get Self. The judge's decision, however, went against the defense. The confessions
would be admissible at trial.

That week in the courtroom, the prosecutor presented jurors with copies of Mike Self's second confession, pictures of the girls' remains, and photos of the accused at the scene pointing to where the girls' bones had been found. He also put on the stand a witness who said that he thought he once saw Self talking to Renee and Sharon outside a convenience store.

The defense had only one witness, the defendant, who again told his version of how Webster police obtained his confession. On rebuttal, Chief Morris denied that any of it had ever happened, describing Self's confession as Deal had, voluntary. The jury took thirteen hours to deliberate and returned a guilty verdict—the sentence, life in prison.

It was what happened after the trial that would convince many that a nest of crooked cops might have condemned an innocent man to life behind bars.

Months after the trial, Don Morris resigned and returned to DPS to work as a trooper. His friend, Tommy Deal, left Webster a little more than a year later.

Then in September 1975, in the little town of Caddo Mills, northeast of Dallas, word spread that the State National Bank was being robbed. Men carrying guns and paper bags were demanding money out of a teller's drawer. The mayor was called, and he ran to the barber shop, knowing that the proprietor had a rifle. A group of townsfolk, alerted by police-band radios, descended on the bank in time to see two men escaping, one holding the teller, the daughter of the bank president, hostage. The robbers sped off, followed by a posse of twenty-five brave citizens. Outside town, the getaway car slammed to a stop, and the robbers pushed the hostage out the door. That gave the citizens in pursuit the break needed to move in. The robbers jumped from the car and ran, only to find they stared down the sights of a young boy's rifle.

The bank robbers corralled that day were former Webster police officers Tommy Deal and a friend, also a former

DPS officer. The man who was later labeled the ringleader of this band of thieves, which had been active in the area for more than two years, including the time that they were fingering Mike Self, was none other than former Webster Police Chief Donald Ray Morris. An article that ran when they were convicted in 1975 called them the three musketeers. Others described the scene in Caddo Mills on the day of the robbery as a comedy of errors on the part of the two hapless bank robbers.

When Self's appeal came up for review in 1979, Morris and Deal, the two men who'd secured his confession, were serving time in federal prisons. The argument at the appeal hearings, as it had been at the trial, centered on the validity of Mike Self's confession. By then, investigations into the circumstances had yielded valuable new witnesses. Depositions were submitted in which Webster police officers on the scene the morning Self was brought in for questioning recounted how the suspect insisted on his innocence until Morris put the fear of God in him. One officer described Morris as sounding "sadistic" that day. "He scared the daylights out of Mike Self," said another officer.

In the interrogation room, when Self said he was innocent, Morris called him a liar. One man heard the chief say, "Mike, you're not going to leave here until you tell me you killed those girls." What the officer would most remember was how frightened Mike Self appeared.

At the hearing, Morris disputed little of what was said, admitting that he'd come on strong with Self. "I told Mike before he ever confessed that I was going to arrest him for murder, you know, of the girls," Morris said.

Gerald Birnberg, Mike Self's attorney for his appeal, found the history of what had happened to his client abhorrent. "Mike had been basically convicted only on the basis of his confession, and it was bullied," he said. "There was no other evidence linking him to the crimes. Was Mike kind of an odd guy? Yes. He wasn't playing with a full deck. He was the perfect patsy."

Before long, articles appeared in Texas newspapers about the bizarre case of a man whose confession may have been forced by police officers who'd turned out to be bank robbers. When Mike Self explained to a *Houston Chronicle* reporter in 1989 why he'd signed the confessions, he said, "To keep Chief Morris from blowing my brains out . . . He said that if I didn't sign the confession, he'd shoot me and say I tried to escape."

Even after years in prison, Self said he didn't blame the jurors who'd ruled on his fate, insisting that they were just doing their job "based on what they heard."

By 1990, Mike Self had been in prison for seventeen years for a crime that few believed he'd committed. Even the prosecutor assigned to represent the state on the appeal doubted that justice had been served. That August, a U.S. magistrate agreed, ruling that the confessions should have been suppressed at the trial. "Dirty pool abounded in the Self case," he wrote. "Self was illegally arrested without a warrant and no independent evidence . . . was ever developed to establish probable cause." Based on that finding, a U.S. district judge threw out Self's conviction, stating that he should be released, unless the state filed for a retrial. If they chose to prosecute him again, however, the judge further ruled that the state would not have the use of the confessions.

For a while, it appeared that doors would finally open and Mike Self, by then middle-aged, might live outside prison walls. That wasn't destined to happen.

Instead, prosecutors challenged the ruling and continued to fight the appeal.

The final resolution came in 1992. While calling the case disturbing both in claims about the circumstances of how the confessions were obtained and the later convictions of Morris and Deal, the U.S. Fifth Circuit Court of Appeals ruled that the federal district court could not overturn the state court's ruling. The judges concluded that there was sufficient evidence supporting the state court's decision that

Self had been advised of his rights prior to signing the confessions and voluntarily waived his rights. The Fifth Circuit also noted that Mike Self had his opportunity to make his case that the confessions had been coerced at the trial, and the decision of the state court and the jurors had gone against him. That decision ended Mike Self's appeals.

Three years later in 1995, twenty-two years after his conviction, Self became eligible for parole. One day, Dewey Meadows saw his old client at one of the prisons. Meadows approached Self to talk to him. The attorney knew how parole boards worked and that Self had a good shot at being released, if he played ball. "You know, Mike," the attorney said. "You could get out of here. All you have to do is tell the board that you're sorry, that you regret your actions."

"But I didn't do it," Self said in his slow, deliberate speech. "I didn't kill those girls."

Years later, the Texas appeals courts would rule that a confession alone was not enough for conviction; collaborating evidence was required. That decision came too late for Mike Self, who died in 2000 of a heart attack in prison.

Looking back on the case even with the benefit of hindsight, Meadows wasn't sure how he would have represented Self differently. "That he signed those confessions was a big problem. The law then wasn't in our favor," said the attorney. "But then, I never thought the judge would let them in. And I didn't believe a jury would find him guilty when there wasn't any other evidence tying him to the two girls' murders."

"I didn't believe Mike Self was guilty," said Doug O'Brien, a former Harris County prosecutor who for a short time worked on the case. In hindsight, not only the circumstances surrounding the confessions bothered O'Brien but something else; while Self lived locked behind bars, more girls died around I-45 and on Galveston Island. "That was a big clue that we had the wrong man. Mike Self was in prison, and the murders continued."

# Chapter 4

## Lambs to the Slaughter
## The Killing Continues

**1973 through 1978**

In fact throughout the seventies, while Mike Self's fate played out at the hands of Webster police and the court system, girls south of Houston continued to die at the hands of one or more killers. When he talked to his wife, Tom Wilson, the dentist who'd had to identify his own daughter's skeleton, described Colette's innocence and the evil that stalked Texas those years in graphic terms: "It was like sending a lamb to slaughter."

Suzanne Bowers, Kimberly Rae Pitchford, Brooks Bracewell, and Georgia Geer. *(Collage courtesy of Kathryn Casey)*

Michael Lloyd Self was arrested on June 10, 1972. While he sat in jail awaiting trial, on January 3, 1973, a strawberry blond sixteen-year-old with hazel eyes, a sophomore, arrived early at J. Frank Dobie High School in Houston's far southeast reaches for her first day back after the winter break. Kimberly Rae Pitchford enjoyed roller skating at a rink near the house, but not helping her mom clean. She was self-conscious about the new braces on her teeth, and coworkers at a fast-food restaurant where she worked part-time noticed that she covered her mouth to hide them when she smiled.

On that day after school, her learner's permit in hand, Kimberly left the school campus and reported to her first driver's education class. Her father was at work, and Kimberly's mom instructed her to call home when class ended, promising to pick her up.

Later, when police pieced together that day, it would seem that nothing unusual had happened. As she did every day, Kimberly took the bus to school. She attended all of her classes and ate lunch with her best friend. At 3:45, Kim reported to detention, punishment for showing up late to a class. At five she was at the driver's school. At six, wearing a new black coat she'd received as a Christmas gift, she walked out of driver's ed.

Then she vanished.

Although she showed signs of some typical teenage rebellion, Kimberly was a responsible young girl, the kind parents didn't worry too much about. When the phone didn't ring, Elmer and Carol Pitchford called their daughter's friends. When none could tell them where to find Kimberly, the Pitchfords called police. Later that same evening, they filed a missing person report.

The bad news came days later.

The next afternoon, two teenage boys walked by a wooden bridge on County Road 65, a rural lane twenty-two miles from the driving school, and noticed something black billowing against a fence. The following day, curious, they returned to investigate. Parking on the shoulder, they walked toward the object and discovered a black coat. That was odd, but not enough to cause any alarm. It was as they returned to the truck that their attention was drawn to something else, something in a nearby bayou. They cautiously approached. There'd been a recent rainstorm, and whatever it was appeared to be pinned against a bridge in the rushing current.

When they realized what they were looking at, they turned and ran.

The teenagers rushed home to tell one of their fathers, who returned with them to the scene. Once there, he saw what they'd described: a girl's body, facedown, partially underwater. Wondering if it could be some kind of doll, looking for a less horrific explanation, the man retrieved a long branch and poked it. It appeared real. Reluctant to touch anything else, they ran back to the car and drove to a nearby home, where they rang the doorbell and asked to use a phone to call police.

On the scene, police recorded that the dead girl wore a blue-and-red dress, a red bra, and a small gold cross on a chain around her neck. The clothing matched the description on a recent missing person report. By then, however, there was little question. A driver's license application retrieved from the coat pocket bore the name Kimberly Pitchford. At nine that evening, the police arrived at the Pitchfords' house. "They brought us the bad news," said Kimberly's father, Elmer.

The medical examiner assessed the cause of death as ligature strangulation.

Twenty months later, on September 6, 1974, law enforcement in the Houston and Galveston area again searched for two missing girls. That day the youngsters were from yet another I-45 town, Dickinson. Brooks Bracewell, twelve, and Georgia Geer, fourteen, didn't show up at McAdams Junior High School. Georgia's mother called to report the girls missing, telling police that she thought they'd skipped school. For a while, police assumed that this time they might just be dealing with runaways, especially after reports came in that the girls were seen at a motel on County Road 517 near Alvin playing football with a group of unidentified men. Afterward, another witness claimed to have noticed the girls hitchhiking, and yet others said the girls had stopped at a convenience store.

Many couldn't understand what was happening along the Gulf Coast. Some wondered about theories that one man, one lone man, could be responsible for so much death. Was that possible? The following year, the entire country talked about a new phenomenon. The term *serial killer* entered vocabularies and took over headlines with the arrest of a handsome former law student named Ted Bundy. It was in 1975 that he was incarcerated for the first time. Held in Utah on a charge of aggravated kidnapping and attempted criminal assault, Bundy was the prime suspect in a long list of unsolved homicides spanning the nation. In the years that followed, he escaped twice, only to finally be arrested in Florida in 1978.

"When we heard about Ted Bundy, we wondered if that was what was going on down here," said a woman who remembered the fear that permeated the southern Houston and Galveston areas during her teenage years. "We thought it must have been someone like Ted Bundy responsible. But we thought that since no one had died since the Pitchford girl, maybe it was over."

It wasn't.

On April 18, 1976, yet another devastating discovery turned into banner headlines. On that day, a roughneck working a Phillips Oil site stumbled upon the skulls of Brooks Bracewell and Georgia Geer. This time, prisoners were brought out to help with the search of marshes in Alvin, not far from where Colette Wilson had been abducted nearly five years earlier. Because of floods in the area the previous year, the search proved difficult and more than four thousand man-hours went into collecting bits of clothing, teeth, and pieces of jaw. At that time, none of the girls' other bones were found. Again, dental records identified the dead. Both Bracewell and Geer suffered blows to the head.

Still, Bracewell and Geer had been missing for nearly two years. During that time, no other girls disappeared. The towns along I-45 and the island held on to hope. Assuming the girls were murdered by the same killer, perhaps the man had moved on. Perhaps he'd died. Perhaps he was in prison or jail for another crime. Perhaps, but no one knew, not for sure.

Perhaps he was just lying low, letting the spotlight wander. Perhaps he waited and watched, hoping for another opportunity.

At 10:40 A.M. on May 21, 1977, twelve-year-old Suzanne "Suzie" Bowers left her grandparents' home two and a half blocks off the Galveston seawall. Her plan: to walk a mile home, change into a bathing suit, and grab her bike, then ride three miles east on Seawall Boulevard to meet friends at a popular hangout, Stewart Beach. It had rained earlier in the day, but the sun came out, transforming that Saturday into a good day to work on her tan. Suzie loved the water, worshipped it, swam, surfed, and skied. She'd asked her grandfather for a ride home, but he later said that he thought the

Something of a tomboy, Suzie Bowers posed for this photo in sixth grade.

exercise would be good for his granddaughter and sent her on her way. There didn't seem any reason to worry; Suzie had traversed that same route often, and there'd never been a problem.

The second of four children, Suzie lived with her father and stepmother but stayed many weekends with her siblings at her grandparents' house on Avenue S1/2. The soon-to-be-eighth-grader had shoulder-length brown hair, green eyes, and, at just under five feet tall, weighed approximately ninety pounds. A spirited tomboy, Suzie favored baggy clothes to cover up the fact that she was developing into a teenager.

That afternoon on Stewart Beach, her schoolmate and good friend Sara Groves watched for Suzie. When Suzie didn't show up as she'd promised, Sara wasn't initially worried. Then when she got home later that afternoon, Suzie's grandmother called and said that Suzie had never arrived at her parents' house that morning. They couldn't find her. At first, Sara still wasn't too troubled. "But Suzie's grandmother kept calling. When she was still calling at six that evening, I figured something was really wrong," said Groves.

That same evening, Suzie Bowers's parents reported her missing to Galveston police.

Even with so much recent evidence suggesting that reports of missing teenagers could end very badly, officers at first wrote off the parents' fears, saying that Suzie had probably run away. Groves remembered telling them that Suzie wouldn't do that, that she wasn't that kind of a girl. And Bowers's stepmother told the *Galveston County Daily News* she didn't believe it either: "All the money Suzanne had saved for a choir trip is still here, as are all her clothes. Her friends are all accounted for. She didn't run away . . . We just don't know what happened. It's as if she was swallowed up in thin air. We have no clues. She's just gone."

Suzie Bowers would be the last of the 1970s killings of teenage girls tied to the I-45 mysteries. Nearly two years later, in March 1979, two boys on dirt bikes rode through a field on the mainland, not far from where Colette Wilson, the dentist's daughter, disappeared, and found Suzie's skeleton. What first caught their attention was a training bra and small bits of red, blue, green, and brown cloth.

In hindsight, four of the girls' killings would have ties to Alvin. Colette Wilson lived in the small town and was abducted not far from her home. Suzie Bowers's skeleton and Brooks Bracewell's and Georgia Geer's skulls were discovered in the Alvin area. Another tie was that Bowers's skull, like Wilson's, Bracewell's, and Geer's, showed evidence of trauma.

"A friend called me and said Suzie had been found," said Groves. "I asked if she was okay, and the girl said, 'What do you think?' I knew then she was dead."

"We've been praying for an answer, but we didn't want to hear this," Suzie's grandmother told reporters. "The only relief we can try to feel is that Suzanne is not suffering."

Sara Groves kept in touch with the grandmother over the years, visiting and talking on the phone. When Suzie's grandfather died, his wife told Groves that the last word on his lips was his dead granddaughter's name.

Later, when police circulated through the country taking alleged serial killer Henry Lee Lucas on trips asking about cases, he'd say he thought he remembered murdering little Suzanne Bowers. Yet many would eventually discount his story, as they did those of so many murders he claimed to have committed. Sara Groves would spend her life remembering what happened to her friend, urging police not to close the case. Her impression was that no one was investigating. "Once Lucas confessed, they wrote it off," she said. "It was like it was over, but it wasn't, because the dates, what Lucas said, didn't match what happened."

While Lucas was in prison, Groves wrote him, asking if he murdered her friend. The killer wrote back denying that he had, saying that he'd only claimed he'd murdered Bowers and others to get extra favors from authorities, perks like access to a television and cigarettes. "You ask me if I was guilty of killing your friend, the answer is no. I did give a false confession to the murder, but I was not guilty of it. I was given all the evidence about it," he wrote. ". . . I know that was wrong now, because I hurt a lot of people by making the false statements. I hope you will forgive me."

Over the decades, Groves mounted her own inquiry, including calling the man who leased the property where her twelve-year-old friend's bones were found. He said he'd seen two vehicles in the field about the time Suzie disappeared. One was a truck, but the other—like the last vehicle Debbie Ackerman and Maria Johnson were seen entering in front of the Galveston ice-cream shop on the November 1971 morning they disappeared—was a van.

Often, Sara called Suzie's grandmother and compared notes. "Grandma Bowers never stopped trying to figure out who murdered Suzie," said Groves. "Until the day she died, Suzie's grandmother left the room Suzie slept in the way it was on the day she disappeared. Her clothes and stamp collection were still there. Suzie's grandmother never got rid of anything."

Death was all around Groves during those years. In 1971, when Debbie Ackerman was murdered and her body thrown in Turner Bayou, Groves lived only a block away from the girl's family. Then Groves's good friend Suzie Bowers died, perhaps slain by the same man. Hearing a Bee Gees or Barry Manilow song brought memories flooding back. "Suzie and I were in choir, but neither one of us could carry a tune. We just murdered their songs. We called the local radio station all the time and requested 'Jive Talking,' then sang along at the top of our lungs. Suzie was so much fun."

When asked how her friend's death impacted her life, Groves didn't hesitate: "I never got over it. I've always watched my back."

The seventies ended, and so did the killings. Yet more discoveries remained. In April 1981, the remainder of Brooks Bracewell's and Georgia Geer's skeletons were discovered in a Brazoria County oil field south of Alvin.

In the end, the list of the eleven teenage girls murdered between 1971 and 1977 along south I-45 included: the dentist's daughter, Colette Wilson; the girl found floating near the Pelican Island Bridge, Brenda Jones; Sharon Shaw and Rhonda "Renee" Johnson, who were at first thought to have run away to California; the Kroger bookkeeper, Gloria Ann Gonzales; Galveston best friends Debbie Ackerman and

Maria Johnson; Kimberly Rae Pitchford, who disappeared after driver's ed; Brooks Bracewell and Georgia Geer, thought to have skipped school; and Suzie Bowers, who disappeared while walking home to grab a swimsuit for a day on the beach.

Four of the teenagers died while Michael Lloyd Self languished behind bars.

After Self's trial, no defendant ever again entered a courtroom to be tried for any of the killings. Based on Self's conviction, Sharon Shaw's and Renee Johnson's cases were considered solved and closed. The rest of the girls eventually became the first rows of black-and-white photos in newspapers under the heading MYSTERIES ALONG I-45.

The families grieved, and the girls were never forgotten.

Yet life did go on. Four decades after her daughter's murder, I interviewed Claire Wilson for this book.

From the beginning of our talk, I was struck by how many reasons Claire had to allow life to slip through her fingers. Her second child, Colette, was the first of the eleven 1970s/I-45 murder victims. Then just four years after Colette's murder, Claire's husband died of a heart attack attributed to his overwhelming grief. Sadly, the following year, Claire lost another child, this time in a car accident. So much tragedy. Yet that wasn't what Claire wanted to discuss.

While acknowledging the anguish brought on by Colette's horrific killing, Claire refused to dwell on what could have been, instead preferring to focus on the good in her life. In her eighties, she had ten surviving children, thirty grandchildren, and five great-grandchildren. "I am so blessed," she said. "I have a wonderful family. All the kids turned out to be good people. Did Colette's murder change us? It did. But we never allowed her death to take over our lives. We couldn't."

"If you could find him and talk to him, the man who did this, what would you say to him?" I asked. My assumption was that she would want to retaliate, if not by striking out physically perhaps with her words, attempting to punish the source of her loss and suffering.

"I'm not sure. I've never thought about that. I believe in God, and a long time ago, I put this in his hands," she said. For a moment, Claire Wilson was quiet. When she spoke again, she said, "I guess I'd just ask why. Why did he do this? Why Colette? But I guess I know the answer. Because on that day, she was the one he saw on the side of the road."

A few nights later, I sat in a sushi restaurant with a retired FBI profiler who'd worked many of the cases I was investigating. I told him about my research into the murders of the eleven girls in the 1970s.

"One thing to look at is the timeline," he said. "When the killings start and when they stop, and pair that up with the suspects. An important clue is who was available to do the killing."

Decades after the eleven girls' murders, a lone cop on Galveston Island would pull together all the records he could find and assess just that. He'd construct a chronology of the events as they unfolded. His conclusion? That speculation at the time of the killings was most likely right and all eleven murders—including the two Mike Self died in prison for—could have been committed by one killer. The suspect he'd focus on was one who moved into a house on the island in 1970, a year before the first killing, and disappeared in 1978, a year after the final victim, Suzanne Bowers, died.

# Chapter 5

## The Cop and the Killer
## Fred Paige's Quest

### Galveston, Texas

Alfred "Fred" Paige, believes he knows the name of the Galveston killer. *(Courtesy of Kathryn Casey)*

Between 1970 and 2000, the various versions of the I-45 Mysteries charts would grow to include the photographs of approximately twenty young women. But it all began in the 1970s on Galveston Island with the murder of the first eleven girls. On the day I met with Alfred "Fred" Paige, it was clear that he was haunted by a belief, the certainty that he knew the face, the name, the man behind the brutal slayings of the island's teenage girls. His frustration was that nothing had been done about it.

In his natty Galveston P.D. uniform, Paige had just finished his shift, patrolling the island's streets. With a flat top of graying brown hair, a wide smile, and an inquisitive gaze, in November 2005 the veteran cop was a Galveston P.D. detective working property crimes. Eight years later, he was back in a squad car. Paige didn't say if his belief that he'd unmasked the serial killer had affected his career, but he made it clear that his was a lonely battle. "No one ever connected the dots," he said. "When I started looking at this, it was fascinating how it all laid out. To me, it all seems pretty clear."

The fiftysomething Paige didn't sign on at Galveston P.D. until two decades after the island's serial cases turned cold. The freewheeling seventies were a distant memory when a retired supervisor of Paige's forwarded a letter to him from an elderly woman, an inquiry into the status of the investigations into the two Galveston best friends, Debbie Ackerman and Maria Johnson. The woman had been a friend of Dee Ackerman, Debbie's deceased mother, and she wanted to talk to someone in authority about the killings. Days later, the woman called Paige directly, inviting him to the nursing home where she lived.

In her room, the old woman pulled out a scrapbook of yellowed newspaper articles, the original clips from the *Galveston County Daily News* and *Houston Chronicle* documenting the disappearances of Ackerman and Johnson and the accounts of finding their bodies near the Turner Bayou Bridge. "Please, look into this," the old woman begged Paige, as if she'd carried the horror of what had happened to her friend's daughter with her and never forgotten. "Please try to find out who killed these girls."

That day began a journey, one that took Paige back to a different time, when eleven young girls, six of them in pairs, vanished and died. Over the coming year, the veteran cop put a fresh set of eyes on the old cases and quickly focused on a shadowy figure he believed was the man who once roamed the palm-lined streets, murdering Galveston's daughters.

Carla Costello in her Texas City office, the files on the unsolved cases behind her. *(Courtesy of Kathryn Casey)*

In November of 2005, Paige had never even heard his main suspect's name. That happened a few months later, one afternoon the following January when the fast-talking cop drove across the causeway to the mainland and then north on I-45. Before long, he'd pulled into the parking lot of the Texas City Police Department. Paige was there to see Senior Officer Carla Costello.

The appointment with Costello was a logical place for Paige to start an investigation into Debbie Ackerman's and Maria Johnson's deaths. In the early nineties, twenty years after the first of the Galveston-area girls died, Costello was the one who entered all the 1970s victims into VICAP, the FBI's Violent Criminal Apprehension Program, a national database used to document and compare murders and sexual assaults, in hopes of identifying serial cases. "I'm a big believer in VICAP," said Costello. "We worked hard at that point to get everything organized."

During that process, Costello collected many of the records on the cases, and over the years she became the go-to person for anyone in law enforcement needing information, hence Paige's pilgrimage to her office.

With soft features and tired eyes, Costello had seen much misery over her more than three decades in law enforcement, including the pain of the parents of the murdered girls. Some continued to check on their daughters' cases, calling her or dropping in to ask if anything was being done decades after the killings.

Because of Costello's interest, it was a natural outcome that she became the record keeper, the one who organized the bulk of the cases into white, three-ring binders she kept on the lower shelf of a bookcase beside her desk. In a translucent white plastic file box nestled into a corner, she'd amassed everything from the case that most haunted her: the 1971 double murder of Debbie Ackerman and Maria Johnson, who'd been found in a Texas City oil field, their bodies partially submerged in Turner Bayou. One reason Costello never forgot the girls was that up until her death, Debbie's mom made annual visits to Costello's office. "I'd always hoped that someday I'd be able to tell Mrs. Ackerman that we'd arrested Debbie's killer," said Costello with a slight shrug. "One of the hardest days was the day I heard that Mrs. Ackerman died. I knew then that we'd never be able to give her justice."

That January day in 2006 when Paige walked into Carla Costello's office, he explained his encounter with the old woman in the nursing home and his promise to do what he could to find Debbie and Maria's killer. "Did you ever have anyone you liked for this?" Paige asked Costello. "Anyone you thought might have been behind the killings?"

There was one man, she said. Years earlier the guy, a convicted killer already incarcerated in a Texas prison, had written two letters: one to the Harris County District Attorney and the other to his counterpart in Galveston County. "He confessed," Costello explained to Paige. "But when we tried to follow up, he refused to talk to us. I've always wondered if maybe he's telling the truth, if he could be the killer."

With that, Costello pulled out a copy of one of the man's letters, written from prison and dated January 4, 1998, at a time when the inmate was five years into his seventy-year sentence. The correspondence, addressed to the Galveston district attorney, was disjointed and crudely crafted. In it, the convict contended that he'd murdered all eleven of the girls who'd died along I-45 in the 1970s: seven in Galveston County and four in southern Harris County. Why would he commit such monstrous crimes? In the letter, the man claimed that he'd been brainwashed into committing murder.

Although brief, the inmate's note offered details about two of the crimes: the homicides of the same girls the old woman mentioned to Paige, Debbie Ackerman and Maria Johnson.

In his letter, the self-described serial killer said he'd shot Ackerman and Johnson with a .357 Magnum pistol: Debbie in the neck or the head, and Maria in the neck or back. At the time, he said he stood above the teenagers on a small bridge. Their hands and feet were bound in front with a white nylon string. Knowledge of these facts, the man maintained, proved he was the killer. Yet he added that if he was ever brought into a courtroom he would plead not guilty, laying the blame on the "brainwashing program." In a postscript, the prison inmate said that the "powers that be" knew he had murdered the eleven girls and had done nothing.

The letter was signed: *Yours truly, Edward Harold Bell*

"Does this match the evidence?" Paige asked Costello.

"Pretty close," Costello said.

"Why hasn't this guy been charged with these murders?"

"This is all we have, and he could have gotten it out of the newspapers. We can't prove he did it." Costello said, "He won't talk to us. He could be the killer, or he could just be crazy."

That afternoon, Costello made copies of the letter, the autopsies, investigation records, and other records from the murders for Paige, who thanked her and left.

One of the things Costello told Paige, one of the reasons she entertained the possibility that Bell told the truth in his confessions, was that Bell lived on Galveston Island at the time of the serial killings. "He was part owner in a dive shop on S-Road," she said. That bit of info came to her through the Harris County DAs, who'd briefly investigated after they received their letter from Bell.

Ed Bell was always a good businessman.
*(Mug shot courtesy of the Harris County Sheriff's Office)*

As Costello had said, the Galveston DA, too, had tried to reopen the cases, asking to talk to Bell in prison. He'd refused the requests, and both agencies' investigations were tabled for lack of evidence. The laws had changed. Michael Lloyd Self had died in prison, perhaps an innocent man after being convicted on only a questionable confession. In the decades that followed, court decisions decreed that without corroborating evidence, a confession wasn't sufficient evidence of guilt. What if the confessor was delusional? It wasn't unusual for disturbed people to falsely claim they committed sensational crimes. Some did it simply to attract attention.

Despite such doubts, Paige was intrigued. Eleven murdered girls. Ed Bell claimed to have killed eleven girls. Was the man telling the truth?

Later in his office, Paige reviewed the copies of the old files. The only murders Bell discussed in any detail in his letter to the Galveston County DA were those of Debbie Ackerman and Maria Johnson, so Paige began there, listing the specifics. In his letter, Bell had written that:

1. Ackerman and Johnson were shot with a .357 Magnum pistol
2. Ackerman in the neck, possibly the head
3. Johnson was shot with the gun pointed downward, possibly in the back of the head or the neck from above. "I was standing on a bridge at the time," Bell claimed.
4. Their hands were tied in front; their feet were also bound.

From the evidence records in the case files, Paige pulled together the corresponding details. According to the autopsies, the bullets used to kill Ackerman and Johnson were .38 caliber. That was a type Paige knew could have been fired from a .357 Magnum pistol. There were similarities in the way the girls were dressed when found. Both were naked from the waist down but wore their bras, shirts, and jewelry.

The Turner Bayou Bridge, where Ackerman's and Johnson's bodies were found. *(Courtesy of Fred Paige)*

As part of his investigation, Paige drove to the mainland, to the location where the teenagers' bodies had been found, through a gate and onto the oil field, then down a gravel and dirt road, one that led to Turner Bayou. Once there, he stood on the narrow wooden bridge, imagining what had transpired decades earlier. Paige took a picture, and reviewed what he'd read in the police reports.

In January 1971, the first body found in Turner Bayou was that of Maria Johnson. It was positioned, as Bell had said, close to the bridge. Also consistent with Bell's description, Maria had a bullet hole on the right side and center of her neck, as well as other gunshot wounds around the head. At the scene, Paige stood on the bridge and visualized how it might have taken place as Bell described in his letter, realizing that the killer could have stood above Johnson— perhaps on the rugged wooden slats of the bridge—when he fired his weapon. Also fitting Bell's letter, Johnson's ankles and hands were bound. Could the fishing cord used to tie Johnson's hands have been what Bell called a "white nylon string?"

Paige then considered Debbie Ackerman's killing. When found, her body lay in the water a hundred yards from her friend's remains. Matching Bell's assertions in the letter, Debbie's ankles and hands were tied, but this time by black cords resembling long shoelaces. Like her friend, she had been shot. One bullet tracked through Ackerman's back and out her chest, but the second was—again as Bell had written—in the neck or head region, more exactly on the left side below the chin.

After comparing the evidence to Bell's written description and assessing that he had a match, Paige called the Galveston DA's Office, and one of the prosecutors answered. "There's a letter," Paige said. "Dude, there's a letter!"

The prosecutor hadn't been at the District Attorney's Office when Bell's letter arrived and knew nothing about it. "I told him that I was all over it, and I'd let him know when I came up for air," Paige said. "So then I set about trying to figure out more about who this guy was and could he possibly be the guy who murdered all those girls."

As Paige investigated, a confusing picture emerged of Ed Bell, that of a young man who initially had a bright future but succumbed to dark urges that eventually dominated and destroyed his life.

Ed Bell was born in Houston. His father, Carl Clayton Bell, was an East Texas oil-field worker and his mother a housewife. He had one brother, Larry, who was two years older. They moved often, following Clayton's latest job, but by junior high had settled on a ranch in New Ulm, a small town a little more than an hour west of Houston, outside of Columbus. Young Ed Bell was an amiable young man who focused on his studies and concentrated on bettering his life. "It was a typical American family," said a relative. "The mom was a sweet woman, maybe a little dingy. The Bells had a house in the country, and as boys, Larry and Ed raised livestock."

During Ed Bell's impressionable childhood years, his family witnessed a shocking act of violence, when Bell's cousin reportedly killed his own father. Ed Bell would later contend that their uncle was torturing his wife at the time, forcing water down her throat, and his son shot him to make him stop.

Despite the chaos of his childhood, those who knew the young Ed Bell judged him like pretty much any small-town kid. To family and friends, he was simply "Butch." One of his former classmates at Columbus High School remembered Butch Bell as a close friend, a happy sort of boy. "He was an Eagle Scout, a really good kid. He had a lot of friends. And he was smart."

Other friends agreed, describing Bell as intelligent and gregarious. "The girls seemed to like him. He dated one girl after another in our class," remembered an old school friend. "Butch was just a really nice guy. I never saw him be violent, not in any way."

After his 1957 high-school graduation, Bell enrolled
in one of the Lone Star State's premier universities, Texas
A&M, the home of the Aggies, where he played his trom-
bone in the marching band during football games. To pay
his way, he worked in the dining hall and sold Christmas
cards and fruit in the dorms. "He was a hard worker and a
real entrepreneur," said a friend. "He was one of the most
liked guys in the Aggie band."

At A&M, Ed Bell majored in physical education and mi-
nored in biology. His grades in high school had been exem-
plary, but in college turned average. While there, he learned
to scuba dive, and over one summer he worked as the aquatic
director at a boys' camp. It was in San Marcos that Bell met
his future wife, Bonnie, who attended Baylor University in
Waco. Those who knew her described Ed's young wife as a
pretty woman who was into health food. They dated, marry-
ing while he was still at A&M.

Were there early signs that Ed Bell was capable of violence? Later, no one would recall any. None of his friends
would report seeing any evidence of a volatile temper.
Rather, Bell was someone who tried hard to please, a bright,
outgoing young man who quickly made friends.

Not dark and introverted, Bell had a buoyant personality and a jovial laugh. Larry's wife, Janice Bell, described
her brother-in-law as a big-talking Texan. "Ed was very
friendly, made friends with everyone. He could be very lik-
able. I never liked him, but I can't say why. It just seemed
that he was always tooting his own horn."

Many believed that Ed Bell would one day earn such
bragging rights, by combining his hard work and goals to
become a great success. "I think Ed was a big dreamer," said
an old friend. "And that's not a bad thing."

Over the years, Bonnie and Ed Bell had three children.
The first time he was picked up for exposing himself to
young girls was in 1966 in the rural ranching community
of Sudan, Texas, just west of Plainview. Bell was ordered
into treatment, and would later characterize his stay at Big

Spring State Hospital, a two-hundred-bed psychiatric facility, as a waste of time.

By the late sixties, the family lived in Lubbock, where Bell had a job as a pharmaceutical rep calling on physicians. At the time, he also attended Texas Tech University, working on a master's degree. There, in April 1969, Ed Bell's dark side reemerged when he was arrested for again exposing himself. The repercussions were swift. In response, Bell was kicked out of Tech and a deal was brokered, one in which he escaped prison time by agreeing to inpatient treatment for what were labeled as his "perversions." In his instructions, the judge specified that Ed Bell be treated for nine months in a psychiatric facility, or until a consulting physician deemed Bell cured. About that time, Bell and his first wife divorced.

Ed Bell arrived in Galveston in April 1969 accompanied by his father, Carl Clayton Bell, at the suggestion of a psychiatrist who recommended the University of Texas Medical Branch's psychiatric program. Once there, the two men entered the austere hospital lobby. In the admissions area, Bell and his father answered questions. The reason he was there, Bell said, was because of his "sexual problem."

In response to the interviewer's questions, Bell's father maintained that his son had always seemed a "normal" young man, bright, with friends and healthy relationships with girls. "He seemed to date in a regular manner. Ed never showed any signs of perversions."

When asked about his son's early life, Ed's father responded that his wife had no difficulties during the pregnancy and that Ed suffered no childhood trauma or high fevers, no head injuries to explain his actions. Carl Bell also said that as a youngster, Ed displayed no signs of a propensity toward violence, such as cruelty to animals. He'd played well with other children and was bright, earning good grades.

When it came to Ed's problem, Carl maintained it began in his son's second year of marriage. While still in College

Station, Ed exposed himself at least twice to young girls. From that point on, such incidents escalated, until Ed had been picked up by police five or six times. The most recent offenses were that past April, for which he'd been ordered into psychiatric treatment.

What did the interviewer see in the thirty-year-old Ed Bell sitting across from him that day?

In many ways it wasn't different from what Ed's old friends in Columbus described. When documenting the admission, the interviewer characterized Ed Bell as friendly, a personable man. Yet he did note that the hospital's new patient seemed perhaps *overly* helpful, as if wanting desperately to be liked.

Why had Bell turned from model student and young husband to having what he described as "a sexual problem?" When asked, Bell labeled the root of "his perversion" as a combination of pressures at work and home. He took no responsibility for the incidents that led to his arrest, blaming his actions on others. "Is there anything else going on?" the interviewer asked, seeking information on any signs of mental illness. Was Ed experiencing hallucinations, auditory or visual?

Bell denied both.

On that day in April 1969, Ed Bell entered UTMB's psychiatric program, where he was put on Valium. At the hospital, the physicians eventually came to two diagnoses: a personality disorder and depression. Presumably, his treatment went well, because just three months later, in July, Bell essentially moved out of the hospital on overnight passes although he wouldn't be officially discharged until July 1970. While attending day sessions, he came and went as he pleased.

In Galveston, Bell began a new life. Not long after checking out of the hospital, thirty-one-year-old Ed married again, this time to a twenty-year-old named Debbie, a fellow patient he'd met in the hospital.

The newlyweds moved into a rented second-story apartment in a large waterfront house on Offatts Bayou. "Ed loved Galveston," said an old friend who visited him there. "He loved the water, scuba diving, the casual lifestyle. He seemed to flourish."

On the island, Bell met Doug Pruns, who ran Doug's Dive & Surf Shop in a strip center on Fifty-seventh and Avenue S, next door to a wrecker service. Bell proposed that they partner up. Somehow, he'd pulled together a stash of scuba equipment he wanted to rent through the shop. Pruns and Bell struck a deal. Decades later, when Fred Paige investigated Bell's past and heard about the surf-shop arrangement, it piqued his interest further.

Connecting Bell to the surf shop was an enticing bit of information. "What I learned was that Debbie Ackerman and Maria Johnson (the Galveston girls whose bodies were found near the Turner Bayou Bridge), along with many of the other victims, used to frequent the surf shop. They hung around there." Also interesting was that geographically everything fit. The waterfront apartment Bell and his new wife rented was walking distance to both Doug's Surf Shop, a hangout for the teens, and the Wix Ski Shop, the last place the two Webster girls, Rhonda Johnson and Sharon Shaw, were seen on the August 1971 day they disappeared. Ackerman and Johnson had been at Wix, just down the block from Bell's apartment, skiing the day before they vanished. "Everything is right there," said Paige. "And Ed Bell was right in the middle of it."

While Doug Pruns ran the surf shop day to day, Ed Bell made most of his money selling real estate in Terlingua Ranch in far-west Texas near Big Bend National Park, out of an office in downtown Houston. Later, in the midseventies, Bell expanded his interests, investing in tugboats used to service offshore oil rigs. "Ed always seemed to have a bunch of money, a roll in his pocket," said an old friend. "He talked big and moved around a lot."

There were other indications that Paige interpreted as

confirmation that he was on the right track. An old witness statement from the time of Debbie Ackerman and Maria Johnson's disappearance placed them at the Baskin-Robbins ice-cream shop in Galveston. The last time they were seen, the girls were getting into a white van with a peace-sign sticker on the back window. An unidentified white man was behind the wheel. What made this particularly important, in Paige's estimation, was that just a few months later, in February 1972, Bell was again picked up for exposing himself to yet another young girl. This time he was in Louisiana, and the arresting officer recorded the type of vehicle Bell drove that day: a 1971 white Ford van.

When Paige talked to Glenda Willis, Sharon Shaw and Renee Johnson's friend, he heard something else interesting. In the weeks before her friends disappeared, Shaw and Johnson hung out with two older men, in their twenties or thirties. "It was creepy," Willis said. "What were guys like that doing hanging out with high-school kids?" Just before they vanished, the girls began talking about running away with the men to California. One of them, Willis mentioned, drove a van.

Another source gave Paige more enticing information on ties between Ackerman, Johnson, and Ed Bell. One of Debbie Ackerman's good friends told the veteran cop that the group of friends they ran with that summer spent time at the same waterfront house where Bell lived. They knew the man who owned the property, and some took diving lessons from him.

Working through the evidence, Paige continued to connect the dots linking Bell and the girls as the veteran cop delved ever further into the past and his inquiry into the murders. Some of those Paige interviewed recalled that Bell and his young wife lived at one point in a red trailer that resembled a caboose. At first the trailer sat on land in the Bayou Shores RV Resort, not far from their waterfront apartment. Later, however, Bell moved the caboose onto a rural lot situated two hundred yards from Humble Camp Road.

What made that fact important was that Humble Camp was the road that led to the Turner Bayou Bridge, the site where Debbie Ackerman's and Maria Johnson's bodies were found.

Then there was the timing. The strange events on the island began not long after Ed Bell was released from UTMB's psychiatric program in July 1970.

When Paige expanded his investigation from his initial look at Johnson's and Ackerman's murders to those of the other girls, he again quickly found suspicious links with Bell.

What about Colette Wilson, the dentist's daughter? What caught Paige's attention was her location that final day of her life, attending a multischool band competition. That brought to Paige's mind Ed Bell's own years participating in bands at Columbus High School and A&M. Had Bell gone to the competition and seen Wilson that day? Did he follow her instructor to the corner where she let Colette out of the car?

Brenda Jones, the only African-American victim, also played an instrument. And she was at UTMB visiting her aunt on the July 1971 afternoon of her disappearance, not far from where Bell spent months as an inpatient in the psychiatric unit and where he routinely reported for outpatient therapy.

Was it a stretch to believe that Bell could have been the killer? Paige had ample evidence documenting that in 1971, when the killings began, Ed Bell actively pursued young girls in Galveston.

Two weeks after Colette Wilson's abduction in June 1971, for instance, an island teenager sunbathing in her backyard looked up to see a stranger masturbating as he watched her. The man the girl identified was Ed Bell. The following month, in August, the two Webster best friends, Renee Johnson and Sharon Shaw, disappeared, after last being seen at the Wix Ski School, just down the block from Bell's apartment. Was there any connection to Gloria Gonzales, the grocery-store bookkeeper whose body was found near Colette Wilson's skeleton? During his research, Paige discovered that Bell had business connections in Gonzales's neighborhood and near the Addicks Reservoir, where Wilson's and Gonzales's bodies were found. A month after Gonzales's disappearance, Debbie Ackerman and Maria Johnson were murdered. Both girls frequented the surf shop where Bell was a part-owner and were last seen entering a white van. Perhaps the one Bell owned?

Although 1971 ended, on Paige's list the killing continued.

What happened to Kimberly Pitchford, the sixteen-year-old who vanished after leaving her driving class in January 1973? Had she, perhaps, gotten into Bell's van? Paige had no way of knowing. The following year Bell was again in trouble in Galveston County, this time for exposing himself to two girls he happened upon on a road. That day he drove not the van, but a rented Volkswagen. Not long after, a former psychiatric patient accused Bell of rape but ultimately dropped the charges.

Then the final set of two: Brooks Bracewell and Georgia Geer. Like the others their bodies were found in or near water, this time in a marsh. When Paige ran a records search, he discovered that Bell owned land in the area.

The last of the girls to die, twelve-year-old Suzanne Bowers, vanished near her grandparents' Galveston house in 1977. Here Paige documented a tantalizing connection to his suspect. One of Ed Bell's tugboat captains lived just behind the grandparents' house. "The guy told me that Bell was at his house all the time," said Paige. "It wouldn't be a stretch to think he'd seen the girl."

Then all went quiet. Or at least it appeared to.

The following year, on August 24, 1978, Bell pulled up in front of a house in Pasadena, Texas, southeast of Houston. On the street Bell spied a group of children playing. He got out of a red-and-white GMC pickup nude from the waist down and began masturbating. The girls screamed, and a twenty-six-year-old vet recently home from the service, Larry Dickens, heard his mother, Dorothy, calling the police. His light brown hair swept over his forehead, his mustache trimmed, the former Marine shouted at Bell. Hoping to detain the man until police arrived, Dickens ran to Bell's truck and grabbed the keys out of the ignition.

Furious, Ed Bell retrieved a .22 pistol from inside his pickup. He shot Dickens four times in the chest. Somehow, Dickens managed to run toward the garage, wounded but trying to escape with his life.

Inside the house, Dickens's mother again called police, pleading for help, while outside her son staggered down the driveway before collapsing. Bell grabbed a high-powered rifle from his pickup and walked back up the driveway. As Dickens pleaded for his life, Bell straddled the ex-Marine and pulled the trigger.

Larry's teenage sister, Dawna, pulled up just in time to see Bell fire that fatal shot. "I don't think my mother ever got over losing Larry that way," said Dawna.

Twenty minutes later, after a car chase and gun battle, police had Bell secured in the back of a squad car. They drove him to the Dickens house, where Dawna and her mother identified him as the man who'd murdered Larry. Astonishingly, his lawyer posted bond, and Bell was out of jail in twenty-four hours.

Two months later, Ed Bell was back at UTMB in Galveston, where he admitted himself for another psychiatric evaluation, again for his self-described "sexual problem." After his testosterone levels were deemed high, doctors put him on depro provera, a drug used for chemical castration, one known to diminish male sex drives. What authorities didn't know was that at that same time, Ed Bell was liquidating his assets, including selling all but one of the boats he'd been running to supply oil platforms in the Gulf.

When the next hearing on his case came up, Ed Bell and his remaining boat were gone. He'd jumped his bond and was on the lam with more than $140,000 in his pocket.

In the years that followed, off and on, reports came in of sightings, like one in 1984 from a woman who identified Bell as the intruder who entered her house in Bryan, Texas, near A&M. She screamed when she saw the reflection of a man carrying a large hunting knife in her bathroom mirror. That afternoon, the woman grabbed a gun and chased the stranger from the house.

For fourteen years, Bell was on the run. Based on the brutality of the Dickens murder, in 1985 he was named Texas's most-wanted criminal, his picture displayed in post offices and government buildings across the state. Yet his trail went cold. In Houston, Dawna and her mother worried that Bell would one day come after them, to silence them as witnesses. "Even when I was thirty, I'd look over at the next car on the road and think that I saw him," said Dawna. "My mom did the same thing. We were terrified of him."

Then, on December 2, 1992, *America's Most Wanted* aired an episode including a dramatization of Larry Dickens's murder. A young Matthew McConaughey portrayed the victim, illustrating for the cameras how the courageous ex-Marine attempted to corner and detain Bell. "That was McConaughey's first acting role, playing my brother," said Dawna. "After the program aired, tips started coming in."

Those phone calls led authorities to Panama, where Bell lived under an alias, the name of a dead cousin. He'd married again and had begun a new life, running tourist boats and prospecting for gold on land he bought outside of Panama City. Although he fought extradition, Bell lost and was escorted back to the U.S. by FBI agents.

In June 1993, Bell was finally tried for Dickens's murder. On the stand at his trial, he described the dead ex-Marine as a religious fanatic. "Mr. Bell said he was just sitting there and that my brother attacked him for no reason," said Dawna, who testified at the trial. "His story was so far out there."

While Bell was on the stand, Dawna said he appeared focused on what was going on around him and showed no signs of any delusions or mental illness. "He knew what he was saying."

During his testimony, Bell claimed he shot Dickens in

self-defense and that the fatal shot had been an accident, that he'd tripped and the gun had gone off. According to the autopsy, the bullet traversed front to back through Dickens's forehead.

One day during the trial, Larry Bell, Ed's older brother, approached Dawna. "I'm so sorry," he said, appearing heartbroken. He cried, saying he regretted what Ed had done. "My brother wasn't always like this. He used to be a kind and gentle person. I don't know what happened to him. He just snapped."

The jury rejected Ed Bell's depiction of the events and handed down a seventy-year sentence. In July 1993, Bell disappeared inside the Texas prison system. Five years later, he wrote the letters to the two district attorneys in which he confessed to murdering the eleven teenagers.

After he reviewed Ed Bell's past, Fred Paige believed Bell's claims in his letter. "If you can give me a better suspect, I'd love to hear it," said Paige on the afternoon of our interview, his arms folded defiantly across his chest.

His file on the case in hand, Paige contended that he consulted with the Galveston District Attorney's Office and tried to convince a prosecutor to take his evidence along with Bell's confession letters to a grand jury. "They put me off and put me off. They'll never prosecute it," he said. "They won't because, in a nutshell, the bullets were lost, the clothing was lost, the evidence from these cases is gone. Plus most of the witnesses are gone."

At this point, Paige and I had been talking for a very long time, recounting an investigation into events that were nearly four decades old. For all Paige's hard work, Ed Bell's guilt was still just speculation. Paige had been unable to bring any closure to the cases or the victims' families. "Sure, Ed Bell is in prison for killing Larry Dickens, but Bell killed a lot of other people," Paige alleged, his disgust apparent. "The bottom line here is that Ed Bell will probably never be prosecuted for any of them."

Although Paige couldn't drum up the interest of a prosecutor, he did get the press interested. In May 2006, the first
article ran in the *Galveston County Police News,* a monthly
newspaper that serves the area's law-enforcement community. In it, Paige named Bell as a suspect in the murders and
asked for help from anyone who might have photos of the
white van Bell drove at the time of the Ackerman and Johnson murders. Perhaps he hoped to see that peace sign a witness noticed on the back window of the van the girls drove
away in. Other articles in the *Police News* followed, about
Michael Self's questionable conviction and the evidence
against Ed Bell.

Bell turned down interview requests from the *Police
News,* but five years later, *Houston Chronicle* reporter Lise
Olsen learned of Paige's suspicions. Olsen corresponded
with Bell in prison, and he wrote that he had murdered
eleven girls, five in 1971 and six more in the mid- to late
seventies.

The list Ed Bell scratched out wouldn't turn out to pre-
cisely match the one Fred Paige had drawn up. It wasn't
identical to the names that had run for so many years of
the murdered girls in the chart. Yet many of the cases were
accounted for in the handwriting of a man who claimed to
be a serial killer. For the 1971 murders, Bell left out Brenda
Jones, but included the other murders that made headlines
that year: the dentist's daughter, Colette Wilson, the two
Galveston girls whose bodies were found in Turner Bayou,
Debbie Ackerman and Maria Johnson, and Sharon Shaw
and Rhonda Renee Johnson from Webster, who Mike Self
was convicted of murdering.

Then there were the later murders, the final six. The next
on Bell's list he called simply Pitchford. That bit of information made it easy to peg Bell's sixth victim as Kimberly
Rae Pitchford, the sixteen-year-old who disappeared one afternoon in 1973 after leaving her driver's education class.
In his letter to Olsen, Bell talked of two more girls who'd

died together. The reporter thought this third pair of murder victims was most likely fourteen-year-old Georgia Geer and twelve-year-old Brooks Bracewell. In her article, Olsen recounted what Paige had discovered, that in 1974, at the time of the murders, Bell owned pastureland minutes away from the Dickinson convenience store where Geer and Bracewell were last seen.

In his letter to Olsen, Bell described a dark-haired girl. Was he referring to the Kroger bookkeeper, Gloria Ann Gonzales? It seemed likely, especially since Gonzales's corpse was discovered near the remains of one of Bell's other named victims, Colette Wilson.

In prison, Olsen interviewed Bell, and again he claimed the murders, calling the slain girls "the eleven who went to heaven." That became the headline of Olsen's *Houston Chronicle* article which ran on September 26, 2011. When Olsen asked officials why Bell hadn't been prosecuted, the reply was as Paige had suspected. Current Texas laws stipulated that a confession alone couldn't be used to convict. The courts required corroborating evidence. "I didn't believe we had sufficient evidence that we could proceed to a grand jury with, and without getting into specifics, that's the decision that had to be made, no matter the temptations to proceed otherwise . . . It wasn't for a lack of effort," former Galveston DA Kurt Sistrunk told Olsen.

The day I read Lise Olsen's article, I decided it was time to look into the girls' murders, starting with the oldest crimes, the killings on the island. Before long, I, too, was writing to Edward Harold "Butch" Bell, asking for an interview.

While he responded quickly, he refused to grant me an interview. I kept writing, hoping to convince him to sign the forms that would result in a prison interview. Each time I made my request, Ed Bell declined, instead issuing orders, telling me to do one thing or another and report back to him. Finally, a friend, a trained profiler, suggested I stop writing.

"He's pulling your chain," she said. "Serial killers are big on control. He's trying to control you from inside prison. Pull back for a while. See what happens."

I did, and I waited. Then months later, I wrote Bell again. This time, his answer was the one I wanted. As I prepared for the interview, I wondered if Fred Paige was right. Would I soon meet the Galveston serial killer? Was it Ed Bell? Or was this simply a red herring, an enticing dead end?

# Chapter 6

## The Eleven Who Went to Heaven
## Edward Harold "Butch" Bell

**Brazoria County, Texas**

"If I cut your head off right now, they can't do anything about it," said Ed Bell with a satisfied smirk, his chin jutted out, defiant. "There's nothing anyone can do to me."

Late that morning, I'd traveled south of my Houston home to the Stringfellow Unit, a rambling old prison surrounded by double rows of chain fencing topped by curls of concertina wire in the flat, wooded terrain of Brazoria County. I was there to finally talk to Bell.

Ed Bell in 2012.
*(Courtesy of the Texas Department of Criminal Justice)*

The meeting was the culmination of more than a year during which I'd attempted to interview him. I'd written letters and made repeated requests. In response, I received letters from Bell packed with name after name, people out of his past he suggested I contact. He wanted me to do my research, but not on the killings, rather on what he called the Program, psychological and physical abuse he claimed to have been subjected to since shortly after his birth in 1939.

"I've been in the Program my whole life," he told me. In the prison visitors' room, we talked through a Plexiglas-and-wire-mesh divider. His hair chopped short, his nose and ears elongated by age, brown patches mottling his pale skin, at seventy-four Bell had cold muddy eyes and thin lips that seamlessly transitioned from amusement to disdain to anger. "I believe in free will. But I didn't have it, because of the Program. And I'm not responsible for any of the bad things I've done."

From outward appearances, it seemed that Bell suffered from some form of mental illness. Exactly what, I didn't know, although he repeatedly referred to having been placed in psychiatric hospitals, to people trying to push him into becoming "nuts," and he often brought up paranoid schizophrenia. Was that what psychiatrists had labeled him over the years? He certainly displayed signs of paranoia, insisting that newspapers were being altered to distort his take on reality. In his mind, he was the focus of a large, international conspiracy. He was so important that not only were television shows regularly doctored specifically to mislead him, but he claimed that the FBI had paid off hundreds of people for decades to keep his involvement in the Program secret.

"I have one question," he said. "Who's the president of the United States?"

His hearing nearly gone, he shouted and cupped his good ear to hear my response. "Barack Obama."

Bell frowned and shook his head. "I don't believe it. I'm pretty sure nothing I see on television is true. Those news programs are just set up to play with me."

This wasn't the Ed Bell of 1970s-era Galveston as described by his friends and family. That Bell had been gregarious, a big-talking businessman, and no one had said that they'd noticed any indication that his take on reality was distorted. Rather, he was the kind of guy who always had multiple jobs brewing, who habitually flashed a bank roll. "I was a college graduate. I never had a problem getting a job.

I made a lot of money," he confirmed, with a broad grin. "I knew how to bring it in. No question."

How did his current condition impact the believability of his claim that he was the 1970s Galveston serial killer?

"He may be mentally ill, that doesn't mean that what this man is saying isn't true. It's still possible that he's a serial killer," said Dr. Richard Coons, an Austin-based forensic psychiatrist known as one of the top experts in criminal behavior in the United States. "The problem in this type of situation is sorting out reality from delusion."

Certainly, there have been serial killers with recorded evidence of mental illness: Wisconsin's Ed Gein, who killed two women and tanned the hides of bodies he exhumed to make furniture, one of the inspirations for Hannibal Lecter in *Silence of the Lambs*; Albert Fish, the Brooklyn Vampire, who preyed on children; and Britain's Peter Sutcliffe, a prostitute killer known as the Yorkshire Ripper. So the combination of mentally ill and serial killer wouldn't be new.

Dr. Coons advised that to weed through the maze of Bell's distorted thoughts, solid evidence was needed to determine if Bell told the truth when he confessed to murdering the girls. The best route was through corroborating scientific findings, but that wasn't possible. Fred Paige said there wasn't any DNA available from any of the seventies-era murders. All the evidence had been lost or misplaced decades earlier. "We looked in 1993, when we had a task force on the murders," confirmed another of the investigators. "We couldn't find anything. No clothing. Nothing."

Unless an eyewitness came forward, without physical evidence, the only remaining way to determine if Ed Bell was the man who'd terrorized Galveston Island and the surrounding area was to determine whether or not Bell knew facts about the crimes that hadn't been made public in news reports, the things only the person responsible could know. If not? Perhaps his role was simply imagination, the fantasy in a disturbed mind.

Yet from the moment the interview began, Bell refused to

discuss anything other than what he called the Program. He claimed he was above the law. He argued that his position ensured that he literally could not be punished. It seemed incongruous considering the circumstances. Bell claimed the Program protected him from punishment for any crime. "It means I can't be arrested or charged with anything. I can't be detained. I'm above the law."

Clearly, however, that wasn't the case since he'd been an inmate in Texas prisons for two decades. The contradiction didn't appear to give the dough-faced man any concern. "You just have to understand the Program," he said. "Then it all makes sense."

It was in 1997, the year before he wrote his letters to the two district attorneys, that Ed Bell said he'd figured out that he wasn't responsible for what he referred to as "the bad things I've done." When asked if he meant killing Larry Dickens and the eleven girls, he nodded. Off and on his eye twitched when he talked about the murdered girls. "The twelve people I killed . . . Those bad things." Why wasn't he guilty? Because, Bell said, he'd been an unwitting pawn, manipulated by a government-sponsored experiment.

Bell said he didn't know why he was chosen. But he contended that it might have had something to do with his grandfather, who he suspected personally knew President Franklin D. Roosevelt. The goal, Bell said, was to experiment with a good kid, subject him to abuse and manipulation, to toy with his physiology and determine if he could be made bad. The first step in Bell's definition of turning to the dark side included becoming gay. And the final step centered on belief in a higher being.

"They wanted me to become a homosexual, then homicidal. What comes after homicidal? Suicidal! Then crazy. Nuts. Paranoid schizophrenia. And finally they want to turn me into a Jesus freak," Bell insisted, his arms crossed resolutely across his chest. "Then they think I'll tell them what they want to know."

"Tell them what?" I asked.

"Why people do bad things," he said with an exaggerated frown.

As he talked of the Program, Bell's demeanor appeared increasingly agitated. In his tortured mind, he remained locked in the injustices and horrors of his childhood. "It was a brainwashing program," he said. "The Program has been so absurd and asinine; almost no one will believe it." Although he knew of no one else who'd been subjected to it, Bell contended that everyone around him was part of the charade. Who was behind the plot? Bell described those in charge as government agents, somehow affiliated with the FBI. The vast majority of the time he referred to them as simply *they*. Those in the know included not only the ones pulling the strings but also everyone around Bell. "I think almost anyone on Galveston Island can tell you about the Program," he said.

What did *they* want? Why were *they* doing this?

"To see if they could turn me," he snarled. "I was a good kid, an Eagle Scout. They wanted to see if they could turn me homicidal."

The treatment, Bell said, began when he was a toddler, and at each stage seemed to have been intertwined with sex. At three, he described taking his clothes off and playing show-and-tell with a little girl. The episode was interrupted by Bell's mother, who beat him with a stick. "She really let me have it. No food. Eight hours later, my father comes home. He beats the hell out of me. Again, no food. That's what started it. That caused me to do the bad things."

Bell contended that the beatings accompanied by not being fed forced his endocrine system into overdrive, pumping out hormones. "This was done intentionally. It just threw everything out of whack, all the hormones, including testosterone. It made me oversexed."

Looking back, he said he knew from early on that his sex drive was exceptional. As a teenager, he masturbated five or six times a day. At fifteen, he claimed, his father, an oilfield worker, hired a hit man to kill him. When I asked why, Bell didn't mince words. At the time, his family lived on a ranch: "I was doing things I wasn't supposed to do. Sex with animals."

Looking back, Bell said his one regret was that he hadn't turned the tables on his father by murdering him. "He wanted me dead? I should have killed him. I should have killed my daddy, shot him through the head and buried him in the woods."

Bell had spent the past two decades in prison, and his only news of his contacts on the outside came from family and friends. His older brother had told him that both his parents were dead. They would have been nearing one hundred if still alive, but Bell didn't buy it. He also didn't believe his uncle had died six decades earlier as he'd been told, arguing that the entire episode was a charade staged for his benefit. At the funeral, the dead body in the casket wasn't his uncle's, Bell insisted. "That was a wax figure. It was all part of the Program.

"Why? They wanted me to get ideas. At eight, I could pop a snake's head off at fifty paces. I was really a good shot. What were they trying to get me to do? To kill my father . . . to take me to trial and sentence me to a shot in the arm. Bingo, I'm dead."

His upbringing turbulent, Bell said that when the bad thoughts first came to him, he wondered if it was heredity. While in prison, he came to another conclusion. "My father and my grandfather were both crazy," Bell said, his voice rising. "I thought it was bad blood. Until I got in here. Then I figured out what they'd done to me, about the Program."

When he brought up the "bad things" he'd done, I pushed for details, trying to get him to talk about the girls. "You know the things I've done, the things you're here to talk to me about," he said, referring to the Galveston serial killings he knew I'd come to discuss. As we talked, he became increasingly disturbed. "It was all because of the Program. They pushed me and pushed me. And it kept building inside me. It built and built, until one day, it just blew. I exploded."

"And what happened?" I asked.

"The bad things that you're asking about. I am of the opinion that the Program itself caused me to do those things," he said.

To Bell's mind, this program aimed at testing his ability to turn away from evil had an effect the collective *they* should have predicted. "At six or seven years old, I had enough upstairs to know that if you torture someone, you can get them to do bad things," said Bell. "I don't think it's right that I'm in here. They should be in here . . .

"As a sex offender, because of my hormones, I don't think I was in charge of my free will . . . They tried to get me to kill people. I didn't want to do it. They wanted me to rub people out. They wanted me [to be like] Al Capone."

Why had he confessed to the killings? Bell said it was a way to expose the injustices he'd suffered. Once his fate was known, Bell argued that he would have to be released from prison. "I wrote the letters because I figured out the Program. When I figured out what had been done to me, the pressure came off of me. I realized this was done to me on purpose, so I would do bad things," he explained, absolving himself from any responsibility for the twelve murders he claimed to have committed. "And I wanted people to know about the Program."

Throughout his past, there were times when he said he fought off urges to do bad things. There were times he thought he was supposed to murder people. When he didn't, Bell believed those people rewarded him, giving him ranches, money, even a large office building. "If I come out of here, I'm going to have plenty of money," he contended. "I believe I own much of downtown Houston."

Yet here, too, much of what he said made little sense. For if he'd been rewarded for not killing those on his hit list, didn't there have to be a hit list? "Did *they* pick the girls out for you, the people running the Program?" I asked. "Did they tell you to kill the eleven girls?"

"I don't think they picked anyone out," Bell said, his

twisted mind mulling over the question. "I don't think they told me *what* bad things to do."

Edward "Butch" Bell in the prison visiting room, 2013.
*(Courtesy of Kathryn Casey)*

Over the years, Bell said, however, there were scenarios— or as he called them "setups"—the faceless entities behind his torture set in motion. When he met his first wife on a blind date, he speculated that there was an ulterior motive for introducing them. Off and on he appeared distracted and hummed, and I wondered if he was trying to block auditory hallucinations. He did that at this point in the interview, the hum getting louder and more determined. When he stopped, he said that although he hadn't done as they'd wanted, "I was supposed to rape her. So they could lock me up then."

There were others, including a woman with a young son in 1963 in Paducah, Texas, stranded with a flat tire along a deserted road. As Bell described that day, he was the kind stranger who pulled over and fixed her flat. Looking back he classified it as another of what he calls the many situations the powers that govern his life drew him into. "I wasn't supposed to help that poor lady with her tire. I was supposed to rape her and kill her kid," he insisted, his voice rising. While he fixed the tire, apparently fighting homicidal urges, Bell suspected strangers watched from the woods, monitoring his actions.

When it came to the day he jumped bond on the murder charge, Bell claimed that wasn't what happened. Instead, he insisted that when he was released on bail, those in charge knew he would run and wanted him on the lam. "They wanted to follow me. They wanted to see what I would do. They wanted me south of the Rio Grande River. They thought it would be easy to corrupt me down there," he insisted. In Central America, he adopted the name and identity of a dead cousin but still spotted so many people in bars and restaurants, on the street that he believed were FBI agents in disguise, that he said he made it a point to stop noticing.

In addition to his two wives in the U.S., Bell said he'd married twice more, once in Costa Rica and to a fourth woman in Panama. Yet he contended that none of the marriages, not even those in Texas, were real. Why? The women were in on the conspiracy, Bell suggested, and the marriages didn't abide by the letter of the law, which made them merely masquerades. "They wanted it that way," he said. "So that when I got railroaded into prison on these bogus charges, they could just walk away."

In prison, he said the torture continued. "I've been poisoned in here six thousand times," he railed. "They're trying to make me be a homosexual. I'm not going to do it." Why did they want him to be homosexual? Bell said it was so those in charge of his torture could put him in lockup whenever they wanted.

Now that he'd unmasked the Program, Bell said he was blameless for all he'd done. "My daddy was a total complete fruitcake. Nuts," he said, again referring to his treatment as a child, when he contends his family and a conspiracy of others abused him to turn him into a killer. The result? "I killed twelve people. And maybe a lot of others who committed suicide because of what happened."

What did he hope to accomplish? He speculated that exposing the Program mandated that he had to be released from prison. Once word spread that he wasn't at fault, that he was a victim not a predator, authorities had no alternative other than to set him free. "The people who did this to me belong in prison, not me. Let's expose them for what they are. Who belongs in prison, me or them? They do."

Once he was out? Ed Bell said he'd then answer all the questions about the girls he claimed to have murdered. "But not until I'm out on the street where I belong."

Would he hurt anyone again? No, Bell insisted. Now that he understood the Program and why he'd murdered the girls, he didn't feel drawn to violence. Besides, at seventy-four, he argued that he no longer had the sexual urges that drove him. "If Elizabeth Taylor was in her prime right here, I'd be afraid to even kiss her. Because that might be all I can do," he said, with a curt laugh. Once released from prison, he mused that maybe he'd settle in southern Spain. "I don't want to live in this country, not after what they've done to me."

Why did he kill the girls?

"It was an accumulation from when I was three years old. It built and built, and I exploded. I finally just exploded. It was an explosion. It wasn't the bad blood. It wasn't being oversexed. The buildup is what caused it."

When asked again why he killed those particular girls, he answered, "I can't tell you why they wanted me to do individual things. *They* wanted me corrupt. They wanted me Al Capone. Baby Face Nelson. Bonnie and Clyde. I was a good boy, and they did this to me."

"Did it bother you, Ed?" I asked.

"What?"

"What you did to those girls? Did it bother you?"

He looked at me, then stared down at his hands on the

counter in front of him. Whether he meant it or not, for a moment, he looked repentant. "Of course."

Ed Bell saw proof of the Program's existence all around him. He'd repeatedly confessed to murdering eleven teenage girls. Why hadn't he ever been prosecuted? It was all part of the conspiracy. "Because if I get in front of a judge, and I tell them that I was on a U.S. government program from birth, he'll have to let me out. So they don't want me in another courtroom."

A lull, then Bell went on, explaining his view of faith and eternity. "I don't believe in heaven or hell. I don't believe there's a God or Jesus or Mohammad or somebody. I don't believe it. Jesus Christ was a con artist . . . I don't think there's a god. That throws the whole religion thing into the street."

So there would be no day of reckoning, as Bell saw it, not on Earth or after he died. And why should there be? Even if hell existed, Bell maintained he'd done nothing to ensure that was the road his soul would travel. As the interview wore on, he became defiant. "If people tell you that I'm incompetent, they're the ones who are incompetent!"

At times, Bell displayed his gregarious-salesman side, laughing and telling jokes. "When I die, here's what I want you to do," he said at one point, his tone conspiratorial. "You'll get the word. I want you to tell them to bury me nude in the casket. I'm an old flasher, so I want to be nude. And I want to be facedown. That way, when all those people who don't like me walk by the casket, they can kiss my ass."

What happened on the day he shot Larry Dickens? "I think the whole thing was a setup that went bad," Bell said. "I was coming up from Galveston. The traffic snarled in front of me on I-45. They forced me off the road to go to Pasadena, Texas, for the setup."

As he talked, Bell's voice became increasingly agitated. "I'd been flashing people all over Houston for years. The police knew my license number, what I looked like. But they told everyone, my daddy, the others, they told them, 'You caused this . . . we ain't gonna touch him . . . We're not going to prosecute him. We're not going to mess with him. You did this. You fix it.' They channeled me into Pasadena." In Bell's account, he hadn't taken off his pants and masturbated in front of a group of children that day. He hadn't done anything wrong, nothing to explain why Dickens confronted him.

"This guy comes out of his house, he takes my keys. He's yelling and screaming at me . . . I pull a pistol out from behind the seat of my truck . . . I said, 'I want my keys.' He said no. I shot over his head. Boom! I said, 'I don't want to hurt you.' He throws his hands up in the air. This is not what you want to do with an atheist. I'm an atheist. He starts screaming that Jesus is going to save him. He believes in Jesus. He said he's going to kill this man in the name of Jesus. He comes at me. I emptied the gun. Blood starts coming out of his nose like you'd opened a faucet. Whew!

"He goes into the garage. I need my keys. I get the M-1 carbine out of the truck. He's sitting there . . . I said, 'Give me my goddamn keys!' I shoot from the hip."

The twelfth person Bell claims to have killed, Larry Dickens, lay dying. Yet Bell insisted he wasn't accountable. He admitted shooting Dickens with a pistol then a rifle, but he denied discharging the fatal shot through the head, despite Dawna Dickens's painful memories of seeing Bell shoot that final bullet. "Someone else did that," he said. "I don't remember shooting him through the head. I don't. Someone else did that."

So in Bell's world, he was innocent of the girls' murders because he was manipulated to kill them and Dickens's murder because some unseen person fired the fatal shot. An old man, who claimed not to believe in either heaven or hell, appeared determined to wipe away any responsibility for his sins, to clear his earthly record by blaming others.

Yet what little remorse Ed "Butch" Bell might have shown earlier was now gone, and his voice swelled in anger. "I have known since I was eight years old that there is no

God!" he shouted. "I don't think there's any way I could be farther from Jesus Christ . . . when you die, they take you apart. Take your brain out. Take your internal organs. You going anywhere but a hole in the ground?"

Our time together wore on, and I tried again to maneuver him into talking more about the girls' killings. When he balked, I offered to show him a printout of the I-45 unsolved murder chart with pictures of the victims, one I'd brought with me. Many of the girls were those he'd claimed to have murdered. "Would you look at it?" I asked, pulling it out of a file.

"No," he said, spitting out the word. He turned away, angry. "You don't have to show that to me . . . I think the bad things I've done in my life were because of the Program."

At that point, Ed Bell addressed the invisible others he claimed monitored us and recorded each of his words. "They're going to school on us," he said. "They want to know how I think. They keep looking for a weakness. But I don't have any. I'm King Kong!"

Later, one thing Bell said would haunt me: "You've got Frankenstein's monster." Then, referring to his father and himself, he said, "And you have Carl Clayton Bell's monster."

On the drive back to Houston, I thought about Edward Harold Bell, the grandfatherly-looking man with the twisted frown and ice-cold eyes. The self-described monster. I hadn't been able to convince him to talk in detail about the girls, the eleven he claimed in letters to have sent to heaven. But the man I saw accepted no responsibility. He'd abdicated all free will, claiming he was powerless to do anything but kill. The way he referred to the twelve he'd murdered, the way he tried to hide behind calling the murders "the bad things I've done," that so many small clues linked him to the killings, including a white van matching the description of the one two of the girls were seen getting into?

In my office, I later sat down to test the theory that everything Bell had written in his letters could have been gleaned from newspaper accounts of the murders, the reason those in law enforcement I'd queried had said they couldn't prosecute Bell based on his many confessions. It seemed odd to me that so much would have been reported. Usually, police hold back information like the angles of shots and the type of bindings used.

After I'd searched and found all the available articles on the seventies murders, I put them in chronological order. I didn't consider anything after 1993, when Bell entered his first Texas prison. One investigator had speculated that Bell could be looking up the old cases on the Internet from prison and that was how he knew the facts, but I'd inquired and knew that wasn't possible. Texas inmates don't have Internet access behind bars.

Once I had all the articles before me, I realized that the prosecutors were right: Everything in Bell's written confession was present in one or another of the articles covering the murders, from the angles of the shots into Debbie Ackerman's and Maria Johnson's bodies to the types of bindings used on their hands. "Yeah, but he's been in prison all these years," Fred Paige had told me. If Bell had merely read news articles on the cases decades earlier, the investigator contended that Bell wouldn't have been able to correctly recall so many details. Considering our interview, I thought about Ed Bell's description of the rage that built inside of him and the emotional explosions that he said propelled him to commit murder. When he talked about the killings, he appeared swept back to that time and that place, that moment, standing on the bridge in the oil field, a gun aimed at Debbie and Maria as they cowered below him in Turner's Bayou. Could it all have been the fantasy of an unstable mind?

As much as I believed Ed Bell might be telling the truth, I couldn't know for sure. I had no crystal ball into the past. Unless Bell relayed information only the killer knew, his claim that he was the serial killer would forever be clouded in doubt. Was he toying with all of us? Giving us just enough information to believe he murdered the girls but not enough to prove it? Or was that all he knew, just what had been printed in the newspapers? Were we all listening to the deranged fantasies of a man who had created his own reality?

"Ed, why don't you tell me about one of the killings?" I'd asked. "Pick one, and just tell me everything you remember."

"Not until they let me out of here," he scoffed, his face bitter in rage. "They need to let me out and put the people who did this to me in here. Then I'll talk. I'll tell them everything. But not until I'm on the outside!"

A few months later, I interviewed Ed Bell again. By then, he was housed in the Estelle Unit, a prison hospital. As before, he claimed he was being poisoned and complained that his blood pressure was high. Why was he there? He said that the doctors wanted access to him in order to trick him into "becoming crazy," so they could lock him up in a prison psychiatric hospital "for the fourth time." When he said this, he held up four arthritic fingers and frowned pointedly.

That second visit resembled a chess game, Bell consistently ignoring questions about the girls' murders and redirecting the conversation to his hate for the Program. At times, he looked flustered, angry. But then he smiled and moved on, listing resources he thought would help gain access to FBI files with his picture on them that he was sure existed, ones that spelled out his singular position as the subject of an experiment aimed at "taking a good kid and turning him into a killer."

Was Fred Paige right? Was Ed Bell the Galveston serial killer?

Bell admittedly knew a lot about the killings. He also had possible ties to many of the girls. That was true in one case in particular, the murder of Suzanne Bowers. A former employee of Bell's, a captain on one of the boats Bell owned that ran supplies to the oil rigs, lived with his parents just over a fence line from Suzanne's grandparents.

On May 21, 1977, the twelve-year-old left that same house to walk home to get her bathing suit. She never made it. She was never seen alive again. This was the murder Henry Lee Lucas had once confessed to but later recanted. I asked Ed Bell if he had ever gone to visit his employee at the house behind the Bowers family. "I used to go there off and on . . . he lived there with his parents, so I'd go there sometimes. He worked for me, I guess, about two years."

How often was he at that particular house? "Quite a bit," he answered, with a shrug.

Suzanne Bowers's friend, Sara Groves, had written to Bell in prison, asking him if he'd murdered her friend, and Bell said that he hadn't. "I do not remember hearing about your friend," Bell wrote. "I am sorry for your loss. I can tell you that some people do bad things because of life's experiences. I do not believe that humans are born good or bad."

Even beyond the fact that Bell frequented the home behind Bowers's grandparents', there were other factors that suggested Bell might not be telling the truth. In many ways, the Bowers case was markedly similar to those he claimed to have committed. Suzie looked like the other girls, with her shoulder-length brown hair. Like many of the other murdered girls, Bowers frequented Galveston's beaches and surf shops. Debbie Ackerman and Maria Johnson were last seen getting into a van, and the man who leased the land where Bowers's bones were found described seeing a van on the property around the time of her disappearance.

The final connection: Bowers's skeleton was found in an area linked to some of the other cases, murders Bell claimed to have committed.

"You know, Ed," I said. "A young girl disappeared right there, from the house behind the one your captain lived in with his parents."

Ed Bell said nothing, but his eyes turned frigid, and he glared at me.

I asked, "Her name was Suzanne Bowers. Did you murder that girl?"

Bell clenched his jaw and tied his lips into a taut sneer.

He'd been friendly when I'd arrived, but no longer. Although I asked yet again, Bell never answered my question. He neither admitted nor denied murdering Bowers but glowered at me, furious. I had the sense that my knowing about the case had caught him off guard.

Why wouldn't he talk about that particular case? Perhaps because someone else was involved? According to Groves, an informant told Bowers's grandmother that he'd seen another man kill Bowers, that he was with the killer when she died. And along with the van that was spotted in the field where her bones were found, there was a pickup truck.

From that point on in our second interview, Butch Bell talked about the Program, complaining about the medications he was on and that his head felt swollen. "Maybe it's some kind of mind-expanding drug they're giving me," he said. "They don't want to kill me, just make me suicidal. They're hoping I'll blow my brains out."

At that juncture, Bell excused himself. "I have to go back to my room," he said. "I can't talk anymore. I'm having some pain. But don't tell anyone. No one here. They're causing it."

I knew that I would get no more from Ed Bell that day, and I gathered my things. As I left the visitors' area, Bell stood behind the wire-mesh partition watching, staring, frowning. He looked old and troubled and angry. The last thing he said to me was that he wouldn't see me anymore. My sense was that I'd asked one too many questions about the girls' murders, questions he wouldn't then and might never answer.

That was in 2013, the same year Ed Bell became eligible for parole. The board rejected his application, perhaps because he told them about the Program, or they might have heard his claim that four decades earlier, he'd left a bloody swath across Galveston.

In the months that followed, I continued to write, and Bell responded. While I never got definitive proof that he was the killer, over the course of time he included curt facts about the cases, things like "Maria Johnson had a twenty-dollar bill in her purse." The problem was that if it were true, that fact wasn't recorded in the case file. I couldn't confirm it.

In one letter, Bell described driving the white van that day in front of the Baskin-Robbins, the one seen picking up Maria Johnson and Debbie Ackerman, and I came to believe that he probably did just that. At times, I pictured a younger Ed Bell, his brown hair combed to the side, hanging out of the van window, smiling and urging the girls to climb inside. It was either that or he had a truly amazing memory, one that remembered minutiae he'd read decades earlier in newspaper articles.

Forty-two years after her daughter disappeared, Claire Wilson couldn't tell me what Colette wore the last time she saw her, on the day of the band competition, as she stood on the side of the road holding her clarinet case and waiting for her mother. Ed Bell, however, remembered right down to the color of Colette's purple shorts and that the Mickey Mouse on her shirt was on the front. Yet there were no eyewitnesses, none who came forward to say they saw any of the doomed girls drive off with Bell, and no known forensic evidence tying him to the killings.

Such were the frustrations of decades-old cold cases. As logical as it seemed that Fred Paige must be right, that Bell truly was the Galveston serial killer, in the end, nothing was certain.

# THE 1980s

- Heide Villareal Fye: 25, waitress and bartender, left her parents' house to hitchhike to see her boyfriend on October 7, 1983.

- Laura Lynn Miller: 16, the daughter of Tim Miller, last seen on September 10, 1984, using a convenience-store pay phone.

- Jane Doe: third victim found in the Texas Killing Field, unidentified. Her body was found on February 3, 1986.

- Shelley Sikes: 19, a waitress at a seafood restaurant, forced off I-45 on May 25, 1986.

- Janet Doe: fourth victim found in the Killing Field, unidentified, discovered on September 8, 1991.

# Chapter 7

## The Texas Killing Field
## One Father's Crusade

**League City, Texas**

For decades, this clearing in the woods has been notorious, a seeming contradiction for such a quiet site tucked a short saunter off a side road, concealed behind a stand of trees. Little was heard here but the calls of birds, the rush of a breeze through dry winter leaves, and the occasional car on nearby Calder Drive. Yet the spot lay just blocks off I-45, little more than half an hour's drive to the impressive skyscrapers that comprise Houston's high-rise downtown. All around, people were consumed by the pull of daily life. But in this deserted field, time stood still. It was both hallowed and haunted ground, sacred cemetery and blasphemous atrocity, a place that had witnessed all the good and all the malevolence of which man was capable.

Dedicated to his daughter, Tim Miller's Cross.
*(Courtesy of Kathryn Casey)*

trial and a defense attorney talks about his client's childhood, this person who has done something terrible. I feel like, don't play that game with me. I've been there. Adults make choices."

If Tim Miller's shoulders sag, they have reason. The troubles that plagued him began as a small child when his mother suffered a breakdown. As a result, many of Tim's younger years passed circulating between foster homes until a family stepped forward to take him in. Finally, he had a strong father figure, a happy home life.

Still, damage was done. "By twelve, I was smoking and drinking," he said. He married young, and he and his wife, Jan, lived in Ohio, where Tim worked at Ford Motor Company, when their first daughter, Wendy, was born. Laura Lynn Miller was number two, and then they had a son who tragically died of crib death when he was only seven weeks old.

Tim and Jan struggled through, but more adversity waited.

As a child, Laura ran a high fever, one that put her in a coma and landed her in a hospital, yet she recovered and thrived, growing into a good student with many friends. Tim thought their second child had "turned the corner." Laura worked hard in school, getting good grades. Around the house, she was a happy presence, singing into brushes, spoons, whatever was handy as stand-ins for microphones. Laura was a compassionate young girl who ran track in school. One day in the heat of a race, well ahead and in first place, she stopped just before the finish line. Another young girl had fallen and cried out. Instead of forging on to collect the trophy, Laura turned back to help.

Then when Laura was eleven, she suffered a bad bout of the flu. Not long after, she tumbled off a playground slide, and Tim and Jan ended up in a hospital emergency room listening to a doctor explain that their daughter hadn't suffered a simple fall. Instead, a brain scan revealed that the flu's high fever had left behind scar tissue. Laura had a seizure disorder.

"The seizures changed Laura," said Tim. "She didn't feel as if she fit in anymore. She felt different. It was hard on all of us, but especially Laura. She had so many things to struggle against."

Not long after, the family moved to Texas, lured by the flourishing economy. The Gulf Coast was booming, and they settled in Dickinson, not far from the Johnson Space Center. What had been small towns in the seventies were growing. Tim went into construction and dreamed of building a successful company. Yet he worried. As she entered her teenage years, Laura became sullen. "Because of the seizures, she was put in special-education classes at school, and she was embarrassed. She started skipping school," said Tim. "She started hanging around with kids who smoked pot."

Hoping for a fresh start, Tim and Jan decided to move Laura out of Dickinson. In late summer 1984, they found a small, one-story ranch house on Cardinal Drive, a quiet, suburban street, in the nearby town of League City, by car just ten minutes from their current home. Laura would still be able to see her friends, but she'd attend a new school. Shades of brown and beige brick in the front, the house had a garage and a picket fence, an oak tree in the front yard. It was a new beginning for all of them, and Tim was hopeful.

As school approached, Laura registered as a sophomore at Clear Creek High School, and in early September, the family moved into the Cardinal Drive house. Days later, on the tenth, boxes still waited to be unpacked, and the Millers' new home phone wasn't connected yet when Tim rushed off to work. After he left, Laura announced that she wanted to call her boyfriend from a convenience store on the busy corner of Hobbs Road and West Main Street. Jan had to get to work but offered to drive Laura to the store. It all seemed like such a normal morning, but it would turn out to be one they would play and replay in their minds.

At the convenience store, the traffic whizzing past on its way to and from I-45 just a block away, Jan waited as Laura talked to Vernon, her first serious boyfriend. Time passed, and Jan had to get to work, but her daughter didn't want to hang up the phone. "Laura told Jan that she should go on to work," said Tim. "Laura said, 'Mom, it's only a mile. I know my way. I can walk.'"

Laura was sixteen, old enough to drive and get a job. What could happen to her on such a short walk home?

When Tim and Jan returned home that afternoon, Laura wasn't in the house. At first, he assumed she was with Vernon, that they'd gone somewhere together. But then Vernon rang the doorbell looking for Laura. He hadn't seen her. Tim worried but not too much, assuming that his daughter had wandered off with friends. When she didn't come home, Tim and Jan began driving the streets and searching.

When they hadn't found Laura by the second day, Tim became frantic. "I figured then that maybe she'd had a seizure," he said. They called nearby hospitals, and Tim contacted the League City Police Department. The officer who took the missing person report didn't seem concerned; he told Tim that sixteen was an age where teenagers were known to run away from home. The officer insisted that this wasn't unusual, and that Laura would undoubtedly return soon.

Despite the officer's assurances, by the third day anxiety had taken over Tim's life. No longer did he make excuses for Laura's disappearance. He now felt certain that something was very wrong. "I went to see the police again," he said. "I told them that Laura needed her seizure medicine. She didn't have it with her. And she was religious about taking it. She wouldn't not come home."

In response, the officer again told Tim not to worry, that Laura had probably just run off, and she'd be back. "I didn't believe that," said Tim. "I hoped it was true, but I didn't believe it."

That day, Tim's alarm grew when he learned that another young woman had disappeared in League City eleven months earlier, a twenty-five-year-old cocktail waitress and bartender named Heide Villareal Fye.

Pretty with a Farrah Fawcett cut of shaggy blond/brown hair, the mother of a six-year-old daughter, at the time Heide (pronounced Hee-dee) had been staying with her parents, less than a quarter mile from the Millers' new home. Years later, her parents described their daughter as a trusting woman, one who made friends easily. "Heide never met an enemy; everyone was her friend," said her sister, Josie Poarch-Mauro. "She was a carefree sort of girl, and she loved to laugh."

Heide Villareal Fye saw the good, not the bad, in people. *(Courtesy of her family)*

The evening she disappeared, October 7, 1983, Heide told her father, who was watching a baseball game on television with a neighbor, that she'd decided to hitch a ride into Houston to meet her boyfriend.

When Heide failed to arrive at her destination, her family began searching. One of her father's stops was at a place Heide frequented, the same gas station/convenience store Laura Miller would disappear from the following year, the one on the corner of Hobbs Road and West Main Street, just off I-45. The clerk behind the counter remembered seeing Heide that October evening. In this era before cell phones, like Laura, Heide had used the pay phone on the corner of the building, under a jaunty blue awning and separated from the parking lot by blue concrete barriers.

Certain his daughter wouldn't leave her family, Heide's father searched for her every day.

"My dad was partially paralyzed from a stroke and

walked with a cane, but he went out and searched fields in the area, looking for her," said Josie, her voice heavy with emotion remembering the grief that overwhelmed the family. "It devastated our mother, but our father took it even harder. Heide was the youngest of six, his baby girl. He was heartbroken."

Then came that terrible afternoon the following April, six months after Heide vanished, when a dog carrying something in its mouth emerged from the woods bordering nearby Calder Drive, a quiet country road that angled off I-45. A toddler played on the front porch of a nearby house while his parents stared at the animal, wondering what their dog found in the woods, until they suddenly realized that the object wasn't a ball but a human skull.

When police arrived, they fanned out into the thick brush and straggly trees, searching for clues. Ultimately, attention centered on a patch of land three hundred yards from the house, a Humble Oil field with a narrow road cut through the brush to service a single working well. As if posed, a nearly skeletonized body lay on its back under a tree. Heide's clothes and a necklace were found nearby. When dental records were compared, her family was told that they were a match. While the coroner determined no firm cause, broken ribs suggested that Heide may have been beaten to death.

How was it possible that the body lay so close to civilization without being discovered for so long? The site was less than five miles from the convenience store, and once a week for six months, a worker had driven through the field to service the well, failing to see the woman's corpse concealed in the high grass.

That was April 1984. Five months later, Laura Miller vanished.

Tim Miller considered Heide Fye's murder and worried that there could have been a connection with his daughter's disappearance. He didn't yet know that both girls disappeared after being at the same convenience store, talking on the same pay phone. If he had, he would have been certain there was a link, but instead it sounded believable when the officer he talked to insisted that no relationship existed between Fye's murder and Laura's disappearance. One of the differences, the officer said, was that Fye was a cocktail waitress. "He insinuated that somehow Heide was responsible for what had happened to her because she worked in a bar," Miller said. "He made it sound like she'd asked for it."

Still, Tim wondered. He pushed, wanting to know where the field was, planning to search it himself. "I begged him to tell me where it was," said Miller.

The officer was adamant, however, that the cases weren't connected and that a search of the field wasn't possible. "He said the field was private property and all fenced in," said Miller. "And he told me not to bother Heide's family. He kept insisting that Laura was a runaway, and she'd be back home."

The convenience store phone where Fye and Miller were last seen.
*(Courtesy of Kathryn Casey)*

Long weeks followed, then months that turned into more than a year, while Tim Miller waited for what he feared would be bad news. Despite all the reassurance from police, Tim didn't believe that his daughter had run away. His heart sprinted in his chest every time the phone rang or a car stopped in front of their house. He waited and worried. He lost his job, and a deep depression took over.

Seventeen months after Laura's disappearance, Tim checked himself into a hospital. It was there on the morning of February 4, 1986, that his wife read a *Galveston County Daily News* article aloud to him. The day before, the decomposing body of an unidentified woman had been discovered in the Calder Drive oil field, the same clearing in the woods where Heide Fye's skeleton had been found. This time four boys on dirt bikes smelled something rotting, tracked down the source, and notified police. When investigators combed the area for evidence, they happened upon a second set of human remains, bones protruding from the ground.

The badly decomposed body and newly found skeleton both lay within two hundred yards of the tree where Fye's bones were recovered two years earlier. The positioning of all three was similar: under trees, on their backs, facing up.

As much as Tim didn't want his daughter to be one of the two unidentified dead women, he took no comfort in a quote from a League City detective: "no local . . . missing person cases seem to be related."

That day, Jan Miller rushed to the League City Police Station. When police asked, she supplied Laura's dental records and samples of their daughter's clothes, in hopes that hair could be retrieved for comparison. "I think I knew it was Laura before they told us," Tim said. "I didn't want to believe it, but I already knew."

One of the last photos of Laura Miller.
*(Courtesy of Tim Miller)*

That Laura's remains had been found brought some relief. That she'd been murdered was horrific, but they now knew she wasn't being held captive, wasn't hurt or sick, and no longer suffered.

Yet that gave Tim little comfort. As he assessed the situation, Tim blamed the police for the agonizing months of waiting without answers. "The way

I saw it, the police were partly responsible. It wasn't long after Laura disappeared that I asked them to look in that field. They wouldn't do it. Wouldn't let me do it. If they'd gone then, Laura would probably still have been dead, but they might have found evidence to stop the guy. At least we wouldn't have had all those months of jumping every time the phone rang. Instead, the cops did nothing, and now they had a third victim, a Jane Doe. Maybe, if they'd done their jobs, she didn't have to die."

There were other similarities between the three women besides the circumstances of their deaths. Jane Doe, like Laura and Heide, was white with shoulder-length brown hair. At approximately five-foot-six to -eight and weighing about 140 pounds, the unidentified woman was judged to be between twenty-two and thirty years old. Her most prominent identifying characteristic: a gap between her front teeth.

When it came to how the women died, there were differences. Indications were that Heide had been beaten. Laura's cause of death was unknown. The Jane Doe—whom the medical examiner estimated died two to four weeks before the discovery—had a bullet hole in her spine.

When police finished processing the scene and took down the barriers, Tim and Jan Miller went to the field, just two miles from their home, to see for themselves where their daughter had been found. It wasn't as Tim had been told. There weren't any fences. If the police had given him the location, he would have found Laura days after she disappeared. The frustration and anxiety that had eaten away at him for so long didn't subside but was joined by anger and an overwhelming guilt. "I was her father. I was supposed to protect Laura," he said. "I failed."

From that day forward, the field became sacred to Miller. Ten months later, just before Christmas, Tim, Jan, and their only surviving child, Wendy, returned to the scene. Tim carried a cross he'd made, roughly hewn out of wood. He drove it into the ground near the spot where Laura's bones were found, and beside it planted a fir sapling. On white rock he laid at the foot of the cross, the family placed objects representing things Laura loved, small statues of a cat, a horse, a turtle, and seashells. "It was a way to mark the place," said Tim, his eyes red and moist, his voice hushed, recalling that day. "It was something we could do for Laura."

Tim Miller and the cross he erected in the Killing Field, where Laura's skeleton was found. *(Courtesy of Kathryn Casey)*

Faced with the inconceivable reality of his younger daughter's murder, Tim tried to let the police do their work while he attempted to put his life back in order but with little success. "I don't think anyone can understand what something like this does to a parent unless they've lived it."

By then his life was already spinning out of control. His drinking had escalated, and the grief was crushing. At home, Laura's room remained as she'd left it. But Tim took to spending nights in the field, lying in wait, hoping to cross paths with the killer. He brought beer and sometimes a gun. "I'd scream, 'You chicken shit, I'm here. Come and get me . . . Motherfucker, I'm here. Come and take me!"

One night, he heard something in the darkness. Tim both hoped and feared that the man who'd murdered his daughter walked toward him, yet that moonless night he'd forgotten his gun. To his relief, what ambled out of the woods was instead a horse.

Not long after midnight during yet another stakeout, Tim stood in the center of this bleak, solitary site and fired six shots from his .357 into the sky. Then he waited for the police, wondering if they were nearby, like he was waiting for the killer to return. No one came.

In daylight, the field called to him as well. Many afternoons were spent inspecting every square foot, certain he'd find some trace of his daughter, her clothes, the cross necklace she'd worn on the day she disappeared, or evidence that would point to the killer. Every day he thought about Laura and how she'd died, wondering if in her final moments she'd called out for him or for her mother.

News of the bodies found off Calder Drive spread. Months earlier, a new movie made headlines and won a fistful of awards. *The Killing Fields* documented the experiences of Cambodian journalist Dith Pran after he escaped the Khmer Rouge and the finding of hundreds of thousands of his countrymen in mass graves. As many on the Gulf Coast pondered the deaths of the three women, the press began referring to the League City clearing as the Texas Killing Field.

In hindsight, Tim Miller would contend that police expended little effort to investigate the three Killing Field murders, and he wondered if some of the reason was political. At the time, the nearby Johnson Space Center flourished with large, expensive homes springing up around it, including in League City. The population in the area swelled, and prosperity brought jobs, stores, and new schools. The small mainland towns around I-45 were spreading, growing so fast with new houses and schools that they grew together to form a contiguous patchwork. "I think politicians and such didn't want people to know what was going on here," he said.

Six months after Laura's remains were found, Tim and Jan divorced. "I can't say that we were a happy family," he said. "There were issues. A lot of guilt. We blamed ourselves."

The years came and went, and Tim tried to pull his life back together. Three years after her body was found, police finally released Laura's remains, and a funeral was held. On a gray granite gravestone, the Millers chose a heart etched with three words inside: DAUGHTER. SISTER. FRIEND. Below Laura's name and dates, her parents included a phrase from an iconic Led Zeppelin rock song, ". . . and she's buying a stairway to heaven."

Walking away from the services that day in the cemetery, Tim looked at nearby graves. One hundred and fifty feet from where he'd buried his daughter, he noticed a gravestone bearing the name Heide Villareal Fye. "It gave me the chills," he said. "They were both out in that field, and they were buried so close."

After the divorce, Tim lived in a house in Dickinson. He worked construction and tried to overcome the pain of Laura's murder. One evening, he walked in and saw her framed photo. Anger overwhelmed him, and he shouted, "Damn you, Laura," picking up the photo and hurling it to the floor, where the glass shattered. Immediately regretful, he fell to his knees and sobbed, begging, "Laura, I'm sorry. Please forgive me. It wasn't your fault."

Then the unthinkable happened, on September 8, 1991, seven years after Laura Miller's disappearance, a couple cantered on horseback on a path cut through the Calder Drive oil field and stumbled upon yet another victim. The badly decomposed body was in the same clearing, again under a tree, three hundred feet from the first three. This time the unidentified woman was dubbed Janet Doe. Fitting the profile, she was white. The ME surmised she was twenty-four to thirty-four years old. Janet Doe was five-foot-three and 130 pounds, and, again recalling the other cases, she had long, light brown hair.

Animals had been tearing away at the corpse, and Janet Doe's skull wasn't with the body but was found three days later a short distance away. At the morgue, the medical examiner found evidence that the woman had been struck on the right side of the face with a flat object. Her cheekbone and jaw were both broken, and the blow had damaged a cheaply made partial upper denture. Yet there were differences with this fourth killing, including that this victim, unlike the others, was placed facedown in the field. For a cause of death, the medical examiner settled on strangulation.

As quiet as the investigation into the Killing Field murders had been for five years, suddenly it was all over the newspapers. "Police officials not giving up on murders," Galveston's *Daily News* reported. In a quote, police talked about the problems with the cases, that the women had apparently been killed elsewhere and dumped in the field. "This is the hardest type of homicide to work and clear," a League City lieutenant said. "We have a murder, but we don't have a crime scene."

*America's Most Wanted* aired a program on the newly discovered body, and leads poured in from across the nation, many from families with missing loved ones hoping to claim Janet Doe. To try to identify the woman, the medical examiner attempted to rehydrate her decomposing finger tissue to get prints, then used cameras and lights to expose the ridges. The effort failed, and like Jane Doe, whose body had been found with Laura Miller's skeleton in 1986, Janet Doe had no family or her real name.

Many tried to give the Jane and Janet Doe their faces, including these by forensic artist Lois Gibson.

Over the following years Lois Gibson, a well-known Houston forensic artist, and others, used their talents to try to give back to the women some of what the killer and death had taken, their faces and their identities. Despite the hard work and good intentions, no one stepped forward to claim them.

Obsessed with his daughter's death, Tim continually contemplated who could have killed her. At times, he had theories, including one in particular, a former neighbor with a shady past. But it was only after Janet Doe's discovery in 1991 that a serious suspect emerged in the eyes of law enforcement. Robert Abel was a retired NASA engineer, one with a top-security clearance who'd been with the space program since the early sixties, a brilliant man who helped engineer the Saturn rocket that carried astronauts to the moon.

Bearded, paunchy, and slight in stature, Abel leased acreage on one side of the Calder Drive oil field beginning in 1983, the year Heide Fye disappeared. Early on, he'd shown a keen interest in the cases, at times lending horses to the investigating officers and giving unsolicited advice. In 1990, the year before Janet Doe's murder, Abel purchased the eleven acres directly adjacent to the Killing Field and opened the Stardust Trail Rides, clearing away brush for paths through the woods and installing picnic tables.

To police, Abel appeared inordinately interested in the murders. Did that mean he was involved, or rather was it simply geography, the proximity of having the bodies found so close to his home?

One reason authorities focused on Abel was that he fit a profile drawn up by the FBI Academy in Quantico, Virginia. Based on a review of the evidence, the feds surmised that the man using the Killing Field as his private dumping ground was a methodical, organized sexual serial killer, one with high intelligence who probably had a history of abusing animals.

Married three times, fiftysomething Abel had a past filled with rocky relationships, and two of his ex-wives told police that their former husband had just such tendencies, that he beat horses with pipes until the animals kowtowed to him. The women described Abel's temper as violent, contending that he flew into rages. One grisly comparison to the way the women's corpses were left to rot in the field came from one of Abel's ex-wives; she said that Abel didn't bury horse carcasses but left the remains on the land, where they'd be picked clean by vultures, coyotes, and other scavengers.

Based on the similarities between the FBI profile and Abel's alleged history, the League City police gained a search warrant for his property in November 1993. For twelve hours, they combed through Robert Abel's land and house. When they left, they took with them .22 caliber guns and bullets, the same caliber used to murder Jane Doe, a gold cap from a tooth, human teeth, newspaper clippings about the murders, and boxes of photos. The teeth and gold cap, they reasoned, could have been souvenirs taken from victims. They vacuumed the rugs, looking for hairs or fibers linked to the killings.

One of the final lines of the search warrant read: "Robert William Abel . . . committed these offenses . . ."

In the end, the search produced no evidence tying Abel to the Killing Field murders. One disappointment was that the bullet removed from Jane Doe, either due to being exposed to acid while the body was being defleshed at the ME's office or from weathering in the field, no longer bore identifying marks that could have indicated whether or not it had been fired by one of Abel's guns.

Yet Abel remained law enforcement's primary suspect, and based on the assertions in the search warrant, Tim Miller discarded his theories about other suspects and instead focused full attention on the brilliant-yet-odd former NASA engineer who walked with a stiff gait. "After I saw how Robert Abel fit the profile, I didn't have a doubt," said Tim. "And from that point on, I made his life miserable."

Spurred on by the belief that Abel was the killer, Miller left angry messages on the man's telephone and confronted him when their paths crossed. Before long, Miller began driving to Abel's house in the evenings and parking on the street, waiting for the man to walk out to pick up his mail. In response, Abel complained to League City police, writing in January 1994: "It has occurred to me that the possibility exists that Mr. Miller has decided to personally vindicate the death of his daughter."

While his sights were set on Abel, Tim Miller continued to search for evidence, hoping to succeed where police failed. In 1998, he leased the property that comprised the Killing Field. At the suggestion of the Galveston County Sheriff's Office, he then brought in heavy equipment, back-hoes and pumps, to drain a pond on the land. Keys and change had been found near the water, and there was a theory that perhaps the killer had thrown Janet Doe's purse into the water. The work went on for two days, but all that was ultimately found were scraps of fabric from what appeared to be a woman's blouse, edged in lace.

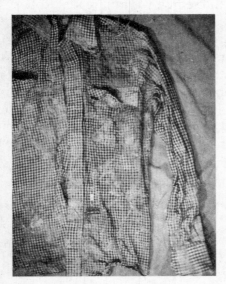

Could the stains on the Killing Field shirt be blood?

*(Courtesy of Tim Miller)*

Frustrated, wanting to know what evidence police had that they weren't sharing with him, Miller filed a lawsuit for records from his daughter's case and received pictures of evidence from the investigation. One was of a blue-checked, Western man's shirt that bore Laura's case number on a tag. Tim wondered if stains visible in the photo could have been blood. In 1986, when the shirt was found, DNA testing had yet to be put into use in criminal cases, but by the late nineties, that had changed. Tim would later say that he went to the League City police station, asking to have the shirt tested, only to be told that it had disappeared.

Disappointed in the way the case was being handled, grieving for his daughter and carrying the guilt of failing her, Tim's life continued to unravel. He married again, but Laura's murder preoccupied him. One night in the Killing Field, he pleaded, "Laura, please do not hate your daddy, but it's time for me to put my life back together. I need to say good-bye."

Walking toward his truck, he heard his dead daughter's voice yet again, "Dad, don't quit. Please, don't quit."

"Damn you, Laura," Tim answered. "Just damn you!"

In 1999, Robert Abel told a *Texas Monthly* reporter that the damage done to him by the cloud of suspicion was all-encompassing. "My life has been destroyed. My reputation ruined. I didn't kill any of those girls. I wouldn't know how to kill."

Meanwhile, Tim Miller didn't stop his quest for justice. He consulted a Native American spiritualist and hired a private investigator in attempts to find the man responsible for his personal hell. Consistently, nearly every lead appeared to point to Robert Abel.

Over the years, Miller again took to parking on Abel's street, waiting for him. At times, Abel walked toward him shaking, angry. One night, he shouted at Tim, "All those girls were whores anyway."

Miller jumped from his truck with his gun and came at the man he despised, throwing him on the ground and holding the barrel to Abel's head. "I could murder you now, and I probably should. But if you're dead, they'll probably never find out who Jane and Janet Doe are," Miller said, holding back his rage. "They say you're a serial killer, and you don't have a conscience, Robert. But I'm going to remind you every day for the rest of your life."

Trembling with anger, Tim Miller walked away.

As he drove off in his truck, he judged that he'd crossed

an important line. "I felt like I'd lost my mind," he said. From that confrontation, Miller drove directly to a hospital, where he stayed for ten days. Before long, his preacher began visiting and talking to Tim about forgiveness. "That was one of the healthiest things that I've ever done for myself," said Tim. "The anger was killing me."

After that pivotal day when he'd pointed a gun at Abel, Tim Miller turned his life around.

Over the years, Tim had begun helping in the searches for the missing in southern Houston, including the victims who disappeared on or near I-45 in the years after Laura's death. It was one night in the Killing Field when he made a promise. "I told God and Laura that I wouldn't turn my back on a family looking for a loved one," he said. "I'd always do my best to be there for other families suffering the way we did."

In 2000, Tim Miller began Equusearch, its reputation as a persistent and determined resource to find the missing spreading first across Texas, then the nation. In 2002, he was invited to Washington, D.C., to be in the room when then-president George W. Bush signed a bill setting aside $10 million to expand the Amber Alert program. Miller sat next to Elizabeth Smart's parents at the ceremony, after he and other Equusearch volunteers helped hunt for their daughter. At the time, Elizabeth, who'd been abducted from her Salt Lake City bedroom the previous June, remained missing. "I saw them like I was looking in a mirror," he said. "They were suffering like I had, all those months Laura was missing." The Smart family's story would have a happier ending, when nine months after her disappearance, authorities rescued Elizabeth and arrested her captors.

In 2008, when Caylee Anthony was reported missing, and media across the nation and the world focused on the toddler's case, Tim and Equusearch volunteers traveled to Florida. Looking back, it appeared to Miller that from the beginning Casey Anthony's father suspected that his daughter was involved in the toddler's disappearance. In one exchange, when Miller explained that they'd begun looking for a body instead of a living little girl, Tim Miller remembers George Anthony called his daughter out of her bedroom, and ordered, "Casey, tell Tim where to look."

Instead of helping, as Tim recalled, Casey stalked off.

By then, Tim had transformed, putting aside his anger and the way he saw his old nemesis, Robert Abel. No evidence beyond speculation ever emerged to tie Abel to the killings, and Tim came to believe perhaps police had been wrong and his old enemy wasn't the man who'd murdered Laura. Regretting all he'd put Abel through, one day Tim saw the man on the road and honked. The two men pulled over, and Tim approached Abel and apologized. Admitting that the other man had ample reason to hate him, Tim said he was disappointed in himself for being swept up in the suspicion and tormenting Abel as he had. "Robert, I am very sorry for all the grief I caused you," Miller said.

At that, both men cried.

"I was glad we had that conversation," said Tim. "We finally put it all to rest."

That reconciliation turned out to be especially important in 2005. Tim was in Aruba helping to search for Natalee Holloway, when he heard that Robert Abel was dead. The retired engineer drove an ATV-type vehicle onto railroad tracks and was hit by an oncoming train. Tim heard that Abel was in bad health and rumors circulated that it could have been suicide. In the end, Abel hadn't left a note, and his death was ruled an accident. Miller wasn't certain that was the case. In the small towns around I-45, many continued to believe that the man who ran the stables was the serial killer, and once Abel had that reputation, he'd remained an outcast. "I still wonder if all the suspicion was part of it," said Tim.

Although Abel was gone, the mystery surrounding the Killing Field persisted. That year, yet another billboard went up with sketches of Jane and Janet Doe along a Houston highway. And when Tim returned home after months in Aruba, he discovered a bizarre letter waiting for him at Equusearch headquarters. The words cut out of magazines and newspapers and glued onto a sheet of paper—decorated with demonic symbols including upside-down crosses and the numbers 666—spelled a chilling message: "Abel is not the devil sought by the League City blue fuzz . . . The key to the nightmare field of death . . . Tim Miller it's me you're looking for . . . I was the last man your Laura saw and many more . . . the police won't get me for I am too smart . . . this monster in me . . . more bodies and bones to be found . . ."

That evening, Tim went to the Killing Field and found the cross he'd erected knocked down and broken. He repaired it and stood it upright.

On one hand, Tim Miller's life had turned an important corner, and while he would never forget, he perhaps began reconciling all that had happened. "I know now that Laura's death wasn't in vain. I miss her, and I think about her every day. The holiday seasons are the worst. But because of her death—through Equusearch—we've made a tremendous change in methods used when searching for the missing."

At the same time, he hasn't given up on his quest to give the murdered girls justice. "I've got nearly three decades into this," he said. "We need to get this guy put away."

The Killing Fields murders unfolded over a seven-year period, from 1984 to 1991. Later I would interview a man who said he murdered one of the women, the fourth one, Janet Doe. And he would insist that Tim Miller shouldn't have apologized to Robert Abel, that there was sufficient reason to believe that he was capable of murder. Yet did Abel kill the first three women whose bodies were found in the field? Perhaps not. For as the years unfolded, other evidence came to light, evidence that Tim Miller's instincts might have been right from the beginning and that perhaps he'd known all along who murdered his daughter.

That realization, however, waited in the future. In the meantime, the blood shed during the eighties wasn't confined to that quiet field off Calder Drive.

As the decade counted down, three months after Laura Miller and Jane Doe were discovered, a perky young woman simply drove on the interstate on her way to her boyfriend's house after a hard night's work. Like so many others, Shelley Sikes vanished.

# Chapter 8

## They Couldn't Prove Murder
## The Abduction of Shelley Sikes

### Memorial Day Weekend, 1986

Eddie Sikes holding one of the "Search for Shelley" posters.
*(Courtesy of Kathryn Casey)*

"Lives can change in the blink of an eye," said Eddie Sikes, a sixty-nine-year-old wearing a tropical shirt, jeans, and sporting a trim white beard. We'd been talking for nearly three hours, and it had been a painful voyage back in time, to Memorial Day weekend 1986 and the day his nineteen-year-old daughter Shelley vanished on her drive home from work. "People just don't realize how quickly things can happen," he said, his eyes misting. "Sometimes they forget that stuff like cars and houses don't matter. That what counts are the people they love."

For a moment, Sikes was visibly troubled as he considered what to say next. He was seated in the office of his steel-fabricating plant in Texas City, on the mainland just north of Galveston and not far from League City and the Killing Field. Beside him were thick scrapbooks of yellowing press clippings documenting the tragedy that had shadowed his life for nearly three decades, and in his hands he held a poster produced in the days following Shelley's disappearance. Unlike Tim Miller, Eddie has found some justice—if justice is ever truly possible—but painful questions regarding his daughter's death remain unanswered. And despite the years, closure has never come. "Not a day goes by that I don't think about what happened. It never leaves me. Looking back, it was a crash course in good and evil."

The year Shelley disappeared, 1986, Galveston was in the midst of a building boom, pricey beach communities and condominiums rising on the upscale west end. One of the island's favorite sons, oil magnet George Mitchell, who'd become famous as the developer of The Woodlands, a massive, sprawling, master-planned community north of Houston, had dedicated his expertise and money to helping his birthplace reclaim its past glory. The Strand, the historic district once rotting into disrepair, was renovated, including

Shelley Sikes in her graduation photo.
*(Courtesy of Edward Sikes)*

repurposing an abandoned warehouse into the latest incarnation of the historic and posh Tremont House hotel.

Despite the face-lift, relatively little had truly changed

on the island in the decade since the eleven girls died in the 1970s. As always, the beaches dominated, and it was in summers that the population swelled. Ranked high on a list of local landmarks were the aged Victorians that survived the great storm of 1900 and Gaido's seafood restaurant, founded in 1911. For many, any stay on the island required at least one dinner at Gaido's to be complete. Tourists and locals alike used the restaurant as a meeting place.

In August 1971, Glenda Willis had picked up her friends from Webster, fourteen-year-olds Sharon Shaw and Renee Johnson, in front of Gaido's. Farther down Seawall Boulevard, Willis said good-bye, as Shaw and Johnson walked off promising to return later that afternoon. It would be the last time Willis saw her friends. Months later, she identified Shaw's and Johnson's jewelry to help police ID their skeletons.

Shelley loved working at Gaido's, a Galveston landmark.
*(Courtesy of Kathryn Casey)*

Fifteen years later on the Saturday of Memorial Day weekend 1986, at 11:34 P.M., Shelley Sikes stood at the time clock inside Gaido's punching out, after a busy shift serving fresh oysters, broiled and golden fried seafood, steaks and drinks.

At just five feet and weighing only ninety pounds, Sikes was petite with a wide smile and big brown eyes. After graduating from Texas City High School, where she'd been pretty much Miss Everything, including most congenial and an assistant drum major, Sikes had gone on to attend the University of Texas in Austin the previous fall. "She'd taken three classes," said Eddie, smiling at the memory. "Music and two dance courses, and I asked, 'What about English and history?' But Shelley really wasn't interested. Her plan was to open a dance studio."

It was a logical strategy for Shelley. She'd been a fixture in ballet, jazz, and tap classes since grade school, and she'd choreographed routines for her high school's drum majors. Loving dance and being center stage, Shelley had a spark about her, a playful nature and a spunky attitude.

Remembering Shelley, Eddie would say that he didn't believe she had an enemy in the world. Instead, she laughed and made friends easily, and she had a penchant for adopting animals, such as the pink Easter chick he gave her and an armadillo he caught that Shelley named Lone Star. She nurtured it for more than a year before it died, then she insisted Eddie dig a hole in the backyard to bury it.

Before Christmas 1985, Shelley called her dad from Austin asking if he'd be

An early photo of Shelley Sikes with her dad. *(Courtesy of Edward Sikes)*

angry if she took time off from college to rethink her future. She was homesick, and he'd later surmise that she missed her boyfriend, Mark Spurgeon, whom she'd been dating since high school. A year behind her, he wouldn't enter college until the coming fall. "I was driving to Austin every weekend to see Shelley," said Mark.

"Not mad but disappointed," Eddie remarked to Shelley about her change of plans.

Shelley in Austin, where she attended the University of Texas. *(Courtesy of Edward Sikes)*

That month, Shelley moved into the Texas City house Eddie shared with his second wife, Denise. Days later, Shelley was hired as a waitress at Gaido's. Eddie wasn't particularly happy about his daughter's new job because it was on the island. "I've always thought of Galveston as kind of a Sin City," he said. "Especially in the summers. There's the beaches, people drink, and there are always guys looking to pick up girls."

Yet Shelley did well at Gaido's and particularly liked working the dinner shifts, when tips were the most plentiful. After work, she routinely arrived home just before midnight. Eddie waited up, and they watched *M*A*S*H* reruns before bed. But on what would become the fateful evening of May 24, 1986, Eddie had taken a holiday-weekend fishing trip to the family lake cottage outside Austin.

That Saturday night, Shelley walked alone through Gaido's door into the parking lot, and climbed into her 1980 dark blue Ford Pinto, intending to drive north onto the mainland to her boyfriend's house, to watch movies. Mark had called about nine thirty, inviting her. "She said she was tired and really didn't want to go out," he remembered. "She said it had been busy at work, and her feet hurt."

Later, the irony of the situation troubled Eddie. On most nights, Shelley would have had a pistol in her car. He had taught both his daughters, Shelley and her older sister, Dana, how to shoot when they were teenagers. But the gun he bought for Shelley was too big for her small hand, and just a week earlier he'd taken it back, intending to replace it. That, however, hadn't happened yet. So on that night, as Shelley drove through Galveston, the Pinto's glove box was empty. It had rained earlier in the evening, leaving the roads slick.

At first, nothing seemed out of the ordinary. On her way to Mark's house, Shelley made a brief stop, driving through a fast-food restaurant and grabbing a burger, then pulled out onto Broadway Street, heading toward the causeway and the mainland. Yet as she traversed the darkened streets, something went terribly wrong.

When Shelley didn't arrive at her boyfriend's house, Mark called Gaido's, and a waiter answered the phone. "Shelley left a long time ago," he said. His next remark would later haunt Spurgeon; with the holiday weekend upon them, the waiter added, "There are a lot of crazies out there tonight."

Not understanding why Shelley hadn't arrived at his house, worried that she could have had car trouble, Mark drove on I-45 toward Galveston, back and forth between his house and the island restaurant, but didn't see Shelley or her car. Increasingly worried, he returned home. At the house, Mark explained the situation to his father and enlisted his help with the search.

This time, when the two men retraced what would have been Shelley's route, Mark searched out the window while his father drove. On the first loop as they left the island and drove north off the causeway, Mark spotted a car parked on the feeder with its dome light shining. Shelley's light sometimes stuck on. "Pull off here," he told his dad.

The car mired in the shoulder's sandy loam was the blue Pinto, and it was empty. Shelley was gone.

Mark's pulse quickened as he looked over the scene. The Pinto's driver's-side window was smashed, glass shards covering the front seat. Inspecting the damage, Mark and his father noted what looked like blood running down the outside of the driver's-side door. The inside, too, was stained with a spray of red on the seat and the front window. Examining the area around the car, Mark noticed the imprint of a bare foot in the dirt beside the roadway. At first, he thought perhaps Shelley had been in an accident, but the blood pattern perplexed him; the way the spatter was scattered about didn't seem right. "Shelley, where are you?" Mark cried out into the darkness, as the occasional car streamed past on I-45. No one answered.

When police arrived, they talked with Mark and his dad. Quickly, it became apparent that the responding officers assumed they'd been called to an accident scene and that Shelley had probably wandered off, perhaps hurt and looking for help. Not appearing overly concerned, the officer wrote up a report. When he finished, he asked if Mark wanted to take Shelley's car and get it off the side of the road. Mark agreed, but his father stepped forward.

"We're not taking that car anywhere," the older man said. "Something's happened here. You need to get someone to pick that car up." Worried that what they were looking at wasn't an accident but a crime, when the tow truck arrived to remove Shelley's Pinto, Mark's father asked the driver to secure the vehicle, locking it to protect any evidence inside.

By then, Eddie was speeding through the night on his way toward Galveston, knowing only that his daughter was missing, her car found, the window broken with blood on the door and inside. A five-and-a-half-hour drive, he stopped halfway and called his wife, Denise, only to be told she had no new information. She'd contacted area hospitals, but none reported treating a girl matching Shelley's description. When Eddie arrived at the scene, fifteen to twenty deputies and police officers milled about. "What happened to your daughter?" one asked.

"I don't know," Eddie answered. "I hoped you'd know that."

Hours passed, without any information coming Eddie's way. When it appeared there was nothing to do at the scene, he drove home to be near the phone. No news surfaced, and by sunrise, Eddie and Denise were at the steel-fabricating plant he owned in Texas City manning the copy machine, running off reams of flyers with Shelley's photo on the top. Word spread, and volunteers arrived and grabbed stacks to post throughout the area. Shelley's mom, Erin, secured a promise through her employer, Amoco Oil, for a five-thousand-dollar reward for her daughter's safe return, and that was added to the posters and flyers. But by then, police had disturbing information that suggested Shelley's situation could be dire.

In the sheriff's office the afternoon following their daughter's disappearance, Eddie, his wife, and ex-wife filled out paperwork to file a missing person's report. In another room, two people who'd driven on I-45 the night before, described to detectives how they saw Shelley's car being pursued by a pickup truck. The first witness, a man, was in his station wagon a little after midnight when Shelley's Pinto pulled up on his right. A pickup hovered behind her, driving recklessly, as if the driver were trying to force her off the road. The Pinto and the pickup barreled past the witness's vehicle. He saw Shelley slam on her brakes and swerve off at an exit, apparently attempting to get away. The maneuver didn't work. While the pickup driver missed the exit, he responded quickly, jumping the grass-covered earth between the freeway and the service road, in pursuit. A short distance down the road, the Pinto spun and slid off onto the shoulder, its wheels mired in the wet earth. That first witness on the scene saw the pickup driver jump from the cab, pull his shirt off and wrap it around his hand, then pound on the car's window.

By the time the man stopped to investigate, the pickup driver had broken the window and was dragging Shelley from her car. To the man witnessing the action, Shelley looked barely conscious. Appearing in a near frenzy, the pickup driver shouted at the passerby that it was a domestic spat and ordered him to get lost. He reluctantly complied when the man put his hand to his back as if he had a gun.

The second statement backed up much of what the first witness had said, but that woman believed that as Shelley was dragged from the car, she was conscious and grasping the car door frame, fighting to prevent the pickup driver from taking her.

When the deputy assigned to update the family explained the situation to Eddie, the reality of what had taken place struck him. There was no longer any possibility that what had happened was an accident, that Shelley wandered off and waited in a hospital bed. Eddie's daughter had been taken by someone who obviously meant her great harm.

At the police station, a forensic artist worked with the witnesses to draw a composite of the pickup driver. The face that emerged was that of an unshaven man with long-ish brown hair, dark eyebrows, and an angry pout. Based on the blood found in the Pinto, they assumed that he'd cut his arm and could be wearing a bandage. Yet while investigators now had an idea of what the man who'd taken Shelley looked like, they didn't have a name or a license number for his pickup truck.

That day and the next, Eddie and the rest of Shelley's family waited impatiently for news, but none came. Not knowing what to do or how to find help, Eddie approached someone he thought would understand what the family faced. He picked up the phone and called John Walsh, whose six-year-old son, Adam, had been abducted from a Sears store in Hollywood, Florida, five years earlier in 1981, his decapitated body found days later. At the time Eddie called him, Walsh was gaining a reputation as a staunch victims' advocate with a special interest in abducted and exploited children. Later he'd go on to become the host of the television show *America's Most Wanted*. "I didn't know if I'd get through, but I did," said Eddie.

Sympathetic, Walsh listened. What he then advised Eddie Sikes to do became an outline for the painful months to come. Walsh told Eddie to do whatever he could to get publicity and pressure the investigators. He said to "keep the case in the headlines to keep the cops out of the coffee shops and out on the street looking for Shelley."

Heeding the advice, Eddie Sikes hired a publicist to promote Shelley's case, and Eddie kept churning out those posters, in English, and later in Spanish, giving them to neighbors, family, friends, total strangers, anyone willing to spread the word. "I think we printed somewhere around three hundred thousand flyers, and we had them in forty-six states," said Eddie. "One friend got them on the backs of eighteen-wheelers that traveled all over the country."

Meanwhile, Mark Spurgeon not only grappled with the uncertainty and fear of what had happened to his girlfriend but also felt as if he were under a magnifying glass. Called in repeatedly to talk to police, he gave statement after statement. Unmarked cars trailed him each time he drove out of his driveway. "I understood why they were doing it," he said. "But at the same time, I wanted them to stop watching me and go find Shelley."

If at first Eddie and the rest of Shelley's family assumed she'd be found quickly, that didn't happen. Instead, days, weeks, then months passed without news. Leads came in and were followed, polygraph tests given, but nothing led to Shelley or her abductor. On his own, Eddie drove every route he could think of off I-45, hoping to find something to shed light on the mystery of what had happened to his daughter.

At times, his thoughts drifted to the Killing Field off Calder Drive. It had been only months since the remains of the second and third victims, Laura Miller and Jane Doe, were found. Was it possible that the man who'd abducted Shelley was the Killing Field's serial killer? Had the evil that stalked that desolate oil field claimed Shelley, too?

The suspicion tormented Eddie, and for days, alone, he walked the field off I-45, searching, hoping yet fearing he'd find Shelley's remains. "I memorized every square foot of that field," he said. "I never found anything."

Desperate to uncover his younger daughter's whereabouts or, if the worst had happened, her remains, Eddie went so far as to hire a plane to fly him close to the ground, crisscrossing the area, looking for a body or an area where the ground appeared to have been recently disturbed. But with no positive results, his mission ultimately appeared hopeless. Shelley had vanished without a whisper.

Months passed, and Eddie's relationship with police soured. Before long, he began following investigators when he heard they were interviewing suspects, sitting outside on the street, watching. "I wanted to make sure they were doing their jobs," he said. And Eddie, his wife, Mark Spurgeon, and Shelley's mom continued to hand out flyers. While Eddie refrained from talking to the press, Shelley's mother and stepmom took on that role, keeping Shelley's name in the news.

At times, the phone rang with tips, sometimes from psychics who claimed to know where Shelley was buried. Although disbelieving, Eddie investigated, not waiting for authorities to follow up. "The police don't always want families to be proactive," he said. "But I was going to do whatever I could to find Shelley. If I had to get crosswise with the police, I was willing to do that."

Time passed until finally, eight months after the abduction, another witness from that horrible night talked to police. Authorities didn't tell Eddie until later what the man said, that there'd been not one but two men in the pickup, and that one of them beat Shelley in a rage before he pulled her from the Pinto.

It was about that time, unable to sleep at night, grieving and frustrated, that Eddie called one of the higher-ups at the FBI and asked him if he had children. The man said he did. "Have you ever been with them in a store and suddenly they disappear? You look for them, and they're gone? You holler for them, but they don't answer?"

"Yeah," the man said.

"I've been doing that for eight months now," Eddie said. "I need help."

The following day, the FBI supervisor called local police, and two agents were assigned to the case, but in hindsight it did little good, because even with the renewed investigation, no answers came. The result was that Eddie Sikes learned a hard truth. "Texas Rangers, FBI agents, detectives, and such, they're all just people," he said. "They're just regular folks, and they can't always solve the cases."

Throughout that year, Eddie and the rest of Shelley's family continued to keep on the pressure with the "Search for Shelley" campaign. Donated billboards on I-45 with Shelley's picture and the composite of the suspect prominently displayed asked for information. And as the one-year anniversary approached, Shelley's family redoubled their efforts, and local newspapers ran updates on the case, more flyers went out, and the reward grew to $12,000. A rally was held in Texas City, and volunteers who attended took home posters to deliver to restaurants, stores, or tape to light posts. Yet there were still no leads.

Then a month later, on June 22, 1987, a remarkable thing happened just over the border in Ciudad Juarez, Mexico; a shaggy-haired man with a beard entered a cantina and saw a poster in Spanish with Shelley's photo. Troubled and drunk, he stumbled back across the bridge over the Rio Grande, to the rundown El Paso motel where he was staying. Hours later, at 4:00 P.M., he called 9–1–1 begging for help, saying that he'd tried to hang himself and slit his wrists. When police arrived, they found the distraught man with two suicide notes, one written on the back of his auto insurance card, in which he claimed to have been involved in the kidnapping of Shelley Sikes.

A still photo taken from the police video of King's first confession. *(Trial exhibit)*

The man in the hotel was John Robert King, a twenty-nine-year-old unemployed laborer. Because he was suicidal, King was taken into protective custody and transported to a hospital. The following day, El Paso police returned, read King his rights, and then took an oral statement from him in which he said that he'd been involved in the Galveston abduction of a woman named Shelley Sikes. During that statement, King implicated a friend, a drinking buddy he'd done drugs with, Gerald Pieter Zwarst.

When King checked out of the hospital after a three-day stay, police waited. They brought him to a judge to have his rights read yet again.

Afterward, El Paso officers transported King to the station, where two Galveston detectives, Wayne Kessler, a sandy-haired man, and Tommy Hansen, dark-haired and bearded, waited to interview him. Both had been working the Sikes case for more than a year, and both were eager to hear what King would say. Again, the man who was now the main suspect in the case was read his rights, this time while a video camera recorded every word.

On the video taken that day, King at first rarely looked up at either Kessler or Hansen, instead staring at the wall or the floor, as he recounted in a hoarse voice the events that took place thirteen months earlier. He and Gerry had been fishing in Galveston that day, drinking and smoking pot laced with PCP—phencyclidine—an animal tranquilizer also called Angel Dust known to cause hallucinations, numbness, paranoia, and to contribute to violent outbursts. That night, around midnight, they were in Zwarst's pickup driving off the island, when King saw Shelley in her Pinto.

"I gave her a friendly wave," King told Kessler and Hansen. Was that all he'd done? Whatever transpired between them, Shelley lost patience. "She shot me the finger."

In King's account, Zwarst was behind the wheel. King said he told his friend what the girl had done, and Zwarst "flipped out," forcing Shelley off the road, then breaking the window and pulling her from the car. For the most part, King claimed to be so out of it from drugs and alcohol, that he was barely involved. Yet he admitted helping Zwarst carry Shelley to the pickup truck and putting her on the front floorboard. What were his intentions? King said he did it because Shelley was hurt, and Zwarst said they were taking her to the hospital.

Yet that made little sense. If King only wanted to help Shelley, if Zwarst was the one who pursued Shelley, why did King say he climbed on her in the back of the truck? "I got on top of her. I don't know if I had intercourse with her. Then I heard her whimpering and crying. I backed off."

Later, King said they ended up at his parents' house in

Bacliff, twenty-six miles north of the spot on I-45 where they'd left Shelley's Pinto. At that point, King said Zwarst disappeared with Shelley and a shovel out of the elder Kings' garage.

Only later, King said, did he happen upon a place in the woods behind his parents' house, one where it looked like something had been buried. "I knew there was something bad there, but I didn't want to know what it was." Throughout the entire episode, from abducting Shelley through burying her, King said he was in a drug-and-alcohol-induced haze, in and out of consciousness.

What caused his suicide attempt that brought King to the attention of law enforcement? The constant publicity. "I wanted to deny it. It couldn't have been us. It must have been us. I was going to run from it, get a job somewhere."

Instead, King ended up in that drab hotel room, attempting to hang himself with his shoelaces and slit his wrist with a blade from a disposable razor. When he called his mother, she asked him to call 9-1-1 for help.

"I can't believe I didn't stop Gerry," King said. "He busted the window out . . . or maybe I did? . . . Now that I look back, it seems like a bad dream, a nightmare."

When it came to hitting her, King said he hadn't done that. "I know that for a fact."

"What caused her death?" one of the detectives asked.

"It must have been the shovel," King answered, suggesting that Shelley may have been alive when buried.

There were many contradictions in King's statement, among them that he had no intention to abduct Shelley but that he might have been the one who'd broken out the window. He claimed that he believed they were taking her to a hospital, yet when she moved on the floorboard in front of him, he pushed her down with his foot. In his account, his primary crime was that he didn't prevent his friend from abducting the teenager. "I didn't know what was going on," he said. "It was like I was in a daze or possessed or in a blackout or something."

"You and Gerry were in the truck that night, and he was driving?" Kessler asked.

"Yeah," King answered. He looked up and at the detectives when he said that he worried that Zwarst would try to put the blame on him.

"Do you want to go back to Galveston?" Kessler asked.

"Yeah," King answered.

**F**our days after his suicide attempt, King was in Galveston being outfitted with a concealed recorder. That afternoon, he met with Zwarst, a thirty-two-year-old unemployed pipe-fitter. A lanky man, Zwarst had brown hair with sideburns and a mustache. King tried to bait his friend with questions about the abduction, but Zwarst denied knowing what he was talking about. Later that night, Zwarst was arrested and brought in for questioning by Kessler and Hansen. At first Zwarst denied any involvement, but the two detectives kept challenging him, saying, "You're lying."

Finally, Gerald Zwarst admitted he remembered that night. His story paralleled King's in some ways but varied in key facts, including who was driving the car and who forced Shelley Sikes off the road and abducted her.

In his statement, Gerald Zwarst agreed that they were in his truck that night. When it came to who was behind the wheel, however, he disagreed, insisting that King was the driver who forced Shelley's Pinto off the road. After the abduction, they took her to a

Mug shot of Gerald Pieter Zwarst. *(Courtesy of the Harris County Sheriff's Office)*

park, where King put her in the pickup's bed and climbed in on top of her. But Zwarst wasn't sure if his friend had raped her. "The last time I heard any sound out of her was when she was on the floorboard," Zwarst said. "She tried to get up one time, and he kicked her back down."

Neither admitted responsibility for Sikes's murder or confirmed if she was dead or alive when buried.

At two that morning, the four men were in an interview room in the Galveston County Sheriff's Office—Zwarst, King, Hansen, and Kessler—with questions and allegations flying.

"What was obvious from talking to them," Lieutenant Tommy Hansen would later say, "was that it went from flirtatious to bullshit to murder because anger set in. They were flirting with her, and finally she'd had enough. She flashed them the universal signal at that point, and it went from play to, 'Okay, bitch!' It escalated until it was, 'Oh, shit. What have we done?'"

During the interrogation, from left, Hansen, King pointing at Zwarst, and Kessler. *(Trial exhibit)*

"Discuss this so we can find this girl's body and know exactly what you did and how she happened to be dead," one of the detectives ordered at the double interrogation. But that didn't occur. Instead, the two men blamed each other.

"Neither one wanted to take responsibility, which isn't unusual when there are two involved," said Hansen. "And what was really obvious was that Shelley was just in the wrong place at the wrong time."

The interview continued, and King claimed that Zwarst had taken a shovel and the body to the woods. In response, Zwarst countered by saying he didn't even know there was a body, that he was "out of it" most of the time.

"Bullshit!" King charged.

"I don't know anything," Zwarst insisted.

"One of you or both of you know where she's buried," Kessler charged.

In response, King kept pointing at and accusing Zwarst, who did the same in kind until Hansen ordered, "Somebody's lying . . . we want to know where she's at . . . Her family has the right to bury her!"

Yet by that interview, five days after King's suicide attempt, the detectives weren't simply at the mercy of what King and Zwarst wanted to tell them. They had lab results that pegged the blood inside the Pinto as King's, not Zwarst's. Kessler pointed out to King that he was the one who had scars on his arm from breaking the window and the one identified by witnesses as both the driver of the pickup and the one who'd pulled Sikes from the car.

"No, man," King shouted, again pointing at Zwarst. "He knows, man. I swear to God, he was driving."

The bickering continued until Hansen removed Zwarst from the room.

Once they were alone, Kessler talked calmly to King, telling him that the likelihood was that he wasn't remembering everything because he'd been so high that night. "I know you didn't go out that night intending to kill this girl. But what happened happened, and it got out of hand," Kessler said. "Tell me where she is."

Gradually, it appeared that King started to understand that it was likely he'd been the force behind the abduction, and he began wailing like an injured animal, "Oh, man, I couldn't have," he sobbed. "I couldn't have."

"Tell me what happened," Kessler said. "Tell me where she is."

"I can't remember, man," King cried.

"You can't hold it in. Will you tell me?"

Over and again, King insisted he didn't remember anything from that night other than what he'd told them, that Zwarst was behind it all, but the detective wasn't buying the explanation, instead saying that wasn't how it happened, but rather what King wanted to believe. "Clear your conscience, John," Kessler said. "Is she back there [on your parents' property]?"

"She must be," King finally said. "I don't remember burying her . . . Gerry helped me . . . I can't remember."

"Do you remember digging? You say he helped you?"

"I think he did . . ."

"Where did you bury her?"

"Right there out in the back of my mom's house," King said.

"What finally killed her?"

"The shovel, maybe," King said. ". . . Seems like I remember, unless she was already dead, jabbing her with the shovel . . . She was in a grave and the dirt was on top . . . I can't remember doing it, but I can just picture myself doing it."

When he was later read his rights again, a judge would say he heard King mumble something on the order of: "I have to get this off my mind. I done it. I done it. I can still see her body moving when I hit her with the shovel."

The day after the interview ended, Eddie and the rest of Shelley's immediate family met at the sheriff's office to hear what investigators had learned. "I lost it," said Eddie. "I just broke down and cried."

When Eddie first saw the two alleged killers, it was in a courtroom where they were being read their rights. His thoughts were "dark," he said. "I wanted fifteen minutes alone with them."

Believing the case was finally coming to an end, Shelley's mom, Erin, wanted to buy a casket, but Eddie reminded her that they didn't yet have their daughter's body. By then, King had agreed to take Hansen and Kessler to Shelley's grave, to allow them to recover her remains.

Why didn't they ever take that trip? Tommy Hansen would say that he remembered getting ready to take King to his parents' house to look for the burial site when King suddenly asked to talk to a lawyer. "At that point, everything stopped," he said. "Once he said 'lawyer,' we couldn't take him. And after he talked to the lawyer, he was no longer cooperating."

"We were that close to finding Shelley's body," Tommy Hansen said, holding up his thumb and index finger an inch apart. "If King just hadn't asked for a lawyer, he would have taken us to the site, and we would have been able to dig her up. But once he did ask, it was over. It was all over."

In the weeks that followed, Kessler and Hansen obtained a search warrant and six hundred officers, deputies, and volunteers searched in chest-high brush in the woods behind the King house. Cadaver dogs were brought in based on King's claims that he and Zwarst had buried the body there. Helicopters circled overhead, and a forensic team manned gas-emission equipment that was designed to detect vapors released from decomposition. Eddie, his then-wife, Denise, and his ex-wife, Erin, waited and watched, but nothing was ever found.

Speculation built. John King's parents had a new driveway, and rumors circulated that Shelley was buried beneath it. But Hansen and Kessler found records that indicated it was poured a short time before, not after the kidnapping.

Meanwhile, the Galveston County District Attorney at

the time, Mike Guarino, prepared for trial. The main discussion revolved around the charges. Eddie hoped that King and Zwarst would be tried for his daughter's murder. Yet Guarino worried that could be difficult to prove without a body. Instead, he favored aggravated kidnapping. The police had eyewitnesses and multiple confessions from King and Zwarst detailing how they'd driven Shelley off the road and taken her hostage. "We had a good kidnapping charge and an iffy murder charge," said Guarino. "And the truth is that they're comparable charges, both first-degree felonies carrying maximum penalties of life."

One more consideration: There was no statute of limitations in Texas law for murder. If Guarino held back until authorities found Shelley's body, he could go for capital murder and perhaps get death penalties. Without a body, he worried that the odds of a jury's voting for death weren't in his favor.

"But I thought we had a really good case," said Guarino. "I felt good about it."

That didn't change when King's and Zwarst's defense lawyers fought the admissibility of the confessions. The attempt failed, and Guarino pulled together the evidence for the trials. Both were shifted to courthouses outside the Houston-Galveston area, to seat impartial juries. The Sikes case had made headlines for so long, Guarino didn't even fight defense motions to move the trials. "It ensured that it wouldn't be an issue they could raise on appeal," he said. "We just went along with it."

As he prepared, Guarino assessed the men's confessions. In his eyes, he didn't fully believe either King's or Zwarst's accounts. "It seemed more likely to me that they were both in on it," he said. "If it wasn't Shelley, it could have been anyone that night. They were both out of control. All drugged up and drunk. When I looked at what we had, I thought the evidence was overwhelming."

Not long before the first trial, other witnesses came forward, this time men who'd been jailed with Gerald Zwarst the year after the abduction, when he was arrested for public intoxication. They said that during jailhouse conversations Zwarst described helping to pull Sikes into the truck and said that he watched as Sikes was buried. At one point, Zwarst said Shelley Sikes regained consciousness and moved, and that King, as he'd said in the presence of the judge, hit her with the shovel.

Meanwhile, Kessler and Hansen had tracked down Zwarst's truck, the one they were in the night of the abduction. In it, a crime-scene unit found hairs compatible with those taken off of Sikes's brush. In the days before DNA testing, it couldn't be identified as her hair, but it was classified as a possible match.

When Guarino looked at the case, he marveled at the way King had come forward and confessed. The district attorney had never seen a case like it in his twenty-eight years as a prosecutor, and he credited Shelley's family for making it happen by keeping the case in the headlines. "Shelley's family really solved this case. If King hadn't felt the constant pressure, if he hadn't broken down, I don't know that we ever would have figured out that he and Zwarst were the ones."

In the end, John King was tried first, then Gerald Zwarst. In his opening statements, Guarino told jurors that on that night Shelley Sikes could have been anyone's daughter, a good kid who had bright plans for her future. She was simply driving to her boyfriend's house after work when she became an unwitting victim of violence. "There was nothing to tarnish her image, just minding her own business," said Guarino. "There were a lot of things about Shelley that the jury could identify with. It was evil that exists that caused the series of events that took her life."

Witnesses, one after the other, identified King as the one who pulled Shelley from her Pinto, beating her before he even got her out of the car. On the stand, King said that he wasn't a kidnapper and that it was Zwarst who'd abducted

Sikes. Guarino pushed to try to recover Shelley's remains, asking, "Where's the body? Where's the body?"

"I don't know!" King insisted, burying his head in his hands.

"Did you and Zwarst dig up her bones and dispose of those bones?" Guarino asked. "Dispose of them as garbage?"

"No, that's a nightmare!" King said. When Guarino pressed, contending that King abducted, raped, and killed Sikes, he became infuriated. "No! No! That wasn't me, man. I swear. It wasn't me."

"Where's Shelley?" Guarino asked again.

"I don't know!" King answered.

During the breaks, Shelley's boyfriend, Mark, and her family cried together.

Zwarst's trial was similar in many ways, except that by then Zwarst was no longer saying that he remembered King abducting Sikes or much of anything that had happened that night. Instead, he said he'd made that up under pressure from police and that he was so drugged up and drunk that he'd spent most of the night passed out. Guarino described Zwarst's memory as "selective."

"No, I'm telling the truth," he said.

When he took the stand to describe finding Shelley's car along the side of the road at both trials, Mark Spurgeon would remember feeling as if "my blood was boiling," when he looked at the two men. King never looked up at him, while Zwarst impressed him as cocky.

At the conclusion of their trials, King and Zwarst were both convicted and given life sentences on the kidnapping charges. When the jurors gave interviews, they all agreed that they believed that the men had not only abducted but also murdered Shelley Sikes.

Once both men were in prison, Guarino attempted to make a deal with Zwarst, offering him immunity on a murder charge if he would take them to Shelley Sikes's remains.

"We'd consulted Shelley's family, and they wanted to give her a proper, Christian burial," said Guarino.

Zwarst and his attorney agreed, and in September 1990, the convicted kidnapper was hypnotized. Afterward, a massive three-day search was mounted in a park near a power company where King's father worked, one where the family often fished and camped. It was an area John King knew well, so it made sense that he might have taken Shelley there. A white blouse was found, but no bones. Some members of the family looked at it and surmised from its small size and the fact that it had been hand altered—something Shelley did often—that it was hers. Eddie wasn't sure although he did remember that the uniform she wore to Gaido's, the one she would have been wearing on the night she disappeared, had a black skirt and a white blouse. Cadaver dogs also hit on the area, as if there had once been remains buried there.

"I think she was probably moved," said Hansen. "We don't know. They had plenty of time between the abduction and the arrests."

King and Zwarst have both been eligible for parole since 2007. Each time it comes up, the Sikes family protests, wanting them to serve out their sentences. Under Texas law at the time of the offense, a life sentence was a maximum of forty years.

Would Shelley's family stop objecting to parole for the two men in exchange for learning where she's buried? "I think Shelley's mom would," said Guarino. "Families will do things for closure, and it's part of our culture that we bury our dead."

Eddie Sikes disagreed. While he wanted to bury Shelley, he also held firm that Zwarst and King needed to serve the full forty years. And Sikes hadn't given up on the prospect of finding his daughter himself. Thirty years after Shelley's death, her father kept a shovel in the back of his car, and off and on still occasionally stopped and searched deserted fields. "I just have these feelings sometimes," he explained, with a shrug. "I pull over, and if it's someplace I haven't looked before, someplace where it looks like it could be, I start digging."

In the years since the trial, the family has held a service for Shelley at the Baptist church were Eddie was baptized, and on the ten-year anniversary of her daughter's disappearance, Erin placed a marker carved with Shelley's name in a cemetery. "This is the first time I've ever been able to bring flowers anywhere," she said at the time.

At his Hill Country lake house, Eddie built a memorial of his own, fencing in a section with wrought iron and stone and mounting two eagles on posts, dedicated to his lost daughter.

Eddie Sikes holding his scrapbook of clippings on his daughter's disappearance. *(Courtesy of Kathryn Casey)*

In the years following Shelley's death, Eddie Sikes and his second wife, Denise, divorced, and Eddie married Sally, who worked with him at the fabricating company. On the day

I interviewed Eddie, she was at his side, patiently prompting answers to questions when the memories crowded him so that he couldn't think of a name or an event. At one point, he sat in his chair and paged through his yellowing scrapbooks of clippings on his daughter's case. His eyes grew red, and he appeared near tears. Before long, he put the book to the side, as if to try yet again to push it all into the past.

Eddie Sikes was aging, but as I gathered my things to leave, he confessed that he had unfinished business. "I'm not ready to die yet," he said, stroking his full white beard. "There are still things I want to do with my life. The biggest one is that I want to find Shelley's remains. I want to bury my daughter."

# Chapter 9

## The Bone Doctors
## The Trial of Clyde Edwin Hedrick

### Galveston County Courthouse

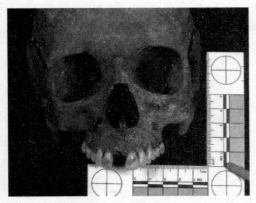

A photo of Ellen Beason's skull taken in 2012. *(Trial exhibit)*

Trials rarely bring true closure, because there is no way to erase the agony when a loved one is lost to violence. Yet the legal system is all we have, the only mechanism available to even attempt to administer justice. Parents of murdered children long for answers and that the persons responsible will be identified, exposed to the world for their atrocities, and convicted of their crimes. They want the killers to pay the price the law deems for such heinous acts.

As I worked on this book, I met mothers and fathers deprived of even basic knowledge of what transpired during the most life-altering events of their lives, the murders of their daughters. For most, there were no arrests, no judges' gavels pounding in courtrooms to signal that it was permissible to attempt to put the nightmares behind them and pick up their lives. The system failed them. Destined to live wondering and regretting, they could only pray that someday the answers would come.

For many, the unknown shadowed them. Eddie Sikes trusted that his daughter's killers lived behind bars but searched for Shelley's remains. Tim Miller buried his daughter but never stopped pondering the identity of Laura's killer.

Only on rare occasions, when it seemed the very stars aligned to light the way, did hope of a resolution emerge undiminished by bitter memories of past disappointments.

Those were the circumstances in late 2012, when Tim Miller voiced a renewed optimism, believing his long journey of uncertainty might have an end. "I think you've come to see me at a good time," he said, a twinkle in his eye. "Can you keep a secret until it becomes public?"

When I agreed, he explained, "We may finally be putting this thing together."

The conversation transpired on the first day I met Tim in his Equusearch office. That afternoon, he sat at his desk and talked, bringing me back to the first years after his daughter's death, when his sights were set on one man, his initial suspect in the killings, a neighbor.

They no longer lived in the same houses. Tim resided on a rural spread, and the man in question had also moved on, eventually landing in the nearby coastal community of San Leon. On his front lawn that Halloween, this man built a macabre cemetery display, one populated by four graves with make-believe stones etched with the names of horror-movie killers. "Four, like the four girls whose bodies were found in the Killing Field," Tim told me, with a disgusted shake of the head. "Like he was saying, there it is. I did it. And no one got me."

Actually, Tim didn't speculate that the man in question murdered all four girls whose bodies were found in the Killing Field, but the first three: the waitress and young mother Heide Fye; Tim's daughter Laura; and the first of the two unidentified women, Jane Doe. The last victim found in

1991, known as Janet Doe, had so many differences, including body positioning, those investigating theorized that she was most likely the victim of a separate killer. "The first three, including Laura, I always thought that maybe this neighbor of mine did them," said Tim. "When the police said it was Robert Abel, for a while I thought it was him. I lost my focus. I now believe that I may have known the man responsible for Laura's killing from the start."

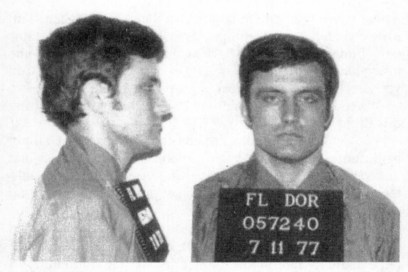

1977 Florida mug shots of Clyde Edwin Hedrick. *(Trial exhibit)*

The man Tim Miller referred to was the first suspect he mentioned to police, an ex-convict named Clyde Edwin Hedrick. In 1977, Hedrick was convicted of attempted arson and sentenced to five years in Florida. In 1984 when Laura disappeared, the construction worker with the prominent forehead and cold, deep-set eyes lived just down the block from the house the Millers had recently moved out of in Dickinson.

What made the man stand out was that Hedrick was the

last person seen with a woman named Ellen Rae Beason. They left a bar together one night in July 1984, and Beason vanished. A year later, her body was found, but based on the evaluation of the evidence at the time, Hedrick wasn't charged with her killing.

After Tim Miller discarded his belief that Robert Abel was Laura's killer, his attention repeatedly centered on Hedrick. Although he had never met him face-to-face, Miller speculated about the man's possible connection to the Killing Field from the moment he heard about Hedrick's link to Beason's death. In Tim Miller's eyes, he saw too many coincidences to be ignored.

First there was the timing: Heide Fye disappeared in October 1983, Ellen Beason in July 1984, and Laura in September 1984. Then Jane Doe died sometime in late 1985 or early 1986. Secondly, the Texas Moon Club, the joint Beason left with Hedrick that night, was the same bar Heide Fye patronized. The place booked local bands, and Hedrick was a regular, spending his nights on the dance floor. Since they both hung out at the Texas Moon, it seemed logical that Hedrick and Fye knew each other. Third: Hedrick's proximity to the Millers' prior home. Finally, on his recurring searches of the Calder Drive field, Tim Miller discovered piles of discarded tiles stripped off roofs. Clyde Hedrick worked for a roofing contractor. "I thought maybe Hedrick used the field to dump garbage from his jobs and visit where he'd left the girls," said Miller.

Yet he had nothing conclusive. In fact, Miller didn't have any direct evidence branding Hedrick the killer, and when Miller relayed his theory to League City police, he said they scoffed. "They told me it wasn't so, that it was crazy," said Tim. "They wouldn't listen."

Despite the disinterest of League City police, Miller continued investigating. He had the club connecting Hedrick with Heide Fye, and before long he had something linking the man to Laura. Not only had Hedrick lived near the Millers, but also Laura's friends said she'd been inside the man's house. They'd gone there to buy pot, and Laura had gone with them. With that information, Tim Miller proved that Clyde Hedrick, who admitted he'd been with Ellen Beason when she mysteriously died, also knew two of the three victims whose bodies were found in the Killing Field: Heide and Laura.

Eager to share what he'd learned, Miller returned to the League City Police Department. Again, he said, the officers brushed him off. "They didn't want to hear it," said Miller. "I knew there was something there, but they weren't interested. I was irate. The police wouldn't listen to me about Laura's being in the same field as Heide, and I'd been right. Laura was out in that field the whole time. I knew Clyde Hedrick was somehow responsible for Ellen Beason's death."

Miller didn't give up. Off and on he stopped at the League City Police Department, looking for reassurance that Laura's case was progressing. "Why is eight years old middle-aged?" he asked a detective one day. When the man asked what Tim meant, he said, "Laura died at sixteen. For her, eight was middle-aged."

Another day when he pushed for an investigation into Clyde Hedrick, Miller said the officer he talked to appeared irritated. Rather than a promise that he would investigate every lead, the man eyed him, and asked: "Why did you kill your daughter and those girls and put their bodies out there in that field?"

"I nearly jumped over the desk to get my hands on that man," Tim recalled. "I had to hold myself back."

The decades passed, and no answers came. Then something happened in 2010. Something that gave Tim Miller his opportunity. Galveston County Sheriff's Lieutenant Tommy Hansen, who more than two decades earlier was one of the investigators on the Shelley Sikes case, made plans to retire. Yet Hansen, by then an affable, white-haired man who wore wide, wire-rimmed glasses, didn't plan to completely leave law enforcement. He had unfinished business to attend to, investigating the area's abundant cold cases. For the first time in the history of the Killing Field murders, an investigator had the opportunity to concentrate on the embarrassment of unsolved cases, and Hansen had help. He would function on a part-time basis as part of a task force that included FBI Special Agent Richard Rennison, working out of the agency's local satellite office. A tall, muscular man with short dark hair and a goatee sprinkled with gray, Rennison had a knack for working cold cases. "I enjoy them," he said. "I like the challenge."

A dogged investigator, Special Agent Richard Rennison sought out cold cases. *(Courtesy of Kathryn Casey)*

Even before Hansen made his change, his attention never completely left the Killing Fields. For decades, he'd kept a blowup of the I-45 Mysteries chart behind his desk. He knew the girls' faces and names by heart. Hansen could recount all their stories. The murders troubled him, as they had so many others. Rennison felt the same way. He'd come up through the ranks, beginning his career as a League City policeman. And of all the cases, the Calder Drive slayings were among the area's most notorious.

Lieutenant Tommy Hansen kept a blowup of one of the I-45 charts behind his desk for more than a decade.
*(Courtesy of Kathryn Casey)*

So in 2010, as Hansen prepared to retire from his full-time job and start working part-time on the cold cases, Tim coincidentally asked Rennison to stop in at the Equusearch offices. Once the FBI agent arrived, Tim brought up the Beason case. Patiently, Rennison listened, appearing interested. When he left that day, he told Miller that he would talk with Tommy Hansen and get back in touch.

The following day, Rennison and Hansen spent the entire day at Miller's office going through his files and talking to Tim about Ellen Beason and the Killing Field murders. "It was an emotional meeting," said Miller. "I was crying, talking about Laura, and they teared up, too. I told Tommy and

Richard that I always suspected Clyde. I suggested they look into Ellen Beason's death. I said, 'Start there.'"

**S**unday, July 29, 1984 was the last day of Ellen Rae Beason's life. A receptionist for a real-estate company, the pretty twenty-nine-year-old, once married, lived at home with her parents and a brother. Friends described Beason as dependable, hardworking, a good cook, yet a free spirit who loved to party and dance and sometimes drank a bit too much. On that night, she walked into the Texas Moon at about 6:00 P.M. The event was a fundraiser to help pay funeral expenses for a local family who'd lost a child in a car accident.

Was Ellen Beason's death an accident or a murder?
*(Trial exhibit)*

The evening proved a difficult one. After Ellen arrived, her good friend Candy Gifford introduced her to Hedrick. At first, all went well. A disc jockey played rock and roll, and Gifford danced, sometimes with Hedrick. But by nine, a disagreement had erupted between Gifford and her husband. The issue was Hedrick, who Gifford would later describe as hovering around their table. "My husband left, and I followed," Gifford would recall years later.

Not long after, Clyde Hedrick and Ellen Beason walked out the door of the Texas Moon together.

The following morning, Candy Gifford drove past the bar and noticed her friend's car in the parking lot. Ellen should have been at work, and Gifford worried enough to call Beason's mother. The family hadn't seen Ellen since the day before. She hadn't returned home from the club. Days passed, and Ellen remained missing.

"I started asking Clyde what happened, where Ellen was," said Gifford. Hedrick's responses were less than helpful. He claimed that after he and Beason left the bar, they drove around looking for Candy. Later, he took Beason back to the Texas Moon, where she walked off toward a truck, got inside with someone, and drove away. Hedrick said he couldn't describe the truck or the person. That didn't satisfy Gifford, who thought Hedrick must have known something that would help solve the mystery of her friend's disappearance.

Time passed, and Gifford continued to prod Hedrick for answers he didn't supply. Finally, one night four months after Ellen's disappearance, Gifford and Hedrick were again at the Texas Moon. Still determined to find her friend, Gifford asked Hedrick more questions about Beason. This time, Hedrick turned to Gifford, and asked, "Do you want to see where she's at?"

In the darkness, Hedrick drove Candy Gifford toward the Galveston Causeway. Before they entered the bridge, he veered off, toward an open field that ran along a railroad track. There, he guided her on foot through tall brush and weeds, down into a ravine strewn with garbage. He stopped at tires piled on a soiled and torn abandoned couch, pulled the tires off, then tipped the couch back. Gifford recoiled as she stared down at a decomposing body. She spotted a small gold necklace Ellen always wore, and Gifford knew it was her friend.

The account Hedrick gave Gifford that night was that after he and Beason left the Texas Moon, Beason wanted to go to a local swimming hole. Once there, he stayed in the truck, drank a beer, and smoked a joint, while Beason shed her clothes and ran into the shallow water. She invited him to join her, but he refused. Time passed, and when he began calling out to her to return to the truck, she didn't answer. He turned his truck lights on the water, and he saw Beason's body floating. Hedrick said Beason had drowned.

After walking out and pulling her body from the water,

Hedrick said he panicked, thinking others might not believe Beason's death was an accident. Instead of taking her to a hospital, he drove around, eventually dumping her body in the ravine and piling the couch and tires on top of her.

Then Gifford said that Hedrick told her not to tell anyone what she'd seen, a statement she interpreted as a warning that if she did, she or her family could be in danger.

For seven months, Gifford kept Clyde Hedrick's secret, she contended out of fear. Then in July 1985, he trashed her apartment, and she went to the police. The next day, she took officers to the ravine near the railroad tracks, where they moved the couch and exposed Ellen Beason's skeleton.

A macabre find: Ellen Beason's remains in the ravine. *(Trial exhibit)*

When interviewed by police, Hedrick repeated the same account of Beason's death he'd given to Candy Gifford. Days later, his fate rested with Galveston County's chief medical examiner, Dr. William Korndorffer, the man conducting the Beason autopsy. What Korndorffer ruled could have either corroborated or contradicted Hedrick's story. But when the report was filed, it did neither. Instead, Dr. Korndorffer concluded that after examining her remains, he was unable to decide how or why Ellen Beason died. On the autopsy form, the physician wrote "not determined" for both cause and manner of death.

In the end, Clyde Hedrick was put on trial and convicted of abuse of a corpse, sentenced to one year in prison and a $2,000 fine. And Ellen Beason's remains were in a plastic bag inside a casket beneath a granite monument that read, WITH THE LORD.

Yet many continued to believe that Clyde Hedrick had gotten away with murder.

In 1993, although they hadn't indicated any interest in the case to Tim Miller and appeared to rebuff his suspicions, the League City Police Department must have been troubled by the Beason case. That year they exhumed her remains to be reexamined. Instead of sending her skeleton back to Dr. Korndorffer at the Galveston County Morgue, however, her bones were transported to Denton, Texas, to the laboratory of Dr. Harrell Gill-King, director of the University of North Texas Institute of Forensic Anthropology. Gill-King, one of the nation's top forensic anthropologists, spent his career searching skeletons for clues.

Soon after the package arrived, Dr. Gill-King opened the clear plastic bag holding the skeleton to begin his assessment. But he was taken aback by the condition of the bones. In morgues across the nation, it was common procedure to clean bones before examination, removing tissue so indications of trauma can be seen. Apparently that hadn't been done at the Galveston ME's office, because according to Gill-King, when he received Beason's bones, they remained coated with debris and thick layers of connective tissue.

Assessing the task, Gill-King knew any conclusions he came to had to be based on cleaned bones. How else could he see any concealed injuries?

To be sure he had access to the entire skeleton, Gill-King had Beason's bones carefully washed and all remaining tissue peeled off. Once that was accomplished, he started his examination. On the newly exposed surface of the skull, it didn't take long to discover a crack so large that it ran downward from one cheekbone all the way to the other. To have resulted in such a major fracture the skull, one of the thickest bones in the body, had to have sustained a tremendous blow.

To judge when the injury occurred, Gill-King examined the edges of the break. Living bone breaks with rough edges, like a branch off of a tree, while dead bone breaks smooth, like a ceramic plate. On Beason's skull, the edges of the fracture were rough. The patina of the break also matched that of the rest of the skull, suggesting it had aged the same period of time. Those considerations led the forensic anthropologist to decide that the massive fissure occurred at or around the time of Beason's death.

Documenting the injury, Gill-King compiled his report, listing the cause of Ellen Beason's death as blunt-force trauma and the manner as homicide.

For a second opinion, Gill-King then sent Beason's skeleton to Dr. Marc Krouse, the deputy chief medical examiner and principal "bone man" at the nearby Tarrant County Medical Examiner's Office. Like Gill-King, Krouse had no difficulty finding the fracture on the newly defleshed skull, and he, too, judged it was perimortem, inflicted near the time of death. That finding, combined with the way Beason's remains had been found hidden beneath the couch, led Krouse to agree with Gill-King that Ellen Beason had been murdered.

Perhaps the League City police assumed that under such circumstances Dr. Korndorffer would reconsider his opinion. Instead, when the remains were returned to Galveston, the county's chief medical examiner grew angry. The fracture, he insisted to the district attorney, wasn't the cause of death. In fact, the physician asserted that the damage hadn't even been present when he examined the bones a decade earlier. Arguing that it was insulting that Gill-King and Krouse would accuse him of not cleaning the skull and missing a fracture so large a fledgling doctor would have seen it, Korndorffer stood by his original findings.

At that juncture, Galveston's district attorney faced a quandary; if he filed murder charges against Clyde Hedrick, Galveston's own chief medical examiner would testify for the defense.

In October 1997, a crew reinterred Ellen Beason's bones beneath the granite marker. There they waited, until that day in Tim Miller's office, when he suggested FBI Special Agent Richard Rennison and Galveston County Sheriff's Lieutenant Tommy Hansen reinvestigate her death.

Both men remembered the case, and they knew that many shared Miller's suspicions that Hedrick was responsible. "It was one of those cases people didn't forget," said Rennison. "There was the sense that there'd been a killing, and someone had gotten away with it."

With busy schedules it took time, but in November 2011, Hansen and Rennison began looking into the Beason case. Once they did, they learned of the 1993 exhumation, and Gill-King's and Houser's findings, that Beason's death was a homicide. At first, the investigators wondered why nothing had been done, but then realized that it all came down to the conflicting autopsies.

By then, Dr. Korndorffer had retired after three decades as Galveston's top medical examiner, and there was a new district attorney in Galveston County. Hanson and Rennison met with the chief prosecutor in the felony division, Kevin Petroff. "We began talking about exhuming the body again," said Petroff.

On March 28, 2012, for the second time, a backhoe dug into the sandy soil in Forest Park East Cemetery, uncovering a small casket, the size of a child's, holding Ellen Beason's bones. The following day, a captain in the sheriff's department drove north to Denton, to again bring the bones to Dr.

Gill-King for analysis. DNA had already been collected from Ellen's brother Ross, and a specimen was taken from the bones for comparison, to confirm that they were in fact Ellen's. And for a second time, Dr. Gill-King wrote a report documenting the skull fracture, labeling it as the cause of death, and listing his opinion for manner of death as homicide.

Soon after, around noon on April 4, 2013, Clyde Hedrick was arrested for the murder of Ellen Rae Beason. When an officer put the handcuffs on him, Hedrick appeared irritated, saying, "I already done my time for that."

As the events unfolded, and news cropped up on the cold case heading toward a courtroom, Tim Miller watched with interest, wondering if Hedrick was connected to his daughter's death. Then, as the investigation continued, something remarkable happened.

Two months after Hedrick's arrest, a lawyer for an inmate in the Galveston County jail contacted Kevin Petroff at the District Attorney's Office. The attorney had something he wanted to discuss. In the jail, while looking at a newspaper article about Equusearch and Tim Miller, three inmates claimed Clyde Hedrick made damning confessions: nonchalantly commenting that he'd had sex with and murdered Tim's daughter, Laura. During that same conversation, Hedrick allegedly also admitted killing Heide Fye and clubbing Ellen Beason to death with a table leg.

At first, the claims were kept secret. But then that fall, while preparing for trial, Petroff filed a list of extraneous offenses and allegations with the presiding district court, notifying the defense of any additional issues that could come up at the trial. Included was a long list of accusations against Hedrick, everything from drug use to the sexual abuse of a minor. At the end of the documents filed with the district clerk, Petroff included the assertions made by the inmates that Hedrick had confessed to not only killing Ellen Beason, but also Heide Fye and Laura Miller.

Once reporters discovered the official document on

the county clerk's Web site, newspapers and TV stations throughout the Houston area ran pieces naming Hedrick as a suspect in the infamous Killing Field murders. In response, reporters made their way to the county jail, requesting interviews. When questioned, Clyde Hedrick insisted that he'd never confessed to killing anyone and that he was being unfairly accused.

When Miller heard that Hedrick had reportedly made self-incriminating statements involving Laura's murder, Tim was furious. Although he'd believed for many years that Hedrick was a possible suspect in Laura's murder, the allegations of a confession shook him. "It feels like it's happening all over again," he said one day. "It feels like it's ripped the bandages off all the wounds."

As Hedrick's trial date approached, with the published claims circulating that he might be the Killing Field serial killer, it seemed that even more rested on the upcoming proceedings.

Yet despite Gill-King's and Krouse's assessments that Ellen Beason was murdered, the case against Hedrick wasn't an easy one, with Kevin Petroff, Rennison and Hansen repeatedly running into complications. Predominantly: the inability to find much of the evidence.

Over time, records had vanished, including the 1985 autopsy file with all Dr. Korndorffer's photos. League City couldn't find its file from the 1993 exhumation and had yet to locate Dr. Gill-King's photos from that examination. While disappointing, this wasn't unexpected in decades-old cases. "It's not unusual to have missing evidence," Rennison would later say. Records could be misfiled, sometimes systems changed, and data was misplaced, and on the Gulf Coast, evidence could be lost to the flooding brought by hurricanes. "In these old cases, it's really the norm."

Yet it would turn out that the Hedrick case was anything but ordinary.

Perhaps the most surprising twist: Petroff had been requesting that 1985 autopsy file for nearly two years. Although Dr. Korndorffer had retired, his daughter, Brenda Williams, still worked for the ME's Office. She'd repeatedly searched, but it hadn't been found. Then in January, just two months before the trial, Williams asked her father, ill and in a wheelchair, if he knew where the Beason file could be. To her surprise, he responded that he'd taken it home. It was in his storage unit.

"We went to his house," Petroff recounted. "Dr. Korndorffer was pleasant enough, but he was still arguing that he hadn't made a mistake." Despite Gill-King's contention that the bones were encased in tissue when Beason's skull arrived at his office in 1993, and it was his staff that cleaned them, Korndorffer insisted that wasn't true. Instead, the former ME claimed that his assistant cleaned the bones before the first autopsy. And Korndorffer remained adamant that the skull fracture hadn't been there when he first examined Beason's skull in 1985.

Back at the district attorney's office, when Petroff combed through the newly retrieved file and the photos, however, what he found appeared to contradict Dr. Korndorffer. The retired medical examiner had handed over pages of neatly labeled thirty-year-old, 35 mm slides, intended to be slipped into a projector and displayed on a screen. The problem was that based on the numbers on the cardboard frames, sixty-five slides were missing. Of the images Petroff did have, only two were of the skull. Seeming to confirm what Dr. Gill-King contended, in both surviving views of the skull included in Dr. Korndorffer's 1985 slides, the bone remained concealed under a thick layer of tissue, dirt, and debris.

As they prepared in the weeks leading up to the trial, Petroff and his second chair on the case, Kayla Allen, understood that they faced the identical situation to the one that had tabled the case in the midnineties; by then, Hedrick's defense attorney had subpoenaed Dr. Korndorffer. In the courtroom, the two Galveston County prosecutors would be forced to confront the county's former chief medical examiner, who would testify against the state.

Prosecutors Kayla Allen and Kevin Petroff with the skull replica used at the trial.
(Courtesy of Kathryn Casey)

Clyde Hedrick's trial began on the morning of Tuesday, March 25, 2014. Throughout the five days of its duration, Tim Miller sat center stage, in the front row, next to the aisle, behind the prosecutors. Surrounding him filling the first two rows were friends, all Equusearch volunteers, who came to support him. From the defense table, Hedrick glared at Miller, who stared back, refusing to avert his gaze from the man he believed murdered his daughter.

Other interested parties—those with a personal stake in the proceedings—filled the third row: Heide Fye's family, her sisters, one of their husbands, and their daughters. They, too, had come to watch the trial of a man they considered a

prime suspect in the murder of their loved one. Often their thoughts trailed back to the day in 1983 when Heide disappeared. "Heide was so full of life, so loved," said Josie Poarch-Mauro, one afternoon. "We want to know who did this, to see the man punished. It's been too long."

Of Ellen Beason's family, her brother Ross appeared anxious and overwhelmed by the drama as it unfolded in the courtroom. He hadn't told his aged mother about the trial, not wanting to bring her back to the time when his sister died. "Ellen's death tore our family apart," Ross said, tears in his eyes.

Yet the missing evidence and the conflicting medical opinions made the case far from certain. Another concern was Hedrick's defense attorney, Jeremy DuCote, known as a hard fighter and an able opponent. At the defense table, his partner and wife, the noticeably pregnant Leigh Love, sat between DuCote and his client. No longer resembling the strapping construction worker who'd left the Texas Moon with Beason on that fateful night, at fifty-nine Hedrick was a heavily wrinkled man who'd lost much of his chin to cancer. Yet his eyes, pale, cold, and empty, hadn't changed.

2013 booking photo of Clyde Hedrick.
*(Courtesy of the Galveston County Sheriff's Office)*

As in most trials, much of the prosecutors' initial efforts painted the picture, depicting the case's journey. "A woman walks into a police station," Petroff said in his opening statement, dramatically recounting how Candy Gifford first told authorities in 1985 that she knew where to find Ellen Beason's body.

For the defense, Jeremy DuCote didn't disagree. Ellen Beason died, and his client was with her when it happened. Yet it wasn't murder, he said, but an accident followed by a mistake, one Clyde Hedrick had already been convicted of and served time for. "The fracture in 1994 [the one seen by Dr. Gill-King] did not exist" in 1985, DuCote contended. "It wasn't there . . . You will find Clyde Hedrick not guilty."

Through Beason's friends' descriptions, Petroff and Allen introduced the dead woman to the jury, describing the fun-loving twenty-nine-year-old who never aged another day because she'd met a terrible fate that July 1984 night. When Candy Gifford took police to the ravine, they pulled back the couch. "I saw the skull first," the officer who'd accompanied her reported.

From the day the bones were recovered, prosecutors detailed the convoluted course the case had taken, including the 1986 trial, the 1993 exhumation, and the interest of the FBI's Rennison and the sheriff department's Hansen that laid the foundation for finally charging Clyde Hedrick with murder.

Among the first things Petroff did when Rennison took the stand was read Hedrick's testimony from the 1986 abuse of a corpse trial into the record. Once completed, Petroff asked Rennison if anything in Hedrick's description of the night Beason died concerned him. "Yes," the FBI agent answered.

Just the evening before, Rennison prepared for trial by reading Hedrick's testimony, when the FBI agent suddenly had what he considered an aha moment, when a picture crystallized. What he'd noticed was Hedrick's description of finding Beason's body in the water. "He said he saw Ellen Beason floating," Rennison pointed out. "People don't float when they drown. Their lungs fill with water, and they sink."

A murmur ran through the courtroom, like breath escaping as the audience filling the benches recalled headlines of drowning victims being pulled from the bottoms of pools, ponds, and rivers.

The second thing Rennison noted was Hedrick's own description of the area where he claimed Beason swam, so shallow that he said he walked out to retrieve her body. How could Beason have drowned in water she could stand up in? If she had gotten in trouble, she could have walked to the shore.

The final thing Rennison found unbelievable was Hedrick's claim that Beason had gone skinny-dipping, then tried to coax him into joining her. Instead, Hedrick testified that he drank a beer and smoked a joint in his truck. "A beautiful woman takes her clothes off and tries to get him to swim with her. He doesn't go?" Rennison remarked. "As a man, I thought that was strange."

Gray-haired with glasses and a beard, Dr. Harrell Gill-King resembled the professor he was, when he took the stand and recounted his credentials. While medical examiners most often saw newly dead or decomposing bodies, Gill-King's examinations took place farther along in the death process, when little remained but evidence of trauma recorded on bone. Knife marks, gunshot holes, and as in this case, fractures.

On the Elmo, the document projector that displayed images on a TV screen, Kayla Allen loaded the only two photos marked as coming from Dr. Korndorffer's 1985 autopsy that showed the skull. For the jurors, Gill-King pointed out a thick layer of tissue obscuring the bone. "Is this the way you received the skull?" Petroff asked.

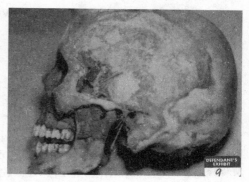

One of the only two known 1985 views of Ellen Beason's skull, still covered in tissue. *(Trial exhibit)*

Gill-King answered that it was. "The skull had not been cleaned . . . there was connective tissue, soft tissue, it covered the bone." After recounting how his assistants soaked the skull in warm water and peeled off the tissue, the anthropologist explained that once the skull was uncovered, the fracture became easily visible. He then used a stereomicroscope to examine the break, noting the rough surface and the fracture's consistent patina that matched the overall discoloration of the skull. Those two findings, he testified, indicated that the injury occurred at or near the time of Ellen Beason's death.

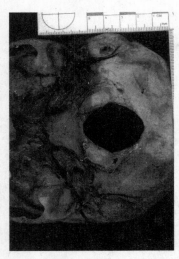

The cleaned skull from beneath, taken in 2012 and showing the fracture.
*(Trial exhibit)*

"That is some of the hardest bone in the body. It survives fires," Gill-King testified. Such a substantial fracture could only have been caused by "a tremendous blow."

Asked if the damage could have resulted from anything but homicide, Gill-King scoffed, "The possibility that this type of injury occurred without help from someone else is right up there with monkeys typing Shakespeare."

Dr. Krouse agreed when he took the stand, diagnosing that the fracture was the result of substantial blunt-force trauma, and that it couldn't have happened when the couch was put on top of Beason's body, after she was dead. In that scenario, the couch "would have caused damage to the more delicate bones in the face and body, and there is none."

Yet DuCote vigorously challenged both doctors, reminding jurors that Gill-King and Krouse didn't do the original autopsy, and neither had seen the remains when first recovered in 1985. Repeatedly, the defense attorney directed the testimony back to the missing evidence, including autopsy photos and the police report from the first exhumation. Even the fourteen photos Gill-King took of the skull during his first examination had disappeared. "Don't you wish you had your photos . . . those slides, to see if the fracture is there?" the defense attorney asked.

In response, Gill-King maintained he had all he needed to form his opinion.

In his cross-examinations, the defense attorney reminded the jurors of the many things Krouse and Gill-King couldn't tell them, including identifying the alleged murder weapon. Rather than homicide, DuCote suggested that without toxicology reports and a full body to examine, the doctors couldn't rule out the possibility that Beason had drowned or died from an overdose.

While Dr. Korndorffer had been adamant with the lawyers when they met before the trial, neither appeared prepared for the retired ME's stormy demeanor on the stand. Even DuCote, who'd subpoenaed the eighty-four-year-old, handled the feisty old man carefully and struggled to direct his testimony. In the end, he appeared frail in his wheelchair and continually turned to talk directly to the jurors, ignoring the attorneys and the judge who attempted to reel him back in. Yes, he said, his assistant had cleaned the skull, contradicting Dr. Gill-King's testimony. No, Korndorffer said, he didn't know what happened to all the missing autopsy photos including, presumably, many of Beason's skull.

In 1996, the physician had been so insulted by being second-guessed by Gill-King and Krouse that he'd made a video arguing his case. Although the other experts told jurors that signs of hemorrhage weren't useful in this type of a skull fracture, that there often wasn't evidence of bleeding and if there had been any the blood would have deteriorated and disappeared with decomposition, Korndorffer, his voice shaking with anger, insisted that the fact that he'd seen no bloodstains in 1985 was positive proof that at that time no fracture existed.

Cross-examining a fragile octogenarian presented considerable challenge. Kevin Petroff needed to prove his case, yet it wasn't good for the jury to judge that the prosecutor was attacking an old man in a wheelchair. While Petroff proceeded cautiously, Korndorffer sputtered angrily. After the retired ME admitted that the Beason file was the only one he'd removed from the office, Petroff asked why he'd made an exception with that particular case. "Because I was dealing with dirty policemen!" the physician shouted. "They were going to do away with my autopsy report!"

When Petroff asked Korndorffer if he thought Dr. Gill-King was part of a conspiracy, the retired physician speculated that the anthropologist was being used "to convict an innocent man."

Other testimony followed. Another forensic pathologist took the stand, one hired by the defense who initially backed Dr. Korndorffer's views but then retreated when told that Dr. Gill-King's office reportedly cleaned the tissue off the skull and that Dr. Korndorffer had not initially seen the bone defleshed. "If the skull wasn't cleaned, he wouldn't have seen the fracture," she said.

It was late in the trial when the witness Tim Miller waited for finally entered the courtroom, Max Stephenson, one of the inmates in the county jail who claimed to have heard Clyde Hedrick not only confess to killing Ellen Beason but also Heide Fye and Laura Miller. Yet on the stand, Stephenson, handcuffed and wearing his jailhouse uniform, wasn't allowed to talk about anything other than what he said Hedrick told him about Ellen Beason. To do otherwise, to bring up Hedrick's possible involvement in other offenses, could have caused a mistrial or resulted in a conviction, if the jury came back with one, being overturned on appeal.

Clyde Hedrick "told us that he thought [Ellen Beason] drowned," said Stephenson. "He said when he was putting her under the couch, she woke up, and he hit her with a table leg."

On cross-examination, DuCote's second chair, Leigh

Love, implied that perhaps Stephenson lied to get a deal from the state. "You told the FBI guy you wanted your case dropped," she accused.

Stephenson, serving a three-year sentence for evading arrest, admitted that was true but said that Special Agent Rennison had offered him nothing for his testimony.

At the end of the trial, Kayla Allen began closing arguments, reminding jurors of who Ellen Beason was on that final day, a young woman with her life ahead of her. What was important about Stephenson's testimony, she said, was that it matched the scientific opinions, those of Gill-King and Krouse, that Beason's death was caused by being struck with tremendous force by a heavy, blunt object.

"This is a wrongful prosecution of an innocent man," Leigh Love countered. What Clyde Hedrick had done was reprehensible, but he'd been convicted and served his time for abusing Ellen Beason's corpse. Her husband followed, agreeing, arguing that the state wanted it both ways. For decades, prosecutors relied on Dr. Korndorffer's testimony to convict defendants of murder; now they wanted the jurors to ignore his testimony, not to believe him when he said Ellen Beason's skull wasn't fractured in 1985. "It's hard to buy the story of the state that the Galveston ME's Office was so incompetent that it missed a fracture a first-year medical student could find," DuCote said. ". . . Agree with Dr. Korndorffer that the cause of death is undetermined."

The last one to speak was Kevin Petroff, who repeated what the FBI's Rennison had said, that Clyde Hedrick's description of the way Ellen Beason died was illogical. Drowned bodies don't initially float. At first, lungs fill with water, and they sink. Only later will such victims rise to the surface, the result of gases formed by decomposition. Petroff also asked how likely it was that Ellen Beason died in water so shallow she could have stood up and walked to shore. Even more important, Petroff said that the jurors knew that what Dr. Korndorffer said wasn't true, he hadn't cleaned the skull, because Dr. Gill-King had testified that when the remains were exhumed the skull arrived at his office with tissue still covering the fracture. "This is what a government cover-up looks like," Petroff said. "Someone screwed something up and tried to hide it. . . . [Dr. Korndorffer] took the file home . . . put it in his storage area."

After a pause, Petroff reminded jurors, however, that despite all the medical testimony, the case wasn't about the bone doctors or any of the experts. "What we're talking about is the life of a twenty-nine-year-old in 1984 . . ." he said, holding up Beason's photo. "Did she drown in water that just came up to her waist, or did this man who hid her under the couch crush her skull from side to side?"

While murder was the first option on the paperwork, when they returned with their verdict that wasn't the jury's decision. Instead they found Clyde Hedrick guilty of a lesser charge, involuntary manslaughter. While they judged him responsible for Ellen Beason's death, their verdict suggested that they weren't certain that he intended to kill her.

The following Monday, the punishment phase began, and more witnesses testified, mainly family members pleading for mercy for Hedrick. Yet it was one witness in particular who made the greatest impact. A college student who lived with Hedrick as a teenager, the woman initially liked her mother's new boyfriend. That faded, however, as Hedrick exposed himself to her, and she testified she suspected he watched her through a hole drilled into her bedroom wall. She said Hedrick showed her pornography when she was just thirteen, and at fifteen touched her breasts. She cried about a time when she said he gave her something to drink, and she awoke the next morning feeling as if she'd been sexually assaulted. As she voiced her accusations, the jurors stared at Hedrick in disdain, especially the men.

In the end, jurors handed down the maximum allowed, sentencing Clyde Hedrick to twenty years in a Texas prison.

While throughout, the testimony had centered only on Ellen Beason's death, Tim saw the proceedings as his day in court as well, hoping he'd hear Laura and Heide mentioned. When they weren't, he appeared ever more resolute that the matter hadn't ended. One day, he and the rest of Laura's family, along with Josie and all of Heide's relatives, deserved their own trial. But would that ever come?

After listening and viewing the evidence presented at Hedrick's murder trial, Tim talked about two statements he'd heard that took him back to the Killing Field. The source was Hedrick's 1986 testimony at his abuse of a corpse trial, which Petroff read to the jury. First Hedrick mentioned that the field where he'd disposed of Beason's body was one he was familiar with because the company he worked for used it to dump old roofing tiles. In the area around the Killing Field, Miller had also found piles of old, discarded roofing tiles.

Secondly: In his 1985 account of Beason's death, Hedrick had described disposing of her body. On the stand, he said that after he transported her to the ravine, he laid Beason on the ground. Then before he covered her with the couch, he took off the shirt he was wearing, a red Western one, and draped it over her face.

What that brought to mind for Tim Miller was the blue Western shirt he had a picture of in his files, the shirt found near his daughter's remains and tagged with her case number. In the picture, it appeared stained, perhaps with blood. Was it possible that the shirt could be the answer to three decades of questions, that it had the power to finally bring the Killing Field serial killer to justice? Did it belong to Clyde Hedrick? Could it be stained with his DNA?

"Maybe this shirt thing is something Clyde does," Tim mused.

Yet there was a problem. Police had told Tim that the shirt, along with much of the Killing Field evidence, was lost. In the decades since his daughter died, it seemed that like so many cold cases, time and human error had damaged the investigation. What it hadn't diminished was a father's commitment. In no uncertain terms, Tim Miller challenged, "I want them to find that shirt. I want them to keep looking."

In the end, there were indications that authorities could be doing just that. Although unable to comment on ongoing cases, when asked, the FBI's Rennison wouldn't confirm or deny that the investigation continued into whether or not Clyde Hedrick was the Killing Field serial killer. Instead, he smiled, and said, "All I can say is that we haven't closed any of these cases."

While confident that Special Agent Rennison and Lieutenant Hansen continued to look into the murders, in the months following Hedrick's conviction, Tim Miller understandably grew impatient. Five months after Hedrick's trial ended, Miller initiated an action he hoped would push the case forward. On August 25, 2014, he filed a civil action, a wrongful death suit against Hedrick for Laura's murder.

Not expecting to become rich from the suit, Miller had other goals in mind. "I feel like I'm the father to all four of the girls whose bodies were found out in that field. And I want Clyde Hedrick to tell the truth about what happened to them. That's all I want. The truth," Tim said, "and I want him to tell us who Jane Doe is. I want to be able to tell her family what happened to her."

Two weeks after filing the lawsuit, Miller returned to the Calder Drive Killing Field. Surrounded by family and friends, he stood in the center of the clearing during a candlelight vigil. At the ceremony, Tim reinstalled the old weathered cross he'd erected in Laura's memory, repaired and bearing a new plaque with Laura's photo and birth and death dates, to commemorate the thirtieth anniversary of his daughter's death. In addition, Tim and the Equusearch volunteers erected three more crosses in honor of Fye, and Jane and Janet Doe. Then they tied two hundred ribbons to the surrounding trees, each one bearing the name of a missing person.

The very next morning, Tim was in Plano, Texas. A twenty-three-year-old woman was missing, believed to have been abducted, and the family had called asking for help.

# Chapter 10

## "Fear in Her Eyes"
## Mark Roland Stallings
## The Murder of Janet Doe

**Woodville, Texas**

Mark Roland Stallings in the interview room. *(Courtesy of Kathryn Casey)*

At the end of the Clyde Hedrick trial, so many questions remained. Perhaps he was the serial killer who'd made the Calder Drive field his personal burial ground. Perhaps he wasn't. Perhaps Tim Miller would never know for sure. If it were true, it begged another question: If Clyde Hedrick murdered the first three women whose bodies were found posed under the trees, what about the fourth? Who killed Janet Doe?

As I worked through the cases, at first I found no answers. Then one day I read an article out of the *Houston Chronicle* archives about a man named Mark Roland Stallings, who had once been a hired hand on Robert Abel's League City ranch. According to the 2001 reports, while in prison on other charges, Stallings confessed to the Killing Fields murders. Since no charges were ever filed, I assumed police uncovered evidence that excluded Stallings, but I decided to investigate anyway. In the end, I learned that Mark Stallings hadn't been cleared. In fact, he remained the prime suspect in Janet Doe's murder.

"We think Stallings did one of the murders," said Lieutenant Tommy Hansen at the Galveston County Sheriff's Office, the same Galveston Sheriff's investigator who'd worked the Shelley Sikes and Clyde Hedrick cases. "We believe he murdered Janet Doe. But he refused to sign a confession, and so far we don't have the evidence we need to charge him."

Eventually I learned that Stallings not only remained a suspect in the murder of the final Killing Fields victim but also in the murders of two women in Fort Bend County, west of Galveston.

"I was maybe seven or so," Mark Roland Stallings told me, recounting the first time he put his hands on a girl's neck and realized that he felt thrilled by her gasp for breath. We were separated by thick glass and talking via a phone in the maximum security section of a prison just outside the small Texas town of Woodville. Only sixteen men were housed in the unit, those considered the most dangerous and the greatest flight risks. It was an austere place, one where visitors were meticulously searched coming and going, where access was carefully monitored.

In these somber surroundings, Stallings reminisced, describing a time long past when he was still a child, one whose attention was drawn to forbidden preoccupations. On that day when he was seven, Stallings played "husband and wife" with a little girl who might have been eight or so. "For her age, she knew everything about being sexual. She hit on me," he said. Aroused, Stallings experimented. "For some reason, I took my thumb and mashed it in her throat."

At that, Stallings held up his thumb and positioned it against his own neck, to illustrate where he'd pressed, at the base, directly over the girl's windpipe. "I saw her face. She had that fear in her eyes. I pulled it back out. She was crying. I apologized, said, 'Don't tell! I won't do it again. I promise.'"

While he never hurt that particular girl again, it would be a promise that Stallings would fail to keep. For according to his own words, there were many women in his future who would be victimized by this man with the cold blue eyes and soft Texas drawl, including one of the murdered women found in the Killing Field.

Talking about his past, Stallings remained emotionless, except during those moments when he recounted the final seconds of a woman's life. Then he grew excited, his voice rising through a thin smile. For Mark Roland Stallings, these apparently weren't tragedies but cherished memories.

In his account of his life, Stallings came of age in the countryside outside Seguin in Guadalupe County, one of the oldest towns in Texas, a center for farming and ranching. In a family of ten children, he described his upbringing as unruly, saying his parents let their brood run with little supervision. As a child, he said he was sexually abused, starting at the age of six, by a woman he never identified.

Violence, too, entered his life early. At seven, he had the encounter with the eight-year-old girl, the one where he thrust his thumb into her throat. At eleven, he claimed to have stabbed a schoolmate on the playground over a dip of snuff, then threatened to slit the boy's throat to convince him to say the stabbing was accidental. At thirteen, Stallings said he raped a young woman at knifepoint. She was eighteen, a relative, and she begged him "not to do anything crazy."

What made him feel justified? He judged her to be a loose

woman, one who gave her sexual favors away. So he felt entitled to do what he would with her.

In the mideighties, Stallings was in his early twenties, married with two children, and working as a laborer. "I got involved with this guy," he said. "We got to know each other, smoked pot and stuff like that. We'd go out on occasion, get blasted. There was this one prostitute I used to mess with."

Her street name was Champagne, and Stallings described her as a white woman with an olive complexion, "real pretty and real nice." All went well until Champagne decided for some reason that she no longer wanted to service Stallings's needs. Perhaps she sensed something about him that worried her. One night when he was out with his friend, Stallings suggested they look Champagne up for a little fun.

"My thing is, it's not up to you when you want to have sex if you're a fucking prostitute," he said, with a sardonic frown. "You sell your body, you disrespect yourself like that, you ain't got no rights."

That evening, Champagne got in the truck with the two men, and they drove off to an abandoned trailer. Once they arrived, Champagne, possibly realizing something was wrong, refused to have sex. They, however, had other plans. Stallings pulled the woman out of the truck, forcing her toward the trailer, while the other man yelled at him to hurry before someone saw them. Inside the trailer, she still refused to do as they wanted, and they fought. "I slammed her upside the head, and I slammed her upside the wall," Stallings said. He beat her and threw her into a back bedroom, where both men forced themselves on her. This time, Stallings said, he wasn't the one who finished the woman off. Instead, after his second go-round with the woman, his friend emerged from the bedroom saying, "I strangled the bitch."

When Stallings investigated, he said that he found Champagne dead with a red scarf tied around her neck. Assessing the situation, he deposited her body in a closet, then rounded up three stray dogs he locked inside the trailer, assuming they'd grow hungry and consume the evidence. Before leaving, Stallings broke the trailer's door handle off on the outside, to keep the curious out. It worked for about two weeks.

"In the paper, it said that they found a female body, twenty-four to twenty-five years old," said Stallings. "I worried for a while that they'd find fingerprints. I was already on parole. I thought about it two or three days, but no one came to talk to me."

Not long after, in early 1988, he met Robert Abel, the man who for a decade would be the prime suspect in the Killing Field murders. The way Stallings characterized it, the two men quickly bonded. "Robert had a dark side like I had a dark side," Stallings told me, his voice grave. "Before too long, we became more than boss and employee."

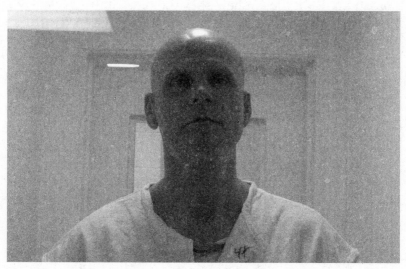

Mark Stallings said he became violent at a young age.
*(Courtesy of Kathryn Casey)*

In Mark Roland Stallings's account, he and Robert Abel came from very different lives but recognized that they were fellow travelers. The job Stallings accepted was that of foreman on Abel's ranch in Bellville, a small town a little more than an hour northwest of Houston. The land just outside town, two adjoining cattle ranches, had been in the NASA engineer's family since before Texas was a state. A small house anchored the property and the adjacent family cemetery, laid in a grove of trees with headstones dating back to the late 1800s.

On the ranch, Stallings's job became less foreman than laborer, as Abel instructed Stallings on his duties, including tending the stock and doing repairs and upkeep. "Robert didn't want to hire anyone else," said Stallings, who waved his hands expressively, emphasizing his words. "I ended up doing pretty much everything."

Abel fluctuated back and forth, living on his land on the edge of the Killing Field in League City and the family spread in Bellville. When they talked, Stallings learned that Abel shared his view of women. "He'd tell me stuff like women always want to dominate the world . . . make the decisions . . . tell when a man can touch them, when he can't. I said, 'I know. I understand.' I could feel the darkness in Robert. I was relating to that. I was thriving off that myself."

If Stallings told the truth about the events that unfolded in the following year, police weren't wrong when they eyed Abel as someone capable of murder. Before long, Stallings rotated between Abel's two properties, working two to three days a week in Bellville, and the rest of the time staying with his wife in a small cabin in the woods on the League City ranch. It was there one day that Stallings said Abel came to him and asked if he knew where to get a prostitute. In response, Stallings drove to one of Houston's well-known red-light districts, Telephone Road, on the southeast side of downtown. Once there, he pulled over at a small, run-down hotel and picked up a young Hispanic woman who spoke English, then drove her out to the ranch. "We do our thing, and Robert said, 'I want to keep her overnight,'" Stallings said. The next day, Abel seemed on edge, and before long Stallings says Abel told him, "Man, I killed that girl."

That evening, Stallings said he drove to the site where Abel left the woman's body. Once Stallings found it, he tied it with a nylon rope onto the back of a hay baler and pulled it with a tractor into the woods. There he stripped the clothes off and dug a grave, shallow enough to partially conceal the corpse but not so deep it discouraged wildlife. "You can sit out on that property at night and hear the coyotes," he said. "They'll tear a body apart. As far as I know, the coyotes probably strung her from League City to Kalamazoo."

Not long after, Stallings said he returned to Telephone Road, this time alone. On the street, he found another prostitute, one wearing a shirt, brown corduroy pants, and tall brown leather boots. "I tell her, 'Let's go out to this ranch and mess around a bit. I'll show you some cows and shit like that.'"

Once back on Abel's League City ranch, Stallings said he screamed at the woman: "All you bitches. You sell your body, then you make a choice. The way I feel, you ain't got no right to speak about what a person does with your body." By then, Stallings had rigged his truck, removing the lever that opened the driver's side door from the inside, so that the window had to be rolled down to use the outside handle. "The reason was to trap my victim," he said, his voice matter-of-fact.

On this day after he got out, Stallings's prey tried to escape out the driver's-side door. She must have been terrified when she realized that the handle didn't work. Meanwhile, he flung open the passenger-side door and grabbed her. "She kicked me in the chest, and I was outraged," he said, furious at the memory. "Halfway out of the truck, I was like, son of a bitch, and I hauled off and hit her." When he grabbed her leg, her boot slid off, and he began pummeling her with it.

"She's groggy, out of it. By the time I start having sex with her, she's coming to. She tries to bite me, so I punch her a couple of times. I took her sock, wrapped it around her neck, and I choked her out."

As he had with the Hispanic prostitute, Stallings said

he then removed all the clothing from this victim's corpse, dug another shallow grave, buried the woman and left. Not long after, he threw her clothes into a convenience-store Dumpster.

Asked if he could identify either of the two women, Stallings smirked. "I didn't ask no names. These women were whores."

The following day, Stallings bragged to Abel about his exploits and the new corpse buried in the woods. Instead of being impressed, however, Abel quickly grew agitated, not wanting to go to the site to see the body, instead saying over and over that there were too many bodies on his land. Stallings didn't know about the first three victims who'd been found in the Killing Field. He didn't understand Abel's concern, telling his boss that there were only two women buried in the woods. Stallings's appetite for sex and violence whetted by the recent killings, he had plans. With all Abel's acreage, the ranch hand saw no worries about disposal, but Abel insisted he wanted none of it. "I'm sending you back to Bellville," he told Stallings.

"Robert was freaking on me," said Stallings, with a disgusted frown that suggested the older man was weak. In the months that followed, Abel looked tired and stressed, and dark circles framed his eyes. Not long after, he fired Stallings. "It never left me about Robert firing me," said Stallings. "Then I thought I was going to get even."

At one point, Stallings described returning to Abel's property, prepared to murder his ex-boss and anyone else he found there. But when he arrived, Stallings eyed a young boy, maybe eleven or twelve, on a tractor. He didn't know the kid, and he decided he didn't want to kill him. So Stallings simply talked to Abel briefly and quietly left. But it didn't dissuade him from his course of action. He was prepared to do what he had to do to bring Robert Abel down. "I was going to get the son of a bitch."

The county housed trucks in a facility near League City, and one night in 1991, Stallings said he borrowed one, intending to use it to carry out his plan. Again he drove to the same section of Telephone Road, with its run-down hotels and stores. There he found a teenager, pretty, with long blondish brown hair—he gauged between sixteen and twenty—standing alongside the road looking for a John interested in paying for sex. She wore a white shirt with a blue stripe, blue jeans, and tennis shoes. He didn't ask her name. After her body was found in the Killing Field, she'd be called Janet Doe. "I'll do you for ten dollars," Janet told Stallings.

"What do you want it for?" he asked.

"Crack," the girl said, a pipe dangling from her lips. Instead, Stallings bargained with a dealer on the street and bought the girl two rocks. They smoked it. They had sex, then they talked. As Stalling recounts it, the young woman was morose, lamenting the state of her life, and looking for a way out. Estranged from her family, she said her father didn't know what type of life she led. "Why do you disrespect your body like this?" Stallings asked her.

"My dad don't care about me. No one does. I really don't want to be alive." Stallings then listened as, he said, the girl recounted a fantasy, saying: "I want to have sex, and I want to be killed during the sex."

"Well, she's talking to the right motherfucker right here," Stallings said, the memory exciting him. "You know what I'm saying?"

"My intention was to get back at Robert," said Stallings, describing how he suggested they take a ride in the county-owned truck. "So we go back out there." They drove toward League City, then exited the freeway at Calder Drive, coming around the corner and continuing on through the gate and onto Robert Abel's property. Parked in the truck, Stallings asked the girl

The hands of a killer?
*(Courtesy of Kathryn Casey)*

if she wanted to have sex again. She agreed. She was still in the front seat, when she took her jeans off, and he ordered her to roll over on her stomach. As he moved inside her, he grabbed the seat belt and struck her once, then again in the head, with the metal buckle.

"Pow, I hit her on the back of the head. Bam. She goes, 'Ow!' I hit her again, and her face kind of goes funny. Then I take the seat belt, wrap it around her neck."

Stallings's voice was tight and excited as he described cinching the seat belt tight, strangling the teenager. When he was done, he left her shirt on her, and instead of driving out into the woods, as he had the others, he transported her to the clearing directly behind Abel's property. He said that he didn't know until later that it was called the Killing Field, and that it was there that three bodies had been found years earlier.

"I laid her out, putting her in an empty spot. The others I was hiding. This one, I wanted to be found. She wasn't buried, and she was meant to be found."

"You wanted them to look at Abel? You wanted to get even?" I asked.

"Yeah," he said. "It worked. It sparked a whole lot of shit."

If his story is true, Stallings accomplished what he intended. It was after that fourth body, Janet Doe, was discovered in September 1991, that authorities focused on Abel. Soon the FBI compiled a profile of the Killing Field serial killer, one Abel fit, and Tim Miller started waiting for Abel when the retired engineer walked to the road to collect his mail.

Later in 1991, Stallings was convicted of burglary. Then in 1996, he was in a Texas prison for possession of a firearm and shooting an old man through a window, wounding but not killing him. While incarcerated serving two fifty-year sentences in 1998, Stallings tried to escape, taking a guard hostage with a smuggled-in gun and holding her for four hours. The result: three convictions for aggravated assault and one for aggravated kidnapping. Sentenced to life and not eligible for parole until April 2021, Stallings devised yet another plan to get out of prison. He decided he had a story to tell, and that it could prove his get-out-of-jail-free card.

From prison, Stallings notified authorities that he had murdered women in Fort Bend and Galveston Counties. Before long, the headlines in the state's newspapers read: "Man's confession could solve 'killing field' case."

"Prisoner claims he committed Calder Drive killings," read another on November 3, 2001, in Galveston's *Daily News*.

"I never told them I killed *all* those girls," Stallings said with a wry smile. Instead, he told authorities from Fort Bend about the woman his friend murdered, the one left in the abandoned trailer. And he talked to League City police about the two women murdered and left on Abel's property off Calder Drive. "I did it to get out of here," he said, glancing around the white walls of the narrow cubicle he sat in, a fluorescent light shining overhead, casting the walls and Stallings in an unnatural yellow glow. "I thought while they had me out there, I could figure a way to escape."

For weeks Stallings traveled outside prison walls, shackled and handcuffed, pointing out where he said he'd disposed of bodies, telling parts but, he said, not his entire story. Then, he said, authorities lost interest. "I think they blew it," he said. "I thought they'd want to talk to me more."

It wasn't, however, that they thought Stallings was lying. In the newspapers, Fort Bend and League City authorities agreed that Stallings knew more than he should have about the killings, suggesting he might have been involved. When I called League City and talked to a detective, I was told that Stallings was "a prime suspect" in Janet Doe's murder.

When I pressed further, the man said, "We think he probably did it."

When I reached out to the other jurisdiction where Stallings said he'd been involved in a murder, Fort Bend authorities said the same thing, that they considered Stallings a viable suspect in a murder in their jurisdiction.

The League City detective contended that all the murders of the girls whose bodies were left in the Killing Field remained active investigations. Yet Stallings insisted no one from either jurisdiction had talked to him in more than a decade.

Weeks after I left the prison, trying to determine if Stallings told the truth, I brought Janet Doe's autopsy and the description Stallings gave me of her murder to be reviewed by a friend, a retired assistant medical examiner. After he compared the two, the physician nodded. "It could have happened that way, the way he said he did it. There's not enough here to say for sure that he did it, but it's certainly possible."

Was Stallings telling the truth? He did have a reason to lie. A possible motive: hate for Robert Abel. Although Abel was long dead, perhaps Stallings abhorred the man enough to want to tarnish his memory. But if that was his motivation, Stallings could have added so much more to his tale.

In prison for sixteen years at the time of Hedrick's trial, Stallings didn't know about the allegations against the man. To see what he'd say, if he'd try to implicate Abel in other murders, I asked Stallings if he thought his ex-boss killed the first three victims found in the field behind Abel's house: Heide Fye, Laura Miller, and Jane Doe. Rather than grow his accusations against a man he clearly despised—one who was deceased and couldn't defend himself—Stallings didn't take the bait. Instead, he shrugged and frowned, admitting, "I don't know. Robert never told me he did them. I didn't even know about those girls . . . But I know he did have a dark side. He could have done it."

After Stallings made his claims about the murders in 2001, Abel talked to reporters, describing his ex–ranch hand as "too dumb to string a fence," saying he was relieved that Stallings had come forward, and maintaining that the man's confession cleared him of suspicion in all the Killing Field murders. Others, however, told me that Abel appeared to not believe his own press, and that rather than calm the matter, the former space engineer became increasingly peculiar and obsessed with the cases. "Robert got kind of squirrelly at the end," said one person who knew him. "He started acting oddly. Lots of times, he looked like he was afraid of his own shadow."

Perhaps an explanation lies in something Stallings recounted that happened a few years before Abel died. While in prison, Stallings said he received a letter from a mutual friend. In it, the writer said that Abel was spooked, claiming that the spirits of the dead women, the murder victims, stalked him.

When Stallings got the letter, he was perhaps amused but not surprised. "I believed him," he said. To the ex–ranch hand, the field behind Abel's League City home had always felt haunted. "My wife and I used to go out and sit on the porch of that little cabin in League City. It was so dark out there, no lights, couldn't see two feet in front of you. She starts getting chills and wants to go inside. She said, 'I feel something.' I could feel it, too. It's like you could feel the presence. You can feel the tension staring at you, like the women were trying to say something."

Through the friend, Stallings sent a message back to Abel, telling him that he understood, and that Abel wasn't imagining things; the girls watched him. The theory Stallings proposed was that the girls had moved on to the next world and weren't afraid of Abel any longer since he couldn't hurt them while he remained in this world. The only way to quiet them, Stallings suggested, was for Abel to die and cross over into the next world, where the women would again fear him. Stallings suggested Abel's only recourse was to "join them in the spirit world."

Near the end of our interview, Stallings ruminated that perhaps his suggestion to Abel hit home, since a few years later he drove his ATV onto the railroad tracks and into the path of an oncoming train. "I like to think maybe I had something to do with that," said Stallings, smiling broadly. "Maybe not, but who's to say Robert didn't decide I was right? Maybe that was enough to push him over the edge."

# THE 1990s

- Krystal Jean Baker: 13, left her grandmother's house on March 5, 1996, to walk to a friend's house.
- Laura Kate Smither: 12, disappeared on April 3, 1997, while jogging on a rural road near her home.
- Jessica Cain: 17, left a cast party after appearing in a play on August 17, 1997.

# Chapter II

## Marilyn Monroe's Kin
## Krystal Jean Baker

**Texas City, Texas**
**March 5, 1996**

Krystal Baker not long before her death. *(Courtesy of her mother)*

**K**rystal Jean Baker was certainly pretty enough to have been related to Marilyn Monroe. The iconic actress, of course, wasn't always the fabulous MM. As a young girl, she was simply Norma Jean Baker, a child born to a troubled mother. The future actress shuttled between foster homes and relatives, then married while still a teenager. Years after Krystal's death, a paternal uncle would say that he researched the Bakers' heritage and discovered the family, including Krystal, was distantly related to Monroe. Was Krystal a great-niece of Monroe's, as the family legend stated? Krystal hadn't been named for the actress; that they shared a middle name was a coincidence. "I don't know," admitted Krystal's dad, Johnny Baker, a trim man in his fifties. "But my uncle said it was true."

None of that would matter to young Krystal, for she'd die years before Johnny Baker's uncle made his claims. Something else out of the past would prove vastly more important than celebrity ties in the context of Krystal's short life: the stories of the girls who over the years mysteriously met their deaths south of Houston. Johnny, in his soft Texas twang, recounted how even as a boy growing up in Galveston, he'd heard tales of the murders of young women in the area, told in hushed tones as if speaking of the unmentionable. Did he worry about his daughter? "It's not the kind of thing you think could happen to your kid," he said, a painful catch audible in his throat. "By the time you realize it can, well, it's too late."

The heart displayed outside Jeanie Escamilla's home.
*(Courtesy of Kathryn Casey)*

It wouldn't be difficult to imagine that passersby on the road in front of Jeanie Escamilla's home in Dickinson quickly surmised that the woman who lived inside had a broken heart. From the street, a memorial heart with a young girl's photo was visible, and leaning against a wall stood a cross with Krystal's name and the years of her short life, 1982 to

1996. Jeanie's younger daughter was only thirteen on the day she died, a rambunctious, sometimes headstrong teenager with much to learn and the prospect of a lifetime ahead to do it.

Inside the house, Jeanie and I sat at a table in a corner of a wood-paneled living room. Her long, dark, reddish brown hair fell softly around her shoulders. Dressed in black pants and sweater with a lacy pink top, a heavy cross on a chain around her neck, she initially seemed eager to tell her story. Once the time had come, her hands shook slightly, and she appeared openly apprehensive, whispering that it still hurt to talk about her lost daughter even though it had been more than a decade since Krystal died. The home was decorated in Native American art, paintings, and sculptures, plaques with words of wisdom, and throughout there were statues of angels, including on a lamp table where a figurine of Christ nailed to a cross was positioned beside the Archangel Michael, his sword drawn.

Angels, creatures with the ability to fly away. But for fourteen years, Jeanie couldn't escape the nightmare of her youngest child's disappearance and death. There were no wings strong enough to release her spirit from the despair that filled her heart each time she thought of Krystal's young body, bruised and bloodied. "I've always been tough, all my life," said Escamilla. "When you're a single mom, you have to be. But nothing prepared me for what happened to Krystal. Nothing ever could."

Jeanie Escamilla yearned for her lost daughter. *(Courtesy of Kathryn Casey)*

Spending time with Jeanie, it was evident that her journey had been a long and often painful one. She talked vaguely of a difficult childhood and frequent hard times. Born in Sikeston, Missouri, she came with her mother to Texas. Jeanie married the first time at sixteen, and she had three children, each four years apart. Tonya was eight and Thomas was four when Krystal was born. Pink and blond, Krystal entered the world with a powerful cry and alert brown eyes. When she was three, of all the little girls in her preschool, Krystal was featured in a photo in the local newspaper, dressed as a Thanksgiving pilgrim.

After she and Johnny split, Jeanie and the children lived in a small brick house, while she worked as a hairdresser. Every other weekend, Krystal stayed with her dad in his apartment near the Union Carbide plant where he worked as a chemical operator. In the mornings, Krystal, often reluctant to rise, moaned, begging for more time to sleep, and each year, starting when she was only eight, she took Johnny for breakfast on his birthday. There was something about Krystal that always made him smile. "Just the way she had about her," he said. In the summers, Johnny worked nights, and they lay about the complex pool during the day, Krystal cultivating her tan.

As children so quickly do, Krystal grew up, and for her thirteenth birthday in August 1995, she posed in front of a red car, looking like a Ralph Lauren ad in a hat, blouse, and a skort (half shorts, half skirt), attractive, young and happy.

Although she'd lived near I-45 since childhood, Jeanie hadn't heard of the mysteries in the area involving young girls who'd disappeared and died. As an adult, she'd had little time for gossip or the evening news. "I had bills to pay, and I worked a lot. I was protective of the kids, but the first two were grown-up, and I started not to worry about Krystal as much," she said. "She was a teenager, and I wanted her to be independent. But I watched out for her. She had her first boyfriend, and I talked to him, reminding him that Krystal was only thirteen. He said he understood. It was an exciting time for Krystal. She was giddy in love."

Home in the evenings, the mother and daughter watched TV movies. When they discussed her future, Krystal ruminated about wanting to help people and becoming a nurse. Sometimes Jeanie brought up the pressures teenage girls face. She reminded Krystal that she was there to help, and Krystal promised to come to her before making any decisions that could affect her future. "I was always open with my kids. I wanted them to be able to talk to me about anything," said Jeanie. "At a certain point, you start being not only Mom but friends with your kids."

Yet in many ways, Krystal was still a child, one who needed her mother. One day she wrote Jeanie a letter in which she talked of falling asleep in her mother's arms: "It makes my dreams seem sweeter; knowing the time I share with you is a gift you give me."

That spring all wasn't well at school. Jeanie attended a conference with the principal, when Krystal complained of being bullied. Like Jeanie, Krystal developed early, gaining curves where some of the other girls weren't as yet endowed. The boys noticed, and a clique of girls in the school took note as well. "They were jealous," said Jeanie. "They started verbally abusing Krystal. One day, they cornered her at a park, and some of the girls ganged up on her, pulling her hair." Worried for her daughter's safety, Jeannie called her own mother, who worked for the railroad as a transporter shuffling staff between locations, asking if Krystal could live with her for the rest of the school year. Krystal's grandmother's house was close by in Texas City, in another school district. Moving meant that Krystal would change schools, and her parents hoped that would distance her from the schoolyard bullies. Krystal was less than happy with the situation, not wanting to leave her friends at her old school.

"Just until summer," Jeanie stressed. Looking back, she said, "We didn't know what else to do."

Those were the circumstances in early 1996, when Krystal Jean Baker moved into her maternal grandmother's cottage-like house on South Pecan Drive, a quaint setting with a front porch surrounded by large trees on a street with no sidewalks. The teenager woke up there on March 5, 1996. Since childhood, Krystal suffered recurring ear infections, and that morning she called Jeanie saying she wasn't feeling well. Judging from the gravelly timbre of Krystal's voice that she was telling the truth, Jeanie suggested her daughter stay in bed and offered to arrange a doctor's appointment.

At the beauty salon that day, Jeanie had a full schedule. She went about her work, not worried but planning to make the appointment and pick up Krystal later. Meanwhile at the house in Texas City that morning, Krystal called her dad. "Would you take me to my friend's house?" Krystal asked, explaining that she'd stayed home because of an ear infection. "I need a ride. I left my shoes there."

The shoes were important to Krystal; they were her first pair of heels, not stilettos but heels just the same. Krystal's friend lived in Bayou Vista, a small community south of Texas City at the top of the Galveston Causeway. Krystal's grandmother was at work and unable to drive her, and the teenager sounded eager to get her shoes and see her friend, who'd also stayed home from school that day. Johnny, however, had put in a full night at the plant and needed sleep. Krystal sounded disappointed.

Exactly what time the argument erupted between Krystal and her grandmother would later seem sketchy. Sometime around two o'clock, however, they stood in the driveway quarreling. Krystal's grandmother, upset when she returned home from work and found that Krystal hadn't gone to school, refused to drive her to her friend's house. Krystal, stubborn as teenagers can be, insisted. She wanted her shoes and to see friends who were congregating at the girl's home

after school ended for the day. The conflict escalated, and Krystal indignantly stalked off, heading south on Pecan Drive, toward Texas Avenue, the nearest main thorough-fare. Frustrated, the older woman went inside the house and called the Texas City Police Department, asking for an officer to stop Krystal and bring her home.

A little more than a block later, Krystal stood in front of a tire store on the corner of Pecan Drive and Texas Avenue, a few miles east of I-45, trucks and cars whizzing past. For a moment, she sat on a bench in front of the store and watched the traffic, perhaps wondering *What next?* Then she opened the door and asked to use the store phone. The workers agreed, and Krystal began dialing. The first person she called was Jeanie, asking again for a ride to her friend's house. "I couldn't go get her. I had clients all afternoon," said Jeanie. "I told her to go home to her grandmother's. That I was going to make her that doctor's appointment and pick her up later. Krystal told me she'd go back to the house and make peace with my mother."

After she hung up, Krystal, however, didn't do as she promised. Instead, she made more calls, contacting her brother, her sister, and friends, asking each for a ride. None could help her. She stayed so long in the tire store, phoned so many that a worker finally reminded her that it was a business phone, and she couldn't tie it up.

Disappointed, Krystal walked outside into the bright sunshine where the traffic streamed past on busy Texas Avenue. She might again have considered her dilemma: what to do? Her friend's house was five miles away on a route that consisted of two busy roads without sidewalks. Walking meant picking her way along rough gravel shoulders, while traffic kicked up dust beside her. Perhaps she paused momentarily and assessed her options. Or she might have been so angry that she never considered backtracking to her grandmother's house. Instead, Krystal walked east on foot along Texas Avenue. Trucks and cars flew by, beside the young girl in the short silvery cotton dress dotted with white and gold flowers. Around her neck, Krystal wore a necklace Jeanie had given her for Christmas, one with a teddy bear on a chain.

Meanwhile on Pecan Drive, Jeanie's mom explained to the Texas City police officer who responded that she wanted him to find her granddaughter and bring her home. She told him that Krystal didn't have permission to leave. As the old woman had hoped, the officer agreed. He drove off, only to return, however, a short time later, to report that he'd been unsuccessful. Although he'd circulated through the surrounding streets, he hadn't seen anyone fitting Krystal's description. By then, Krystal had disappeared.

"Krystal wasn't a perfect kid, but she was trying really hard," said Jeanie. "She was loving and kind, just kind of spreading her wings. She got mad at her grandmother and left; and then, she was gone."

At three that afternoon, Jeanie called her mother to tell her that she had a doctor's appointment scheduled for Krystal.

"She's not here," the older woman said. When Jeanie asked where Krystal was, her mother explained, "I think she wanted to go to a friend's house, and I told her that I wouldn't take her. So we had a fight. Krystal left, and she hasn't come back."

The rest of that afternoon as she worked on her clients, washing, curling, and coloring hair, Jeanie trailed over to the shop's phone to call Krystal's friends, looking for her daughter. When that didn't result in Krystal's voice on the phone or anyone reporting having seen her, Jeanie called the Texas City police. It was the station's second call that afternoon about the teenager, but the officer who answered the telephone sounded unconcerned. "He told me not to worry, that Krystal was probably with friends and would be home in a matter of hours," Jeanie said. At that point, she wasn't overly alarmed, assuming they were probaby right.

Late that afternoon when she got off work, Jeanie again called her mother and Johnny; neither one had seen Krystal or knew where she might be. It was then that Jeanie started to worry. She drove to Krystal's friend's house in Bayou Vista, the one Krystal begged her grandmother to take her to that afternoon. There Jeanie found a group of her daughter's friends, but Krystal wasn't among them. "We called Krystal and told her to come. She said she would, but we haven't seen her," said one of the girls.

"I guess Krystal thought it would be more fun with her friends than being at her grandmother's house," said Jeanie, shaking her head.

Not ready to give up her search, Jeanie drove onto Galveston Island. In March, the sun set early, and she wound through the darkened streets but saw no sign of Krystal. That evening, Jeanie reluctantly returned home, hoping her younger daughter would call. Not long after, Krystal's boyfriend, Randall, rang the doorbell, looking for her. "That was when I got really worried. Something was really wrong," said Jeanie. "Krystal wouldn't have gone anywhere without telling Randall where to find her."

Frantic, Jeanie redialed the Texas City police, only to be told once again not to worry, that Krystal would be home soon.

On that same evening, as sunset approached, seventy-four miles northeast of Texas City outside Anahuac, an investigator with the Chambers County Sheriff's Office named Bradley Moon stood under the bridge near where I-10 jumped the Trinity River and gazed down at the body of a young girl awkwardly sprawled out on the gravel shoulder.

The call came in at just after five, approximately three hours after Krystal Baker left her grandmother's house, as Detective Moon, a husky, mustached veteran of the department, was getting ready to call it a day. Although the county seat, Anahuac was a sleepy little place, a no-stoplight town where if everyone didn't know everyone, they knew everyone's family, where they lived, and their reputations. Murders didn't happen often in this bucolic setting.

The couple who stumbled upon the body had been fishing in the Trinity River. Before they called police, they covered the corpse with a thin white blanket edged in a ruffle and a plaid shirt, perhaps more for their own peace of mind than for the girl's sake since there was no question that she was dead and far removed from earthly concerns like modesty. The body lay on its stomach, reddish blond hair fanned out across the pavement, pale legs flung askew. Her short, flowered dress was hiked up to her waist, showing thin white panties. Her feet were bare.

One had only to glance to know that she'd suffered. Scrapes and bruises covered her limbs and face, a particularly nasty one above her left eye. Even her toes were battered. Yet it was hard not to stare at the girl's neck. There a thick, dark band formed an angry red slash.

Rather than heading home to dinner and family, Moon and a group of other officers with flashlights searched the area around the body, which had been sectioned off with orange traffic cones. They looked for evidence, any indication of who the girl was, a purse, something left by the killer, her shoes. They found nothing. All they had was a girl's lifeless body and not one thing that indicated who she was or who'd killed her. About the most they could say was that she was dead and that she'd apparently been murdered.

That evening, with the body still on the scene, the local justice of the peace drove out to take a look. In small Texas towns without a coroner or medical examiner, JPs have the duty of pronouncing death. This elected official inspected the young girl's sad corpse and ordered it sent to Houston, to the Harris County Medical Examiner, the facility Chambers County relied on for autopsies.

As Moon and the others watched, the body was placed in a black body bag, then put on a gurney and slid into a body car, a hearse from a local mortuary. As the wagon with its tragic cargo drove off, the officers resumed their hunt, scouring the surrounding area for evidence.

Around that time in Texas City, Jeanie stood across a

desk from a police officer, filling out a report of a missing person. She brought a photo of Krystal with her, and she answered each question. Acid ate away at her insides, as she described her daughter, aching with each word. Yet the officer seemed indifferent. Jeanie left, assuming that police would begin looking for her daughter; instead, the officer filed the form, listing Krystal as a runaway.

Early the following morning, March 6, Brad Moon drove from his office in Anahuac into Houston, to be at the medical examiner's office in time for the nine o'clock autospy on the unknown female found under the I-10 overpass. By then, the dead girl had a name, but not her own; she was listed as a Jane Doe.

In the autopsy suite, Moon took photos of the injuries on the body, including the heavy bruising across the girl's throat. When he was done, the physician began his investigation. First, the girl's dress and panties were removed and placed into an evidence bag. Next scrapings were taken from under her fingernails. What was found was transferred onto paper then sealed inside a clear plastic bag and slipped into an evidence bag. Both of the evidence bags were marked with the case number and sealed.

Brad Moon was one of the first investigators on the scene the night Krystal Baker died. *(Courtesy of Kathryn Casey)*

Moon didn't usually mind autopsies. He'd been a cop for years and had witnessed a good share of them. "But this one bothered me," he said. "It was the senselessness of it, that it was a young girl."

As Moon stood by, the forensic pathologist cut into the girl's flesh. The head, hands, limbs, and abdomen were examined individually, then described by the physician in detail as he talked into a recorder. Later, a secretary typed up the official report. On it would be noted a one-inch laceration of the vagina. Although no sperm was found inside her, the wound suggested that this Jane Doe had been sexually assaulted. Tiny blood vessels in the girl's eyes, eyelids, and face had burst, indicating suffocation. Homicide, the doctor determined, and the ultimate cause of death was noted as ligature strangulation.

Late that morning, Moon returned to his office in the Chambers County Sheriff's Office and checked the dress, panties, and fingernail scrapings inside the envelopes into the evidence room. He then went to his computer and typed a report on the case describing the Jane Doe as between fifteen and twenty years old with blond hair and brown eyes. Based on lividity, the pooling of blood after the heart stops pumping that turns skin a purple hue, and a lack of rigor mortis, the medical examiner estimated that the girl died not long before her body was found. Once he finished the paperwork, Moon pushed the send button and submitted it to TCIC (the Texas Crime Information Center) and NCIC (the National Crime Information Center) for distribution to law-enforcement agencies.

The case was less than twenty-four hours old, and Moon had a lot of questions. One thing he felt certain of was that the dead girl wasn't local. If she'd been from Anahuac or a neighboring town, either he or one of the other officers on the scene would have been able to ID her.

The days passed. In Texas City, Jeanie dropped in at the police department often, hoping for news on Krystal's case. Each time she did she heard the same assessment, that there was no need to worry, that she needed to just wait, that

Krystal was a runaway, and she'd eventually return home. But Jeanie didn't believe that. One of Krystal's friends had run away the previous year, and Krystal saw the agony it caused the family. Afterward, she'd told Jeanie, "Mom, I'd never put you through that."

Not knowing what to do, Jeanie and her mother searched. They made up flyers with Krystal's photo and began distributing copies to local stores to display in the windows. And they drove the streets of Texas City, throughout the area, looking, stopping at Krystal's friends' homes, hoping to find her, praying that they'd be able to bring her home alive.

Those same mornings in Anahuac, Brad Moon combed through a pile of inquiries about the unknown white female found under the I-10 bridge. He e-mailed out photos and information, but none of the responding departments identified the girl as the one they searched for. Why no one at the Texas City Police Department noticed reports of a Chambers County Jane Doe that fit Krystal's description would be a mystery, but perhaps the reports didn't match up because in Texas City, Krystal was presumed a runaway not a missing person. "That was the way it was back then, standard," said one of the officers. "She was thirteen and she'd left on her own. We didn't have any indication that there was a reason to worry about her safety."

That, however, gave Jeanie no solace. "I was a mother, doing what I could to find my daughter. No one helped me," she said, her voice rising with anger as she was swept back to those days. "No one else was looking for Krystal, so I had to. Every time I called the police, they said she was a runaway. I knew she hadn't run away. I couldn't work. I couldn't do anything. I just kept thinking about my little girl."

One day, Jeanie went to the tire store where the workers told her about Krystal's visit, how she'd stood at the phone calling family and friends, looking for a ride, without finding one. They saw Krystal walk out the door but had no idea where she'd gone.

For sixteen days, each time the phone rang, Jeanie ran to pick it up, hoping she'd hear Krystal's voice. Day after day, Jeanie talked over and again to all her daughter's friends, but heard nothing that helped determine where her daughter could have gone. And Jeanie prayed, she waited, and she hoped.

Finally on March 21, someone at the Texas City Police Department noticed a Chambers County report on the discovery of a dead teenager found under a highway overpass. Photos of the body were pulled up on the Texas City computers. The girl had died just hours after Krystal disappeared. The description of the girl and her clothing matched the report Jeanie had filed. A call came in, and Bradley Moon made his way to Texas City, a copy of the case file in hand.

That morning, Jeanie dressed for work when the phone rang. She'd been at the police department the day before, and there'd been no news on the case, but the officer on the phone said they now had photos to show her. "He didn't tell me that they were pictures of my daughter on a slab," said Jeanie, crying.

At the police station, Jeanie looked at the first picture but either didn't recognize her daughter or didn't want to acknowledge the truth. "That's not Krystal," she said.

The officer put down another, a close-up of Krystal's face taken during the autopsy with a sheet pulled over the shoulders, covering the body. The slash of purple and red around her neck, however, peered out over the top of the sheet. Her heart pounding, Jeanie realized that she stared at her daughter's face. Her eyes trailed down to the ring of welts that extended from under Krystal's chin to her shoulders. "It was horrible," she said. "They pulled out more photos. They were flopping pictures of my little girl in front of me, dead."

Brad Moon would look back on that day and not minimize the pain he saw, yet he insisted they had no choice. Jeanie had to be shown the photos, so she could identify the body. "It was very emotional," he said. "Your heart just broke. I couldn't say the right things. The girl, she was this woman's child."

After identifying Krystal's body from the photos, Jeanie drove home alone. Sobbing, her body shaking, she got out of the car and fell into a ditch that ran along the road. She cried so hard that she couldn't stand up. Her family helped her, carrying her in. Hours later, it was on the news that Krystal Baker, a thirteen-year-old thought to be a runaway, had been found murdered in Chambers County.

That same day, an officer called Johnny Baker at work and told him that his daughter's body had been found. "I thought she was with friends somewhere," he said, his voice a whisper. "I thought that she'd come home."

At one point, Jeanie picked up the phone and called Bradley Moon to ask a question. "Did Krystal have shoes on when they found her?" She didn't. That brought back a memory for Jeanie. Just weeks before she'd disappeared, Krystal had told her mother what she'd do if anyone ever tried anything untoward with her. The teenager looked serious when she said, "I'd scream really loud, kick my shoes off, and start running."

In the days after they learned of her murder, remorse consumed those who loved Krystal. Jeanie, Johnny, and Krystal's grandmother all wished that they'd dropped what they were doing when the phone rang and agreed to pick her up. Jeanie regretted not leaving work, and Johnny that he'd wanted to sleep after finishing his nightlong shift rather than drive his teenage daughter to pick up her shoes. "But how do you know?" he asked. "How could I have known this would happen."

Perhaps there was second-guessing at the Texas City Police Department, too, where officers were now investigating a murder.

In Texas City, Brian Goetschius became the detective on the case, and he began interviewing Krystal's family and friends, documenting the details of the case and looking for a suspect. The reports he heard pegged Krystal as stubborn, perhaps just a little on the wild side. "But she wasn't a bad kid," he said. "Should we have been looking earlier? We did what we were supposed to do. We didn't have any indication that there was anything other than that she walked away."

Brian Goetschius took over the Baker case in Texas City.
*(Courtesy of Kathryn Casey)*

Meanwhile, Jeanie prepared for a memorial service for her teenage daughter. She had little money, but she borrowed what she could and bought Krystal a white wedding dress, one with a high neckline that extended up to her chin, to cover the wound encircling her neck, and long sleeves to hide her daughter's bruised arms.

When the service started, friends and family lined up at the door, including Krystal's teenage friends. Jeanie fought to hold in her emotions, but at times they overwhelmed her. Texas City officers mingled with the crowd, watching to see if anyone acted oddly. They left disappointed; if the killer attended, they saw nothing that gave him away.

After the doors closed, Jeanie stayed, for the first time alone with Krystal's body. She leaned over the casket, and her tears fell on her dead daughter's face, washing away streaks of the mortuary's thick makeup. Jeanie saw the bruises underneath and that her daughter's left eye was circled in black. "I kissed her and cried, and I cried and cried," Jeanie said. "I said, you're in God's hands now."

Lacking the money for a plot to bury her daughter, Jeanie had Krystal's remains cremated.

The next day in Chambers County, Brad Moon checked out the envelopes holding Krystal's dress, underwear, and fingernail scrapings from the evidence room and transported them to the Jefferson County Regional Crime Lab, where Chambers County had a service contract. The material was logged into a long queue. Months later, when the evidence finally came up for processing, a technician examined the clothing under an ultraviolet light, inspecting it for any substance that could be bodily fluids. The dress material proved a problem. The polished, shiny surface distorted the light. In the end, the technician cut off four small sections of the dress she thought might be stains and sent the samples on for further processing. When the results came back, the fabric samples had tested negative for blood, semen, and saliva.

The only remaining possibility was the fingernail scrapings. But there, too, there was a problem. DNA was just coming of age, and few labs had the equipment to handle what was then such advanced forensic testing. In Texas, one was the Department of Public Safety lab in Austin. In such a large state with so few facilities, the protocol was not to analyze DNA until authorities had a suspect. At the time, it made sense. Unless law enforcement had a person of interest, officers had no one to compare with the recovered DNA.

Yet science was moving quickly, and there were potentially more accurate tests and other breakthroughs on the horizon. So the Jefferson County lab took the precaution of freezing the envelope with the scrapings to hold for another time, perhaps a day when a suspect appeared. And Brad Moon made a second trip to the lab, this time to reclaim the envelope holding Krystal's dress and panties. At the Chambers County Sheriff's Office, he stopped at the evidence room and checked it in for safekeeping.

With no evidence and no suspects, before long in both

Galveston and Chambers counties, the investigators moved on to other cases, ones they had the possibility of solving. "It wasn't that we ever forgot," said Moon. "It was that at a certain point, there wasn't anything for us to do on the case. We didn't have any leads."

One thing Moon did do before putting it to the side was to send the case to Quantico, Virginia, to the Behavioral Sciences Division of the FBI, to be analyzed. When the profile on the killer came back, it theorized that Krystal Baker's murderer could be a serial killer, and that—based on statistical probabilities—the murderer was probably between twenty-five and forty-five and white. The racial information came from theories prevalent at the time that killers most often chose victims within their own racial profile.

Eventually, Jeanie returned to work, but she couldn't forget what had happened to her daughter. She thought of Krystal every day, remembering the injuries that covered her body, thinking about how hard her little girl fought to live. She went to the police station often but came away without answers.

As the case stagnated, Jeanie, who'd once received a poem from her daughter, wrote to Krystal, saying that she had disappeared "like a summer breeze" and calling her "my sweet angel above." On her refrigerator, Jeanie built a memorial, Krystal's photo surrounded by religious pictures and tokens of her love.

Off and on, Jeanie drove to the I-10 overpass in Chambers County that crossed the Trinity River, and stood where her daughter's body had been found. She brought flowers and a cross, and she prayed and thought of all she'd lost, the daughter who would never go to the senior prom, never get married, never have children, never again be held in her arms. Each time she felt her anger rise, the frustration of so many days when the police weren't looking for Krystal because they assumed she was a runaway. "Even if they do run away, the police should look for the kids," said Jeanie. "They could be in danger. They have parents who love them."

The montage memorializing Krystal on Jeanie's refrigerator.
*(Courtesy of Kathryn Casey)*

It would be many years before Jeanie would discover that in Anahuac, at the Chamber's County Sheriff's Office, someone else hadn't forgotten Krystal, and that this one woman remembered and cared would make all the difference.

# Chapter 12

## The DNA of a Murderer
## Sherry Willcox Never Gave Up

**Anahuac, Texas**

Sherry Willcox seated at her desk in the Chambers County Sheriff's Office. *(Courtesy of Kathryn Casey)*

"It was the pictures. I couldn't get the pictures out of my mind," said Sherry Willcox, a woman with shoulder-length medium brown hair, kind eyes, and a direct manner who worked as an evidence officer. "Once I had the file in my hands, I couldn't put it away. Krystal's photos bothered me. If it were my daughter, I'd want to know who did this to her.

And I thought there had to be some way to find out, some evidence left behind."

We were in a conference room at the Chambers County Sheriff's Office, and Willcox sat beside Bradley Moon, the main investigator on the murder investigation. Although Moon worked the case at the outset, it was Willcox who took over the quest to answer the question: Who murdered Krystal Jean Baker? "Krystal fought hard to live," said Willcox. "She deserved justice."

"Jeanie was really the one who kept pushing," said Krystal's dad, Johnny Baker. "I tried not to think about it. I didn't want to. But Jeanie kept talking to the police, making sure they didn't forget about the case."

The years had passed, but Jeanie Escamilla's anger and frustration over her daughter's murder never did. She married and moved into the house in Dickinson, placing the pot with Krystal's ashes under a table topped with photos of her murdered daugh-

The container in Jeanie's living room that holds Krystal Baker's remains.
*(Courtesy of Kathryn Casey)*

ter. And Jeanie never stopped considering what she could do to get police to focus on Krystal's murder and search for the man who killed her. "I'd go to the Texas City police station, and they'd just tell me that they couldn't do anything," she said. "To me it looked like they didn't care. I was Krystal's mother. She was my baby. And I couldn't let it go."

In 2002, six years after her daughter's death, Jeanie took action. She hired a private investigator to look into the case. By then, television programs and newspaper headlines routinely recounted the vast difference DNA increasingly made in criminal investigations, including decades-old cold cases. Jeanie had read and seen in news footage and TV documentaries how small bits of genetic material could be used to identify a rapist or a killer. She'd never forgotten the condition of her daughter's body, covered head to toe with bruises and abrasions. "Krystal must have gotten something on her. I couldn't see how there wasn't evidence," said Jeanie. "I thought there had to be something that would help them figure out who murdered my little girl."

As part of his investigation, the PI went into the Texas City Police Department and talked to the investigators who'd worked the case but came away with nothing. Then he sent a request to the Chambers County Sheriff's Office for a copy of the file. Sherry Willcox had just started working as an evidence clerk a few months earlier. She was assigned to copy the file and mail it to the PI. As she paged through, she remembered the case. At the time Krystal died, Willcox was a schoolgirl. She'd never forgotten the body found under the I-10 bridge. She remembered her own mother cautioning her at the time to be careful; someone was murdering young girls.

The copies made and in the mail to Jeanie's investigator, Willcox could have returned the Baker case file to the records department, burying it among other cold cases. Instead, she placed it on the corner of her desk. At times, she felt drawn to it, combing through the notes on the investigation, including descriptions of the night the body was discovered. The crime-scene and autopsy photos hit hard. Krystal had been so young, and her life ended in a vicious attack filled with rage. Something about the girl touched Willcox deeply. And she, like Jeanie, assessed the dozens of visible injuries to Krystal's body and considered what that meant. "Krystal put up such a struggle, this child, just thirteen years old," said Willcox. "What she went through that day, I couldn't get past it. I couldn't forget."

Occasionally when Willcox had a break from her duties, she picked up the file on the Baker case. Assessing the photos, her eyes were drawn to a stain on Krystal's white nylon panties. Had anyone ever tested it? Could it lead to the killer? Willcox perused the lab reports and found that Jefferson County had processed the dress and the panties soon after the murder in 1996 and found nothing. But Willcox knew that in the subsequent years DNA and forensic science had made remarkable strides. What were once bits of DNA too small for testing could be replicated and analyzed. Over time, Willcox repeatedly considered the possibility that the evidence could be retested. Yet there were so many potential pitfalls. Had the items been properly stored? If not, they would be useless. But the biggest question: Did the evidence room still have the dress and panties on file?

It didn't take Willcox long to pull the records and determine that the dress and panties remained in the evidence room. Once she had the envelope that held them in her hands, she filled out the forms to have them resubmitted. The next time she drove to Houston to the Texas Department of Public Safety lab, where Chambers County then had evidence processed, Willcox brought the Baker evidence with her. It appeared the effort would be to no avail when the DPS clerk manning the check-in desk saw Jefferson County's insignia on the evidence envelope and asked if the contents had been previously tested. Willcox admitted that it had.

"We can't test then," the clerk informed her. Protocol ruled that since there was nothing new in the case, no suspects, there was no justification for spending tax dollars to retest. Sherry Willcox felt defeated. There was no option other than to take the envelope back to the office. Once she returned the envelope to the evidence room, Willcox considered refiling Krystal's paperwork. Instead, she again placed the case file on her desk. She wasn't yet ready to give up.

Unaware of Willcox's interest, Jeanie had no idea that a

Chambers County evidence clerk was now her greatest ally. Instead, she shook her head in disbelief when the private investigator went over his results with her, saying that records showed that Krystal's body and clothing had been processed and no forensic evidence found. "I just didn't believe it," she said. "My daughter couldn't have fought that hard for her life and not have evidence on her. A hair. A fiber. Blood. Something."

In the years since Krystal Baker's murder, Brad Moon had left the Chambers County Sheriff's Office. In 2005, he returned. When Willcox saw him in the office hallway, she recognized him as the investigator on the scene the night Krystal's body was discovered. "We started talking about the case," he said. "I'd never forgotten it. I'd always wondered who killed that girl. It was one of those cases that I'd never been able to put out of my mind. I thought about it off and on, wondering what we didn't do that we should have done, wondering what we missed."

"When we had an opportunity, we talked," said Willcox, who by then had had the file on her desk for three years. "We tried to think of something we could do to work the case. But there was nothing."

Again years passed, and the case never warmed up. Sherry Willcox returned to school and became certified, so that instead of a clerk she was licensed as an evidence officer. And off and on, she paged through the Baker file and wondered. DNA retrieval and processing continued to improve. Forensic sciences moved ahead. The time came when Sherry decided to take a chance.

On February 6, 2009, Willcox had evidence from an unrelated case to transport to the Houston lab for analysis. Before she left her office in Anahuac, she took Krystal's dress and panties out of the Jefferson County lab envelope and repackaged both into a brand-new DPS envelope, one that didn't indicate the evidence had been previously tested. On the accompanying form, Willcox asked the lab to test for bodily fluids and the presence of DNA. "I didn't ask if we could. I just did it," said Willcox. At the lab, she dropped it off as if it were a new case. This time the clerk didn't question the submission.

Back in Anahuac, Moon and Willcox talked about the turn of events and waited. Meanwhile, in the DPS lab in Houston, the dress made its way through processing. First it was given a visual examination for bodily fluids. This time around, the technician manning the ultraviolet light found an additional four spots of interest. One twist of luck was that rather than fading, with age semen stains become more fluorescent. The lab tech tested the areas with a chemical to determine if they could have been traces of bodily fluids and got a weak reaction. All were around the dress collar. She collected the samples by cutting them from the dress, finally forwarding the samples to the DNA lab for analysis.

Eight months later in August, the DPS lab called the contact number on the evidence envelope and asked for Willcox. Moments later, she walked into Moon's office, crying. "They found semen on Krystal Baker's dress," she said. "They have a DNA profile."

It had been thirteen years since Krystal's brutalized body was discovered, and for the first time, law enforcement had evidence that could lead to her killer. Days later, Willcox and Moon drove to Dickinson to meet with Jeanie and Krystal's dad, Johnny. The two officers explained that semen had been found on Krystal's dress, and that they had DNA to identify her killer. What they needed from Johnny and Jeanie were specimens of their own DNA to use to exclude Krystal's DNA from the mix.

Krystal's parents agreed and swabbed the insides of their mouths for Moon and Willcox, but Jeanie felt both elation and horror. She hadn't known about the tear in Krystal's vagina. Over the years, Jeanie had wondered who'd murdered her daughter, at times questioning if it could have been the girls who'd bullied her at school. Now that Jeanie knew about the semen, she realized that Krystal had been sexually assaulted. "I was devastated," she said. "It made me mad to realize someone had kidnapped my daughter and killed her for a thrill."

The previous years had been a roller coaster for Jeanie. Now there was hope. But there still wasn't a killer behind bars. That wouldn't happen until law enforcement identified a suspect by comparing DNA with the sample found on Krystal's dress. "Please," she asked Willcox and Moon. "Take this. Do what you need to do. But if you find out, don't tell me who this guy is until you have him in jail. I don't want to know."

Back at the office, Moon and Willcox speculated on what else could be done for the case. They had DNA, but they didn't have a match. They didn't have the name or face of the killer. Yet that potential now existed. There was the real possibility that at some point the case could end up in a courtroom. Moon thought about the I-10 bridge, slated to be torn down and replaced. He decided to return to the scene and draw a more precise chart documenting the exact positions of the columns and the placement of the body, before the bridge was gone and their opportunity vanished.

Beneath the I-10 bridge, looking away from the Trinity River.
*(Courtesy of Kathryn Casey)*

For years, Willcox had been the keeper of the Baker case file. For the first time, she stood where the girl's body had been found. She helped as Moon measured and charted, and she thought about the photos, what Krystal's body had looked like on that awful day. The emotions were overwhelming. Later, back at the office, she paged once again through the file, speculating that perhaps there was something else useful hidden inside. What she found was a notation that fingernail scrapings had been collected. "Would you look this case up and see if you still have the evidence in your freezer?" Willcox asked the clerk at the Jefferson County lab.

"We do," the woman said.

Days later, Willcox walked into the Jefferson lab with a cooler and ice to pick up the sample. As she had with the dress and panties, she transported the envelope with the scrapings inside to the DPS lab in Houston. It was nearly Christmastime, and what Willcox wanted that holiday season was a break in the Baker case.

The year ended, and a few months into 2010, Willcox received more good news; semen had been found in the fingernail scrapings with DNA matching that found on Krystal's dress. An exact match, they came from the same source, an unknown African-American male. Willcox had another piece to the puzzle. By then she'd entered the initial DNA findings on CODIS, the U.S. government's Combined DNA Index System, a database administered by the FBI that included forensic profiles of convicted felons, missing persons, and unidentified human remains.

Finally, on September 15 of that same year, Willcox's phone rang. The caller explained that she had new information on the Krystal Baker case. Willcox's heart jumped when she heard the words, "We have a match."

# Chapter 13

## "I Saw a Girl Walking"
## Kevin Edison Smith

### Chambers County, Texas

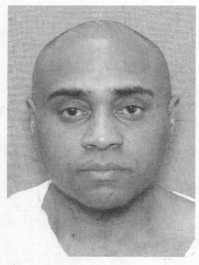

Kevin Edison Smith.
*(Courtesy of the Texas Department of Criminal Justice)*

"There was a lot of excitement in the office the day the call came in," said Brad Moon. "Now we had a name, we knew who the guy was, the one who murdered Krystal. But it wasn't someone we would have expected. This guy, he flew way under the radar."

The hit on CODIS matched both the fingernail scrapings and the semen found on the flowered dress Krystal wore that last day of her life. The reason the suspect's DNA was in the system was that in January 2010, he had been arrested in Pointe Coupee Parish, Louisiana. The charge had been a minor one. Pulled over during a traffic stop because he'd allegedly swerved between lanes, officers found a bag of pills in the car, prescription drugs. He was booked on a felony drug-possession charge. In Texas, DNA was collected only from those convicted of sexual offenses and murder, but

Louisiana law required DNA collection in all felony arrests. This man had only minor skirmishes with law enforcement in the past, including being charged after wrangling with police during a 1994 stop for driving under the influence. There were no sex offenses, no truly violent crimes on his record.

Born in 1965, Kevin Edison Smith was the oldest of four children, raised by his mother and an aunt. Smith grew up in the towns bordering I-45, the family living much of the time around the Texas City area, and he'd earned a degree from Galveston's Ball High School. Over the years, he'd married three times, most recently in 2007 to a woman from Opelousas, Louisiana. A pipe welder, he'd had contract jobs in plants throughout Texas and Louisiana, living a transient life, moving on as one job dried up and another opportunity appeared. "He's a really quiet guy, not the kind who attracts a lot of attention," said someone who knew him. "He wasn't the kind who'd stand out in a crowd."

Once they had a name, Moon called in Texas Ranger Joe Haralson to assist with the arrest. Rangers have jurisdiction across the state, enabling them to cross county lines to move in quickly and apprehend a suspect. Haralson had been working out of Texas City since the mideighties, and he'd been involved in many of the I-45 investigations.

Once on board, Haralson helped write

Texas Ranger Joe Haralson in his office in 2013. *(Courtesy of Kathryn Casey)*

the necessary search warrants to get the information they needed to find Krystal Baker's accused killer, Kevin Smith. The method they used was to determine Smith's cell-phone number. Once they had it, they began surveillance on the phone's activity, watching for it to ping off towers. That should have enabled them to narrow down his whereabouts based on his cell phone's location. The problem was that the phone never appeared to be used. For a week they watched and waited. Nothing. Sensing something wasn't right, they investigated and found they had a wrong number.

On September 22, Haralson and the others received a tip; Smith's latest contract welding job was at the Motiva plant in Port Arthur, Texas. The largest facility of its kind in the United States, the refinery is a massive web of steel pipe and machinery owned by Shell Oil and Saudi Aramco with a six-hundred-thousand-barrel-a-day capacity. At the district attorney's office in Anahuac, Haralson notified the Chambers County DA, Cheryl Swope Lieck, that he was on his way to make the arrest. On the paperwork, Lieck noted something rather ironic. "You know it's Smith's forty-fifth birthday," said Lieck, a sarcastic edge to her voice. "When you put the handcuffs on, tell him happy birthday."

At the Motiva plant, Moon, Sherry Willcox, and Haralson waited for Smith, who'd been called into his supervisor's office. When Smith sauntered in wearing his blue work jumpsuit, unsuspecting of what awaited him, he was immediately read his rights and put under arrest. A muscular man, Smith stared at the group around him but initially said nothing. He appeared stunned.

"You're under arrest for the 1996 murder of Krystal Jean Baker," Moon told him. "Her body was found under the I-10, Trinity River Bridge."

"I didn't kill nobody," Smith said. "You've got the wrong guy."

"Your DNA was found on that girl's clothes," Ranger Haralson said, explaining that the match had been made after his Louisiana arrest.

"How in the world did my DNA get mixed up with that?" Smith countered.

"I knew we had the right guy based on the way he was acting, so cool," said Moon. On the forty-five-minute drive, Smith never spoke another word. Back in Chambers County, he was brought before a judge and again read his rights. His bail was set at one million dollars.

Assessing the bruise pattern around Krystal Baker's neck, thicker on the left than the right, Lieck had theorized that the man who murdered Krystal was left-handed. When she saw Smith signing papers in the courtroom with his left hand, she felt ever more certain.

With Smith tucked safely into a cell in the county jail, another duty waited. That afternoon, Sherry Willcox and Bradley Moon drove to Jeanie's house to tell her that there'd been a break in her daughter's case, and that the man responsible for Krystal's death was under arrest. They brought a photo of Smith, and told her that they had a perfect DNA match. "She cried," said Sherry. "And she said thank you."

Soon, Jeanie's phone began ringing, and reporters dogged her. A press conference was held in which Texas City police explained that there'd been an arrest in one of the cases on the I-45 Mysteries chart. A man was in prison for the murder of Krystal Baker. "It took a while to believe it had happened," said Jeanie. "And then it brought it all flooding back, all the grief and the pain."

At the press conference three days later, Jeanie told reporters she'd given up believing Krystal's murderer would ever be found. Although calling the turn of events a miracle, there was something else she wanted more. "If I had any wishes right now, I wish I could wake up and hold my little girl in my arms."

Weeks passed while Smith waited in jail. Then nearly a month after the arrest, a well-known activist and the leader of the New Black Panther Party, Quanell X, drove from his Houston headquarters to the Chambers County jail to talk to Kevin Edison Smith. A muscular, immaculately dressed man, Quanell X had been commissioned by the family to make sure that Smith wasn't being unfairly prosecuted or mistreated behind bars. Later, Quanell X would say that he told Smith's mother and aunt that if Smith "is innocent I will fight them. But if he's guilty of this crime, I will come back and tell you."

In an interview room in the jail, Smith told Quanell X that he wasn't being abused in the jail, but he was being unjustly accused. At first Smith denied knowing anything about Krystal Baker's murder. Then Quanell X warned him, saying that if Smith cried racism, and it wasn't true, "it could backfire on all of us."

It was then that Quanell X explained to Smith that a second DNA test was being run to verify the results of the first, to confirm that the semen found on Krystal's dress tied directly to him. "Man, my wife is going to leave me," Smith said, hanging his head.

As they talked, Quanell X would later say that he asked Smith something else: "Do you think your DNA is going to be found in other cases?"

What Smith reportedly answered was, "I don't know," indicating that was possible. Then it appeared the reality of his situation hit him, when Smith said, "They're going to give me the death penalty."

The conversation continued, and Smith made it clear that he had a grave concern: being put on trial for his life. With that, Quanell X asked Smith if he wanted him to talk to the district attorney, to see if there was the possibility of tabling the death penalty if Smith was willing to tell the truth about Krystal's murder.

In Texas, for a criminal case to be eligible for the death penalty, a murder had to meet certain criteria: involving a special victim, such as a police officer, or happen during the commission of a second felony. That latter qualifier was met in the case since Krystal was a minor. The semen on her dress and the tear in her vagina indicated she'd been sexually assaulted. There was no evidence to suggest she'd agreed to have sex with Smith—in fact, with so many injuries, it was obvious that she'd tried to fight him off—but even if she had, as a child she couldn't legally agree, and any sexual contact with her was a felony.

Shortly after two that afternoon, District Attorney Cheryl Swope Lieck was in a courtroom waiting for a jury to return with a verdict in another case when she got the message that Quanell X said Kevin Edison Smith was ready to confess to the murder of Krystal Baker, but that he wanted something in return. Reluctant to leave the courtroom, she sent a message back, "Are you sure he's not wasting my time?" When assur-

Chambers County DA Cheryl Swope Lieck outside her office.
*(Courtesy of Kathryn Casey)*

ances came that the offer was a serious one, Lieck left for the jail.

In Moon's office, Lieck talked to Quanell X. "I've explained to Mr. Smith that this is only for this case, not any others," he said.

Lieck was and wasn't surprised. Quanell X had just suggested there could be more cases linked to Smith. "I believe there are others," she said, indicating she understood.

Quanell X said only, "All we're concerned about here today is this case."

A short time later, Moon, Willcox, Lieck, and Kevin

Smith gathered in an interview room, and Quanell X moderated by explaining what the man in question wanted: "Mr. Smith wants assurances that you won't be going for the death penalty."

Once she understood what was being offered, Lieck considered the situation. Like the others, the case resonated for the prosecutor, who'd grown up in the area. At the time of Krystal's death, Lieck had been an assistant DA, and she'd never forgotten about the girl under the bridge. With the DNA evidence, the prosecutor felt confident that she could get a jury to convict and vote for the death penalty. Considering the age of the case she, however, wasn't convinced it would hold up on appeal. And there was something else, that possibility of other cases. She wasn't the only one who thought that there were other victims. Moon and Willcox were voicing the same theories. Smith had been too cool when arrested, and he had a transient past, one where he'd moved from state to state over the years. Lieck wanted Smith alive to answer questions, to have the opportunity to piece together other cases and give other families what relief a confession or conviction could bring.

After a pause to make her decision, Lieck agreed to forgo the death penalty in exchange for Smith telling the truth about his involvement in Krystal Baker's murder. And she reminded him of something Quanell X had already said he'd explained to Smith, that the deal was only for this one case. If there were others, there were no guarantees. "I don't have any jurisdiction over anything that may have happened in another county," she said.

When they explained the situation to Smith, Quanell X said, "She means if there are other bodies that come up with your DNA." When Smith nodded that he understood, Quanell X said to Lieck, "Brother Kevin . . . is not an evil man. A loving family, a wife . . . he was wrapped up in his own personal demons back then as far as drinking alcohol."

"There aren't any do-overs . . . There was a life that was taken," Lieck countered, saying to Smith, "Your DNA was on her . . . I'm not going to bullshit you. You will never get out of prison."

At that point, everyone but Quanell X and Smith left the room so the two men could discuss Smith's options. The death penalty was off the table if he agreed to talk, but would Smith consent to an arrangement that condemned him to spend his life behind bars? A short time later, the others were called back. Smith took the deal. It was then he began talking about the day Krystal Jean Baker died.

In Smith's account, fourteen years earlier he'd worked at the Amoco plant in Texas City, and on that particular day he'd been drinking with buddies after work at Zackie's, a convenience store on Texas Avenue, where he cashed his paychecks. At that time, he said, he'd often get drunk, then pick up prostitutes.

That afternoon, Smith sat on the bench outside the store with other smokers, enjoying a cigarette with his beer when, "I saw a girl walking down the highway." Not long after, he bought a twenty-four-ounce beer for the road and drove off in his green Chevy extended-cab pickup truck.

Approaching the girl, Smith pulled over and lowered his window. Then he started talking, smiling, and offering her a ride, coaxing her into getting into the truck. Krystal must have been tired, her feet sore. She'd been walking for nearly two miles along the dusty highway. Smith was thirty years old, not a bad-looking man, presumably nothing visibly frightening about him. Perhaps he somehow forced her, threatening her with a weapon. But in the version of events he recounted, Smith charmed her, and Krystal ultimately climbed willingly into the passenger seat. Once he had her beside him inside the truck, he turned the conversation to sex. "She said she was eighteen," he told those gathered. "I thought she was a prostitute . . . I was talking to her about some sex . . . oral sex."

The confession continued, with Smith admitting that what Krystal wanted wasn't sex but what she'd been looking for all afternoon, a ride to her friend's house in Bayou Vista. Smith, however, had his mind made up. He drove a short distance, then pulled behind a gas station. He promised Krystal money, but again all she wanted was a ride to her friend's house. Did she try to open the door, to run? Had he somehow locked her in? What Smith said happened next was that Krystal "freaked out . . . just started getting crazy . . . I was trying to restrain her . . . I was drunk."

The teenager, undoubtedly terrified, must have understood the danger. According to Smith, Krystal fought as he tried to force himself on her, hitting and kicking. Quickly, the situation turned lethal. "I grabbed her. I choked her," he said. "The next thing I knew, she'd stopped breathing."

At first Smith insisted he'd strangled Krystal with his hands, but that didn't sit well with Lieck, who'd read the autopsy results. When she said that she knew that he'd used something, some type of a ligature, Smith said, "I had like a strap . . . I kept in my truck."

With Krystal's dead body slumped in the passenger seat, Smith then said he drove nearly sixty miles to the Trinity River Bridge. When asked why there, Smith said he didn't know the place, only that he'd happened upon it and it looked like a lonely location, one where he wouldn't be seen. After he threw Krystal's body out of the truck, he drove off.

The interview continued. A thirteen-year-old girl whose path just happened to cross with his that day was dead, brutally murdered, but Smith voiced no regret, instead blaming Krystal. If she hadn't objected, hadn't fought him, had given him what he wanted, he implied it would never have happened. "I was just playing, and she went berserk," he said.

As she considered his account, the district attorney found problems. It didn't match all of the evidence. The most important discrepancy was that Smith claimed he'd only fondled and ejaculated on Krystal, but that didn't jibe with the tear in her vagina. Still, what Lieck most needed was to know if Smith admitted murdering Krystal, and he had.

The meeting ended for that afternoon. If there'd been

any doubt who they were dealing with, what kind of man, it was settled not much later, when a woman came forward, one who claimed Kevin Smith had been her first boyfriend. She said she'd seen reports about his arrest, and she wanted those in charge of the case to know what Smith had done to her when she was a teenager. Along with another man, she alleged that Kevin Smith raped her at gunpoint. Afterward, he terrorized her, threatening her life, killing her dog to frighten her into keeping quiet.

In the days that followed the Chambers County Sheriff, Joe LaRive, urged law enforcement across the entire Gulf Coast to look into unsolved cases they might have that could fit Smith. By then, the Texas Rangers had used employment records to pin down where Smith lived and when. The result was a web of information, suggesting that if Smith had committed other murders, they could have occurred not just in Texas but Louisiana, Oklahoma, Arkansas, Alabama, Florida, and Arizona.

Not long after his confession, although he'd been repeatedly informed of his rights, Kevin Smith attempted to retract all the statements he'd made, claiming that rather than brokering a deal by getting the death penalty off the table, Quanell X had intimidated him into admitting guilt. Moon attempted to talk to Smith in jail about other victims,

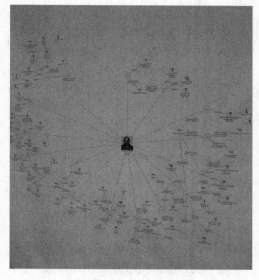

The chart depicting cities where Kevin Edison Smith lived.
*(Courtesy of Kathryn Casey)*

other cases, some on the I-45 chart. Smith denied there were any more to discuss. "No, never," he insisted.

At the jail, Smith's calls were monitored and recorded, and one day he could be heard talking to a family member who couldn't understand why the murder of a teenage girl should land Kevin Smith in prison for life. Rather, she wondered, if seven years wasn't an appropriate sentence. Perhaps she was basing her assessment on the information Smith had given her, his claim that the killing wasn't a murder but an accident.

In jail awaiting trial, Smith's muscles withered, and he lost weight. At hearings, he became belligerent. Not able to pay for an attorney, he was assigned one, Stephen Christopher Taylor, a longtime defense lawyer who'd handled a good share of the county's death-penalty cases.

Months passed, and Lieck wondered if she should prosecute the case, as she'd planned. She wanted to, but there was the possibility that she'd be required to take the stand since she'd been a witness to Smith's confession. In the end, she appointed a special prosecutor, Randy McDonald, who worked both in Houston and Anahuac. McDonald had been the lead defense attorney on a number of high-profile criminal cases, including that of Bart Whitaker, convicted of orchestrating the December 2003 murders of his family. Whitaker's father survived, but his mother and brother died. Faced with the prospect of losing the only remaining member of his family, after Bart's conviction, his father begged for his only remaining son's life. Jurors, however, sentenced Bart Whitaker to the death penalty.

As the Kevin Edison Smith case moved toward trial, Jeanie attended a hearing. Staring at Smith throughout, she thought about all the things Krystal would never do, all the life she'd been robbed of. "He took everything from her," she said. "Looking at him made me feel sick. But I knew I had to be at the trial. I had to be there for Krystal."

# Chapter 14

## The Devil's Face

**Anahuac, Texas**
**April 2012**

The stately Chambers County Courthouse. *(Courtesy of Kathryn Casey)*

In the summer of 2011, vast expanses of the Lone Star State literally erupted into flames. Texans dubbed it the Summer of Fire, as almost 4 million acres burned, destroying nearly three thousand homes. The culprit was drought. That year, even the usually wet spring was desert dry. Months passed without rain, resulting in a parched, brown landscape. A drive through Central Texas passed miles of dying trees, some thick-trunked oaks hundreds of years old. News reports compared the phenomenon with the Great Dustbowl of the 1930s, which attacked the Great Plains. The 2011 drought targeted Texas like an archer sighting a target, including the usually near-tropical Gulf Coast.

As that year drew to a close, weather predictors fretted about the future, forecasting the likelihood of another full year of drought. The state watched helplessly as thirsty trees with no relief shed their bark, their dry trunks splitting and weighty branches collapsing on parked cars and across streets. It felt as if death stalked the state.

This time, however, the experts were at least partially wrong.

Central and West Texas remained dry. But in the new year, the rains came to the Gulf Coast. By early 2012, much of the area appeared renewed, its forests bright with a budding green spring. Backyard water gauges flooded, especially in and around Houston, where storms came heavy and long, overflowing the dammed-up rivers that form the massive lakes that water the vast city. Traveling east from Houston, the landscape was again lush, as I turned off I-10 and drove toward Anahuac in April 2012 for the trial of Kevin Edison Smith, the welder whose DNA had been discovered on Krystal Jean Baker's dress.

A tiny, no-stop-sign town of around two thousand, Anahuac calls itself the alligator capital of Texas. Each year, neighbors celebrate the thick-skinned lizards during Gatorfest. For those passing through, signs along the road ask motorists to be on the lookout for poachers. There was a time when I would have enjoyed the ride, my attention drifting off into the heavily wooded landscape, thoughts of great birds and the morning's first light filtering through a canopy of trees. I instead wondered if undiscovered bodies lay concealed in the water beneath the dense foliage. Startled by my dark thoughts, I shook them off and attempted to focus not on the woods but the road ahead. I kept driving.

The most impressive building in Anahuac was the 1936 Chambers County Courthouse, a grand structure rising out of the flat earth, erected during the Great Depression by

WPA workers for a cost of $276,000. Three stories high, the exterior of the building was ashlar, squares and rectangles of finely hewn stone, with massive art deco lanterns lighting the wide stairs that anchored the main entrance.

Inside the courtroom, the benches were dotted with spectators. Smith's family filled two rows. Many of the other seats were taken by courthouse and law-enforcement workers, weaving in and out, interested in watching what promised to be an important trial. Noticeably missing were Jeanie, Johnny, and the rest of Krystal's family. Texas had what was called "the rule." When enforced, it barred potential witnesses from sitting in on a trial. Usually, the immediate family of the victim was an exception, but for some reason at this trial that hadn't been done. The result was that Krystal's family congregated instead in a nearby office.

At the left front table, Smith sat beside his attorney, an avuncular man with a receding hairline named Stephen C. Taylor. A courtroom veteran, Taylor had experience with high-profile cases. His status as court-appointed, however, rankled Smith, who complained bitterly to his family on recorded jailhouse phone calls that any attorney paid by the state wouldn't have his interests at heart.

Defense Attorney Stephen C. Taylor was well-known throughout the county. *(Courtesy of Kathryn Casey)*

Seated behind the table on the right, the special prosecutor, Randy McDonald, and his second chair, Assistant District Attorney Kathy Esquivel, had case files lined up behind them. Like Taylor, they were prepared and ready to begin.

Gray-haired, mustached, once a Houston prosecutor, McDonald stood before a jury culled from a panel of three hundred of the county's residents at just after nine and began his opening statement, outlining his case. He promised to show that Kevin Edison Smith indisputably murdered Krystal Baker, based not only on DNA but also the defendant's own words, his confession.

From that point on, McDonald relied on witnesses to establish the sequence of events for the jurors. The first called to the stand, Bradley Moon described the scene under the I-10 bridge the evening Krystal's body was discovered. Since she hadn't disappeared from Anahuac or the surrounding area, McDonald had a bit of housekeeping to do. "You observed her body lying in Chambers County?" he asked, to establish that the court had jurisdiction over the case.

"Yes," Moon answered.

On an overhead projector, McDonald displayed photos taken that night. In them, Krystal's brutalized body lay, her legs akimbo. For two weeks, she remained in the morgue, a Jane Doe.

"Were you there when the family identified this girl as Krystal Jean Baker?" McDonald asked.

"I was," Moon said. McDonald then led the investigator through a list of Krystal's injuries, from the gash to her forehead to the bruising on her toes, but concentrating on the hideous wound encircling her neck. On the autopsy table, the teenager looked pale and cold, but it was easy to imagine that before the attack, she must have been brimming with life.

The picture McDonald drew before the jurors described how Smith most likely disposed of the body, pushing it out of his car onto the gravel, then speeding off. "Where the body was dumped, you could drive a vehicle up to that location?"

"Yes, sir," Moon said.

Much depended on the DNA match, and McDonald studiously labored to establish chain of custody for the evidence, confirming that the way it was transported and kept fulfilled legal requirements. In response, Moon described personally transporting Krystal's dress, panties, and the scrapings taken at autopsy from under her fingernails to the lab in 1996 and later picking them up. With that, McDonald handed Moon the evidence envelopes. Wearing latex gloves, Moon opened the first and held up the silver dress covered in white and gold flowers, displaying it before the jurors. In that instant, Krystal became real, not just a name but a young girl in a pretty dress walking down a busy road on a spring afternoon.

When Taylor took over for the defense, he inquired about evidence Moon hadn't produced. Shouldn't there have been aerial shots of the crime scene? Moon said there weren't. Regarding a video taken of the body on the evening it was discovered, Moon said it had been lost over the more than a decade the case remained cold.

On the stand, white-haired Joe Haralson cut an imposing figure, looking the epitome of a Texas Ranger, down to his boots adorned with the image of the organization's badge embroidered in gold thread. Thirty-one years on the job and Haralson had been involved in more than his share of murder investigations, but he still occasionally faced frustration, as in the week during which he helped Chambers County track down Kevin Smith. When they finally found him and arrested him, had it

Texas Ranger Joe Haralson's boot bearing his agency's badge. *(Courtesy of Kathryn Casey)*

been done correctly? Had Haralson or one of those accompanying him read Smith his rights? Since a confession hung in the balance, one the defense attorney, Taylor, objected to being admitted, adherence to the law loomed large.

"I did," Haralson said, verifying he'd made sure that Smith knew he had the right to remain silent and to a lawyer.

Before he gave his confession, Smith acknowledged that he understood his Miranda rights and signed a waiver.

What about the truck Smith drove in 1996, at the time of the killing? It was possible there'd been evidence still inside, perhaps hair or bloodstains tied to Krystal. If her DNA and fingerprints weren't found, however, that could have helped Smith. Haralson said he'd searched for the truck, "but we couldn't find it."

Haralson left the stand and the prosecution's case continued. With the confession groundwork laid, McDonald turned again to the forensic evidence, the all-important DNA match. A series of witnesses verified chain of custody for the clothing and the scrapings, including the former Jefferson County lab tech who initially examined the dress and panties. When Taylor asked if she found any evidence of blood, saliva, or semen on the dress, the woman said, "To my knowledge, nothing was found."

Always, there were reminders of how far science had come, from a time when small quantities of DNA were indecipherable to the present, when tiny amounts of genetic matter could be duplicated and tested.

As the state's tenth witness to take the stand, Sherry Willcox described the hold that the cold case took on her, as she felt drawn to the tragic images of Krystal's body. "It's touching to look at the photos," she said, admitting that she couldn't put them out of her mind. She was the one who refused to file the case away, the one who ultimately found a way to get the evidence retested. "You didn't ask for permission? You just did it?" Esquivel asked.

"Yes," Willcox answered.

"Did your heart jump a little when the DPS lab found DNA on the dress?" Taylor asked.

"Yes," Willcox admitted that it had. The case, it seemed, had become very personal.

"And here we are today?"

"Yes, sir," she said.

It was after Willcox's testimony that something unusual happened. Calling the attorneys to the bench, Judge Carroll E. Wilburn, Jr, asked, "What do we want to do with the skunk in the jury box?"

Trials are emotional, especially for the two families involved, the victim's and the defendant's. In this case, in the old courthouse with few public restrooms, where jurors, witnesses, and family members used the same facilities, perhaps it wasn't surprising that paths crossed. "The skunk" was a juror who'd found herself in the ladies' room with Krystal's mom, Jeanie.

"I don't think we have our witnesses under control," McDonald admitted.

Jurors wear badges, signals that they aren't to be approached or talked to. Any interaction could be deemed an attempt to sway a verdict and cause a mistrial. What had transpired was that the juror in question and Jeanie happened to be in the bathroom together. The woman told the bailiff that Krystal's mom identified herself and showed the woman a photo of Krystal.

As the judge and lawyers talked, Kathy Esquivel was dispatched to caution Jeanie against any future breeches. But the question remained: What was to be done?

An alternate, the potentially compromised juror could simply be dismissed, the trial continued. Yet had that juror talked to the others? Had the contamination spread? The judge mused about how to handle the situation to prevent a mistrial or having the verdict—should Smith be convicted—overturned on appeal. Eventually, the bailiff escorted the woman juror in to personally tell the judge and attorneys her story. In the end, she was released and the trial continued, but only after the judge questioned the remaining jurors, determining that the woman told none of them about her restroom encounter.

At that, the attention returned to the matter at hand, putting testimony before the jurors who would decide Smith's fate. As Esquivel quizzed the forensic scientists, it quickly became obvious that the statistics were overwhelming. The odds that the DNA matched anyone but Smith: one in 332 sextillion for Caucasians, one in 8.591 sextillion for African-Americans, and one in 1.637 septillion for Hispanics. To give a frame of reference, the witness quantified a sextillion, describing it as a trillion billions.

Was it possible that Kevin Smith's DNA had changed over the years? The expert said it wasn't, absent a tissue transplant.

Through it all, a picture emerged of the terror of the last day of Krystal Baker's life.

On the stand, Dr. Dwayne Arthur Wolfe of the Harris County Medical Examiner's Office reviewed Krystal's autopsy for the jury, accompanied by graphic photos. He pointed out the rash of small petechiae, reddish spots and blotches caused by blood pressure rising and bursting capillaries during strangulation. As he described it, Krystal suffered a slow death. Based on the extent of the hemorrhaging, she struggled for life, and Smith fought her, eased up, then tightened the strap around her neck.

"Could this have been done with a welder's belt?" McDonald asked.

"Any kind of belt," the physician confirmed, saying the large abrasions on Krystal's left side were caused from the attacker coming at her from the left rear. When it came to the blunt-force trauma evident on much of Krystal's body, those injuries could have resulted from being pummeled by a fist. The abrasions? Perhaps from Krystal's body hitting the ground as she was thrown from the truck.

"All the injuries look like they were shortly before death," the physician testified, narrowing the time frame to between a couple of hours and minutes before the teenager died. As to the injuries to the right side of Krystal's face, a lack of flowing blood indicated that those happened shortly after death.

The tear to her vagina? The physician identified the cause as an attack with a blunt object. "Could a penis be a blunt object?" McDonald asked.

"Yes," Wolfe answered.

"Or a finger?"

"Yes."

Consistent with the other wounds, the tear in Krystal's vagina happened within an hour of her death.

Yet on cross-examination, Taylor pointed out that there were questions the physician couldn't answer, including where Krystal was when she suffered the injuries and where the dirt came from on her knees. Smith said he'd strangled Krystal in the truck, but could he have taken her to a remote field, assaulted her, and murdered her on the scene? Multiple scenarios were, of course, possible.

Seated in the front of the courtroom, Quanell X made a compelling witness. McDonald led him through the basics, as he described himself as a minister of the nation of Islam and an activist. "Here you were retained as an activist?" McDonald asked. This was an important point. If Quanell X had been in the jail talking to Smith as his minister, the conversation could have been privileged and he could be barred from testifying about its content. But the imposing man on the stand said that wasn't the case.

"Absolutely," he said, limiting his involvement to that of an emissary sent by the family to make sure Smith wasn't being abused or unjustly accused because of his race. Explaining his involvement, Quanell X said he wanted to determine "if this is a case where they picked the nearest brother they could find and threw everything at him including the kitchen sink . . . If I believed he was innocent, I was about to stand with this brother all the way."

Instead, Quanell X said Smith admitted his guilt and wanted to get it off of his chest. The confession was voluntary, he testified, not coerced. "At the end of the day, it's about right over wrong, about justice."

"Did Mr. Smith implicate himself in this crime?" McDonald asked.

"Yes," he answered.

Taylor asked about money Quanell X had been paid by Smith's family, twenty-five hundred dollars, to look into the case. The witness agreed he'd been paid, but he said he'd made no promises other than to find out the truth.

After Quanell X left the stand, the prosecutor recalled Bradley Moon. McDonald had one last thing he wanted jurors to hear, Smith's confession. In a hushed courtroom, the audio played, and Smith described how he'd strangled Krystal Baker. Then, the state rested.

It seemed there was little for Taylor to work with defending his client. Science said Smith was guilty and so did the man's own words. Later, the defense attorney would insist that if he'd talked to Smith first, he would have cautioned him against giving the statement. The forensic evidence might have left some wiggle room, some way to say Smith had sex with the teenager but not killed her. But the confession had done Smith in.

In his opening, Taylor repeated the justifications Smith had given during his confession, that he thought Krystal was eighteen and that she'd gotten in the truck voluntarily, and that the killing hadn't been planned but resulted from events spinning out of control.

The single defense witness was Texas City investigator Brian Goetschius, as Taylor tried to make the point that if DNA hadn't come through, the case might never have been solved. When he asked how Krystal's death had affected the town, the man who by then was a captain in his department said, "I think it was a community event, sir, that one of our children was killed."

The jury cleared from the courtroom, the defense attorney then put before the judge the question of whether or not his client would testify. While Taylor had advised Smith against taking the stand and putting himself before the prosecutor for questioning, the decision was ultimately the defendant's. Agitated and angry, Smith fluctuated back and forth as the judge demanded a final decision. Although he'd indicated both possibilities for months, Smith finally announced that he would not take the witness stand.

The charge was capital murder, and since the death penalty had been bargained away, if Smith was convicted, the sentence was automatically life. In his closing, Taylor never argued that his client was innocent but only that jurors should study all the evidence. "We asked you to come here because we needed somebody to make the decision," he said. "This is Mr. Smith's day in court. You have to determine whether the state has satisfied you regarding those facts beyond a reasonable doubt."

Then he reminded the jurors that the charge read not only that Smith had to be guilty of Krystal's murder but also that he had to have done it while committing the offense of aggravated sexual assault of a child. They had to find both crimes had been committed to come back with a guilty verdict.

"The events of March 1996 were tragic," Taylor said. "All I can ask of you is that you go back, take your time, and do a careful and impartial consideration of the evidence."

"The facts are what they are," McDonald countered, when he stood before the jury. "We are here to ask you for justice . . . It's simple . . . either he didn't do the crime at all, or he's guilty of capital murder."

Reminding the jurors of the forensic evidence and the confession, there seemed little doubt. In Smith's own words, he'd said that he'd put a strap or a belt around Krystal Baker's neck and choked her. "He did it until she died."

The semen proved sexual contact with a child, since Krystal was a minor. And the tear in her vagina suggested that it wasn't consensual. "Justice isn't only for the defendant, it's for the victim," McDonald reminded those gathered. "Convict him by his own words . . . What kind of person . . . blames the victim for her own death?"

When McDonald assessed the injuries, he believed that

Krystal hadn't entered Smith's car voluntarily. The abrasions on her body, he said, were consistent with Smith's having wrapped the strap around her neck while he dragged her to the truck. That was why the medical examiner found dirt on her knees.

Behind the defense table, Smith fumed. "I didn't do it," he could be heard mumbling. "I didn't do it like that . . . I didn't do it like he said I did."

"Can you imagine what Krystal Baker was going through?" McDonald asked the jurors. "What kind of person does this? Someone who has no regard for human life."

The jury came back in only forty minutes. By then Jeanie, Johnny, and most of Krystal's family, Bradley Moon, Sherry Willcox, and Texas Ranger Joe Haralson were all in the courtroom. The verdict: "Guilty."

Once the trial ended, the judge pointed at Willcox, who still had chills from hearing the conviction. "That woman right there solved this. If she hadn't done it, this man would still be on the streets."

When Jeanie stood in front of the courtroom to give her victim

A cross left by Jeanie Escamilla at the site where Krystal's body was found. *(Courtesy of Kathryn Casey)*

impact statement, she felt as if "a roaring mother came out of me."

"You aren't sorry for what you did," she said, looking at Smith. "You're evil. You disrespected my daughter, my family, and your own family . . . Krystal was my sunshine.

Now I hope that when you see the sun you think of her. It's no longer your friend. How can anyone be so evil?"

As the courtroom cleared, deputies escorted Kevin Edison Smith through a back door to a jail cell. The following morning, he'd be transported to a Texas prison, where he'd most likely spend the remainder of his life.

On her way home to Dickinson, Jeanie pulled off I-10 and drove under the Trinity River Bridge. Traffic roared overhead as streams of cars and trucks sped by unaware of the drama unfolding below. At this lonely site, where her daughter's battered body once lay, Jeanie said a prayer then placed a Styrofoam cross covered in artificial pink roses and a small bouquet of flowers. "I wish I could have seen what kind of woman Krystal would have been," she said. "That devil may have taken her body, but God took her soul. I feel like I've walked through hell, looked the devil in the face, and told him off. Thank God they found him so he never hurts anyone else's little girl."

# Chapter 15

## Innocence Betrayed
## Laura Kate Smither

**Friendswood, Texas**

A favorite photo of Laura.
*(Courtesy of Bob and Gay Smither)*

Some families move after losing a child, unable to live in the house their daughter departed from on the day fate ripped her from their lives. Others hold on to the home to safeguard memories, at times designating the girl's bedroom as a shrine, her belongings left undisturbed as if the emptiness awaits an impossible homecoming. To part with a dead daughter's possessions is too hard, too wounding, too accepting of reality, although nothing could convince them that all they've gone through is anything but dreadfully real. For many, the sadness is an unheard voice that ceaselessly whispers of all they have lost.

I wasn't sure what to expect on the day I pulled into the driveway of Gay and Bob Smither's split-level on the west side of Friendswood, yet another of the small towns south of Houston, halfway to Galveston. The community had an interesting past that included devout roots. Founded by Quakers, the Religious Society of Friends, it was settled in 1895. Over the years, the population diversified, and Catholics, Baptists, Episcopalians, and others settled the area, but recalling its beginnings, Friendswood remained the Quakers' Houston-area headquarters. That the horror would unfold in such a place, one founded on a dedication to peace, seemed particularly disquieting.

Like its neighbors, Friendswood was flat coastal plain, the undeveloped areas predominantly pastures where in summers cattle lazily sheltered beneath the expansive branches of oak trees to avoid the harsh Texas sun. Yet where League City and Webster had chemical plants and refineries, Friendswood was a bedroom community, its nearly forty thousand residents for the most part well educated, and relatively affluent, the majority two-parent families with children.

Bob and Gay Smither in front of a tree they dedicated to Laura.
*(Courtesy of Kathryn Casey)*

The afternoon I pulled up to the L-shaped house, a large yellow Lab slumped unconcerned on the front porch. Worried that it might not take well to a stranger, I called Bob on my cell. "Am I at the right house?" I asked. "The pink one?"

His response was a soft chuckle. "I want you to tell Gay that," he said. "I keep telling her the house is pink, and she said it's not."

Moments later, Bob walked out to greet me, as the dog lazily sauntered toward the house beside us. Laura's father was a thin man, with a cap of graying hair and glasses. He had a quiet, intellectual manner, but a bit of a sparkle in his eyes when he asked me to describe the color of the house for his wife. "Well, maybe it's not exactly pink," I hedged. "Maybe salmon?"

Bob laughed, and Gay, the lilt in her voice from growing up in Zimbabwe coloring her response, shot him an amused grin, and said, "Well, it's not a pink, pink."

They were opposites in some ways, it was easy to see. Throughout our time together, Bob remained reserved although his eyes often clouded over with deep sadness. Gay, well, Gay and her wide smile filled the room with a bristling energy. Although it had been sixteen years, they understandably remained devastated and angry. Gay hadn't given birth to Laura, but never thought of her as anything other than her daughter, and she was the most vocal about the tragedy's terrible legacy. Perhaps there was a reason. "My life sentence is that I gave Laura permission to jog that morning," she said. "I will live with that forever."

"Laura was a force to be reckoned with," said Bob, with a wistful smile.

A home-based electrical engineer who worked as a consultant, primarily in the oil business, he was forty when his first child was born. Laura entered the world on April 23, 1984, a loved bundle of energy. "She transformed my life," her proud father said. "From day one."

From the beginning, Laura was an easy child. Bob and

his first wife, Carol, found they could pack up their daughter and take her anywhere. They went to Grand Cayman on vacation and out to nightclubs to listen to music, all with Laura in tow. "She just never fussed," he said. "She was like that from the start."

Yet all wasn't idyllic at the Smithers' Houston home. In 1985 when Laura was still a baby, Carol died of breast cancer. "Those were tough times," Bob said. "Suddenly, it was just Laura and me."

At that juncture, Gay, an English teacher, was on a worldwide expedition. She'd left her home in southern Africa to travel with a friend, and had already been to England and Greece. An adventurer at heart, she'd worked on a charter boat in the Mediterranean and crossed the Atlantic on a sailboat before she landed in Houston, where she took a job as a nanny. That position ended not long after Carol Smither's death. Laura's pediatrician mentioned Gay to Bob, suggesting that she could care for the toddler.

"I hear you're looking for a job," Bob said on the phone that day.

"Oh?" Gay responded. In reality, she wasn't, at least not in Houston. Instead, she'd been eyeing San Francisco as her next stop. So immediately she questioned why she'd agreed to meet Bob for an interview. Later, it would all seem predestined. From their first meeting, Gay, then twenty-six, fell in love with Bob's little girl. "I couldn't help but love Laura straightaway," Gay said. She still carried the image of the first time she saw Laura in her Care Bear rocker holding her Miss Piggy.

"Gay fell in love with Laura first, before she fell in love with me," Bob agreed.

The couple married in 1986, just after Laura turned two, and in 1988, Gay gave birth to a son, David. The year before, Gay had officially adopted Laura. "I figured someday when she was a teenager, Laura would throw it up in my face that I wasn't her biological mother. You know, say, 'You're not my real mom.' I wanted her to know that she was my first child," said Gay. "But Laura wasn't like that. She never got angry with us. She wasn't the kind of child who pouted. It never would have happened."

Even as a child, Laura was precocious, asking Gay to spell "Laura mad at Mozart," so she could write it down when only three. "Mozart was the family cat, and she'd nipped at Laura," Gay explained. "Our daughter was brilliant and adorable. You couldn't help but love her. Everyone did."

At six, Laura began studying ballet. It seemed a good fit for her, since the little girl with the brown hair and wide smile never walked but danced across a room. "She glided down the aisles at the grocery store. She pirouetted," said Gay.

Their daughter also had her serious side. As early as preschool, Bob noticed that other children sought Laura out to settle their squabbles, asking her to mediate their arguments. They knew she'd think the situation through and try to come up with a good solution. "Fairness was important to Laura," said Bob.

In 1990, the Smithers sold the Houston house and moved half an hour south to Friendswood. They wanted more land, and they found it in a rural setting, a house on a gravel road surrounded by cow pastures and only the occasional neighbor. There, Laura and David flourished.

Meeting her new neighbors, Laura often seemed reticent at first. "She was sizing people up," said Bob. "Once she got her footing, you couldn't quiet her down."

"That was how she got her nickname," Gay said, with a wide grin. This was a beloved memory. "We called her Jabber Jaws."

At first, David and Laura attended a public school. But over the years, the Smithers grew dissatisfied, and Gay began homeschooling, with Bob helping out with math and science. In addition to giving their children a more personalized education, Gay and Bob thought it could make their lives more relaxed. "None of us are morning people," said

Gay. "This way, we didn't have to rush around to get the children out the door."

There were happy days learning together, including family events fashioned around the children's studies. When Laura read Jane Austen, for instance, her parents brought her to the stage on which the dramas were set, by arranging a family vacation in England. Exceptionally bright, Laura began talking about someday attending Stanford University.

In addition to their classes, both David and Laura enrolled in extracurricular activities with other homeschooling families. Laura tried sports, including scuba diving and tennis and other types of dance, but her first love remained ballet. "Laura would get upset when they played the Ninja Turtle theme for modern dance," remembered Gay. "She wanted classical music. She wanted ballet."

Perhaps her interest was fueled partly because Laura was an exceptionally talented and determined young ballerina. She practiced five days a week in between her studies. During the holidays, she earned parts dancing onstage in the *Nutcracker*. "Laura was just beautiful," said Gay. "And so happy when she danced."

In 1996, Laura was twelve and entering the seventh grade, and David

Laura in a dance costume at age nine. *(Courtesy of Bob and Gay Smither)*

was eight years old. That summer, Laura auditioned for the Houston Ballet Academy, competing against three hundred children, and won one of only two coveted slots. "She was beyond excited," said Bob.

From that point on, three days a week, Laura trained at the academy. Resolute about improving her performance, when her instructors suggested working out to increase her stamina, Laura initiated her own exercise campaign. Before long, Bob and the children became a common sight on the country roads, Bob jogging while Laura and David rode bikes beside him.

At that point, much of the area around their home was going through a metamorphosis. Subdivisions were quickly replacing what had once been cattle pastures. Contractors fenced in large tracts. Inside the enclosures, they constructed block after block of impressive two-story brick houses on large lots. Even the open field directly adjacent to the Smithers' house was under development, an upscale subdivision in the making. Still, the family felt safe and isolated from the problems of the city. "We didn't even lock our doors," said Gay with a shrug. "We were living family life in small-town America."

On the night of Wednesday, April 2, 1997, Laura stayed up late reading a book called *Fit or Fat* by PBS nutrition guru Covert Bailey, a manual espousing exercise for weight control and strength. "She wanted to hold her arabesque longer," said Gay. "Laura was determined to do well in ballet, as she did with everything."

April 3, 1997, was a Thursday morning like any other. Laura's thirteenth birthday was approaching, and on a whiteboard in her yellow-trimmed bedroom filled with stuffed animals and dolls, she counted down the days. "Twenty days until my birthday," Laura wrote that morning.

"She was so excited about becoming a teenager," Bob said sadly.

Sometime before nine, Bob showered, preparing to meet with a client who was scheduled to arrive at the house in about an hour. Still in her pajamas, Laura popped into the kitchen, where her mother and brother cooked a favorite breakfast, chocolate chip pancakes with bacon. After reading the fitness book the night before, Laura had something on her mind. She worried about her mother. Gay sometimes went on the rotation diet to lose weight. She liked it, since it had recipes and laid out what to eat each day. "The book said you shouldn't go on fad diets. You should exercise to control your weight," Laura said. "Promise me that you won't go on that diet anymore?"

Realizing Laura was genuinely concerned, Gay agreed. Then the almost-teenager asked something that surprised Gay: "Can I go for a jog?"

Busy cooking, Gay didn't believe Laura would really go running that morning since she'd never before gone alone. What Gay answered was: "We're making breakfast."

"I'll be home in time to eat," Laura countered.

Her daughter was growing up. "Okay," Gay said, remaining doubtful that Laura would follow through. Moments later, however, Laura reappeared at the kitchen doorway wearing running clothes.

"When will the pancakes be ready?" she asked. When David said twenty minutes, she responded, "I'll be home in time." With that, Laura, her long dark hair trailing behind her, turned and rushed out the door.

Inside the cheery kitchen, all went on as planned. The pancakes bubbled on the griddle, and David set the table. Soon the steaming circles were on a plate waiting, the bacon crisp, breakfast ready. Bob walked into the room and noticed their daughter's empty chair, and asked, "Where's Laura?"

"She went for a run," Gay said, visibly worried. "She said she'd be home in time for breakfast. She's late. "

The Smithers exchanged troubled glances. They knew their daughter well. Laura was reliable, not the kind of child to be even ten minutes late. Immediately concerned, Bob grabbed his keys. "I'll be right back. I'll drive around and find her."

"We were worried she got hurt, that she'd been hit by a car or something," said Gay. "We knew from the beginning for her to be late, something was wrong."

In his small white car, Bob Smither drove the route he and Laura jogged and biked, thinking that was her most likely course. He assumed that any moment he'd see his daughter. Perhaps she'd turned an ankle and needed help. She could be lying somewhere, unable to walk. There was a light mist in the air, the faint promise of approaching rain as he drove the familiar roads watching for Laura. What began as concern swelled into a burgeoning fear as Bob walked into the house and told Gay that he hadn't found their daughter.

"Well where could she be?" Gay asked.

"I don't know," Bob said. "But I'm calling the police."

"Will they do anything? Doesn't she have to be missing twenty-four hours?" Over the years, Gay had heard of cases where police refused to take a missing person report for a full day, a not-unusual situation throughout parts of the country.

"It doesn't matter. I'm calling," Bob said, dialing 911.

To their relief ten minutes later, at approximately 9:55 that morning, a young officer pulled up in front of their house, responding to Bob's call. The officer took a report and left.

Sixteen years later, the day Laura disappeared would be hazy for both her parents. What they remembered most was how hard the rain fell and how frantically they searched. Bob in his car and Gay and David in the family van, they drove the rural roads hoping to find someone, anyone who might have seen Laura. "Did you see a little girl?" they asked. No one had.

Turning onto the vacant land covered with trees and thick underbrush being cleared for a subdivision on County Road 133, also called Moore Road, the main street that ran not far from the house, the Smithers both stopped and talked to the workers. There were few there. A steady rain fell by then, and the construction supervisor had released most of his crew. Had anyone at the site seen Laura? "No, ma'am," the foreman told Gay. She thanked him and drove away.

Their panic continued to build, and at one point when Bob returned to the house, he grabbed a photo of Laura and quickly pieced together a handwritten flyer. That day, the copier would churn out so many copies, it literally burned out. Before long, neighbors who'd heard the disturbing news of a missing child showed up on horseback, offering help. They took off to search the surrounding fields, while the Smithers and close friends grabbed stacks of flyers Bob had piled on the Ping-Pong table and canvassed the closest subdivisions, knocking on doors, finding no one home.

"It was like Laura had vanished," said Gay. "Our world turned upside down on a dime that day."

On the phone, Gay alerted friends and family, Laura's Scout troop, and her homeschool group. Soon other parents arrived, snatching up flyers and spreading out to the homes in the area, praying and looking, looking and praying. Even the man who arrived for Bob's business meeting pitched in, helping with the search. The police officers told the Smithers not to worry, that children almost always return home, implying that Laura was most likely a runaway. But Gay and Bob knew that wasn't true, and so did an acquaintance of theirs, one who happened to be the chief for the local community college's campus police force. When he heard Laura Smither was missing, he called a Friendswood P.D. captain and vouched for the family, saying Laura would never run away. She wasn't a troubled adolescent but a happy young girl. Something was very, very wrong.

In response, Friendswood P.D.'s chief, Jared Stout, a studious-looking man with thinning brown hair and round, wire-rimmed glasses, immediately reassigned all thirty-nine of his officers to the search for Laura and requested assistance from the F.B.I. At five that afternoon, the special agent in charge arrived at the Smithers' home. By then, more than one hundred neighbors and friends assisted police in the search for Laura, and the rain had pounded down until the gullies and the low-lying areas overflowed. In their living room, the Smithers answered questions, many over and over again.

One of the first things the FBI did was place a tap on the Smithers' home phone, in case Laura had been abducted by kidnappers looking for money. They waited for the phone to ring with a ransom demand, but it never did.

The afternoon blended into evening, when the police informed Gay and Bob that it was too dangerous to continue, and they were calling off the search for the night. Feeling as if their hearts lodged in their throats, the distraught parents knew that despite what the police might do, they couldn't stop, and they continued combing through the fields until well after dark, then returned home only to strategize. All night they paced and talked, off and on standing on their front porch looking out into the darkness, desperate to see their daughter walking toward the house. Around midnight, a man who claimed to be a psychic called, contending that he'd had a vision of Laura in a field near a road. "Any other time, we would have been highly skeptical," said Gay. "But it wasn't any other time, and we were out of our minds with worry."

After listening, Bob and Gay thought they knew the place, and in total blackness with only flashlights to illuminate their paths through the brush, they walked, rain cascading over their faces, calling out to Laura.

"I remember hearing Bob next to me, his voice steady and controlled, like it always is. He was saying, 'Laura. Laura, where are you?'" said Gay. "And I heard my own voice, screaming."

When they returned home at 4:00 A.M., the house buzzed with volunteers and an FBI agent and a police officer who'd been assigned to spend the night. Gay thought it was kind of the authorities to have someone stationed there to protect them, particularly David, in case whoever had taken Laura returned. "We didn't realize yet that we were suspects," said Bob.

By the next morning, a Friday, word of Laura's disappearance had spread like the rainwater spilling over the bayous. David's Cub Scout leader called offering help, and Gay asked him to watch over their son while they worked with the searchers. The house filled with friends and neighbors, while at a nearby softball field, townsfolk the Smithers had never met congregated, eager to help police look for Laura. From there, groups of volunteers fanned out in the continuing rain to comb through the sodden fields. Still, they were resolute. One woman was bitten in the heel by a venomous snake but, when she discovered its fangs hadn't penetrated her shoe, she walked on, eager to help. "We saw the face of God in our neighbors," said Gay. "People we'd never met, total strangers, put their lives on hold and came to help us find our daughter."

At nine that morning, Gay and a friend stood on Moore Road, the main street on Bob and Laura's jogging/biking route, stopping cars, asking the drivers, "Were you here yesterday about this time? Did you see a little girl?"

Many said they had driven that same street around the time Laura had disappeared, that in fact they commuted down that road every morning, yet none said they'd seen Laura. "I handed each one a flyer," said Gay. The drivers sped off, leaving Gay waiting on the road to flag down the next car.

That evening, the local TV stations aired footage of Gay and a friend walking door to door in the rain, handing out flyers. "Everyone wanted to help," Gay said, reliving that moment in her memory, tears clouding her eyes.

When Gay returned to the house, the focus changed, as police again questioned the family, separating Bob, Gay, and David, taking them to different parts of the house. Over and again they recounted the previous morning when Laura vanished. They never refused to answer a question. "We would have done anything they asked, told them anything to bring Laura home," said Gay. "That was all we cared about."

Later that day, Bob grasped what was truly happening. Standing outside of the house, he scolded David for crawling under the deck. When Bob looked over, he noticed an FBI agent watching him with great interest. "I realized we were being observed," said Bob. "But I thought, of course we should be. I told the agent, 'You should look under the deck. And we have a basement. You could search that, too.'" And the police did, over the course of the day removing four large plastic bags filled with potential evidence from the house, much of it Laura's possessions, including her ballet slippers.

At Friendswood P.D., Chief Stout secured a copy of the sex offender registry for Galveston and the neighboring counties. There were more than twenty-one hundred on the list. At the same time, Friendswood P.D. and the FBI compiled the names of men working in the area, including at the nearby construction sites.

Still, the day proceeded without a break. When asked for a comment by the press, Chief Stout remarked about how thoroughly the child had disappeared. "It was as if Laura had been on *The X-Files* and just beamed up."

Another day passed without a breakthrough in the case. The evening of the second day, Bob asked Stout what the plans were for the following morning. The chief answered politely yet steadfastly that the search was over. The police were no longer investing their efforts into looking for Laura. Instead, they would be concentrating on narrowing down the pool of suspects.

As devastated as he felt to think that the official search was over, Bob understood. And as it turned out, that didn't hamper the quest, for the next morning even more volunteers appeared, all eager to help. The media sent out reporters who circulated through the crowd, asking why they were there. Fathers and mothers, grandparents, teenagers,

businesspeople, and blue-collar workers said they wanted
to do whatever they could to find Laura Smither. Some
searched, while others brought baked goods, water, and
food for the volunteers. Local merchants donated money to
provide dry socks, something sorely needed in the continuing rains.

While the volunteers searched, and the community
prayed, Bob and Gay cooperated with authorities. All that
week, the Smithers were asked questions, and they continued to patiently answer. "They were interrogations, but
nice interrogations," said Gay. "That was their job. We understood. But they did it with respect, so we didn't feel attacked."

As the days wore on, Bob fought to believe that their
daughter would be found alive, but it became increasingly
difficult. "After a few days, you kind of run out of stories to
tell yourself that are going to have a good ending," he said,
his eyes downcast and his words hushed. "But I hoped."

Meanwhile, Gay relied on her deep faith. "I went into
denial," she said. "I convinced myself that Laura was being
held captive, and if I prayed hard enough, she'd be let go."
A friend gave her prayer cards, and Gay read them often,
putting her heart into every word, dropping to her knees and
begging God to bring Laura home.

That didn't happen, but they continued to see in Friends-
wood an overwhelming desire to help. At one point, the
Texas-New Mexico Power Company donated a vacant build-
ing to be used as a volunteer headquarters for the search.
When Bob called it, someone picked up the phone and said,
"Laura Recovery Center. Can I help you?"

"It was incredible," he said.

"That so many people cared about our child was huge,"
said Gay. "That was our hope."

In the days that followed, Gay and Bob gravitated to the
search center, where every morning, hundreds missed work,
set aside their own tasks for the day, to search for Laura.
There the Smithers asked what they could do. They were

told to talk to the volunteers and make up lists of who was working and what each person was doing. "At the time, we thought it was busy work, that they were giving us something to keep us out of the way," said Bob. "But we did it. And later on, it would turn out to be useful."

Yet, at the same time, it was confusing and troubling. In the evenings, the Smithers sat in their house doing what the FBI and police asked, making other lists, this time of all the people Laura trusted enough to get into their cars. So while Bob and Gay felt a deep gratitude for all their friends and acquaintances and the legions of total strangers who were reaching out to them in their time of need, they also found themselves looking at everyone around them as if he or she could be the person who'd taken their daughter. "It grew the suspicion," said Gay.

"It was like a cancer," said Bob. "We didn't believe anyone we knew would take Laura, but we just didn't know. We were desperate to find her."

"The one thing was, everyone who knew Laura loved her," said Gay. "We couldn't believe that anyone who knew her could hurt her."

One week blended into the next, and Laura was still missing. A neighbor talked to a psychic who recommended that Gay burn a candle shaped as a cross. If she did, the psychic said Laura would be found. "I did it," Gay said. "I would have done anything."

Perhaps the psychic was well-meaning. Perhaps he genuinely believed that the candle would bring Laura home. There were so many others, including more psychics and just ordinary people across not only Texas but the nation who called authorities, many of them most likely also with good intentions, saying they'd seen Laura or someone who resembled her. Law enforcement splintered off and used valuable time that could have gone toward the investigation, only to hit one dead end after another.

Yet no one stopped looking. Over the course of more than two weeks, somewhere around six thousand volunteers searched for Laura Smither in the fields surrounding Friendswood. They covered nearly eight hundred square miles, most of it rural, through snake-infested swamps, deserted oil fields, and cow pastures, terrain deemed the most likely for the disposal of a body. But nothing was found.

Finally, it was decided that the searching had to end. Too many people had put their lives on hold with no success. Gay and Bob, while not giving up hope, didn't protest when the head volunteers explained that the people of Friendswood had to reclaim their lives. Some hadn't been to work since days after Laura disappeared. They had families to support. It was time. Those leading the efforts and the Smithers agreed on something else as well, that there needed to be an official event to mark the end of the search, to give the volunteers some sense of closure.

That meeting was set for the Friendswood Town Hall on April 20, the seventeenth day after Laura's disappearance. At four that afternoon, three hundred volunteers were greeted and thanked by the Smithers, who showed a video the local NBC affiliate had compiled of Laura and the search. At the meeting, Chief Stout took the stage to speak. But then something happened. As he addressed the audience, thanking those gathered for all the work they'd dedicated to finding Laura, Stout pulled out his pager. Abruptly, he mumbled a hasty thank-you and turned and left, literally running from the auditorium.

"I knew something big had happened," said Gay. "Chief Stout actually went rigid when he looked at that message. I thought they'd found Laura. I thought she was coming home."

That evening, the Smithers held to their practice of not watching the news coverage, but then, at seven, someone called to ask about reports on the local news of a body found, that of a young girl.

"How dare you!" Gay cried. "How dare you call and tell us this!"

Gay didn't believe it and slammed down the phone. But at ten that night, Chief Stout rang their doorbell. It was true. A decomposing body, nude except for tan socks, had been spotted by a father and son training their dog on the banks of a retention pond bordering a residential neighborhood. The pond was fourteen miles north of the Smither house, and while volunteers had ventured close, they'd never made it that far. In three feet of water, the body was wedged inside a metal drainage pipe with water running across its upper half. The current had stripped much of the flesh from the waist up. But there were indications that it was Laura, including braces on the teeth.

Despite the evidence, Gay asked a favor. "Don't tell us it's Laura until you're sure."

That night, their priest and a close friend stayed with Gay and Bob, waiting for news, praying the corpse wasn't Laura's. Yet they also felt guilty, as if by wishing that Laura was still alive, they were condemning another family to the terrible news that their daughter was dead. The autopsy was scheduled for early the following morning. On his report, the medical examiner would note indications of trauma of the neck—as if she'd been strangled—along with blunt-impact injuries, hemorrhages on the lower body and the buttocks. The manner of death was listed as homicide. "Time of death is consistent with the time of abduction or disappearance."

That afternoon, the FBI agent in charge and the chief again drove up the Smithers' driveway. Bob and Gay anxiously awaited them. "They came to tell us that it was Laura," Gay said, wiping away a tear. "It was two days before her thirteenth birthday. I thought about how she'd been counting down the days."

"Even after we heard, we were in denial," said Bob. "Parents aren't engineered to do this. It was a long time before we were able to completely accept it. Maybe, in a way, denial is a gift."

That night, volunteers guarded the Smithers' house to keep interlopers away, and the next day Bob and Gay faced the grim task of making plans to bury their daughter.

Meanwhile, at the recovery site, along the banks of the retention pond where Laura's body had been found, a make-shift memorial came to life, a field of candles, notes, teddy bears, and flowers. Friends and strangers gathered, bringing crosses and staying to pray for Laura, the Smithers, and the entire community, many undoubtedly asking God to bring the person responsible to justice.

When the ME's Office decided to keep Laura's body to have a forensic pathologist run further tests, a memorial was planned instead of a funeral. The service was held at Sagemont Baptist, the largest church in the area, to accommodate the expected crowds, and ministers and priests from all the area churches participated. It rained hard that day as it had every day since Laura had disappeared, as if the very heavens were crying. Yet more than a thousand braved the bad weather to pay their respects, a final coming-together of those who'd worked so hard and so long to try to find Laura. Throughout the investigation, the community had poured its heart into the search, getting to know the family and learning about the little girl lost. In so many ways, Laura had become everyone's child.

In the end, on May 10, 1997, little Laura Smither, who dreamed of becoming a ballerina, was buried near her mother and grandfather.

Time passed, and Bob and Gay tried to go on with their lives, all the while waiting, hoping that Laura's murderer would be found. The memorial continued to grow at the recovery site for more than a year. At times, friends brought the distraught parents statues, teddy bears, notes, some of the things the community donated to memorialize their daughter. While they appreciated it all, none of it truly helped.

"We were broken people," said Gay.

Over the months that followed, his parents say David

began having problems. "He said Laura was the perfect one. I'm the naughty one," said Gay. "Imagine how hard it was for him when she died. And then we found out later that it's common for the siblings, that they nearly always initially kind of self-destruct."

Their house became a shrine to Laura, with photos of her in the living room. Her room was left untouched, the whiteboard in it still bearing her handwriting as she counted down the days to her birthday. Initially, the door was kept closed. "Here was this room that had always been filled with joy," said Gay. "Now it was like a tomb. And we gradually came to see that David was suffering. He'd lost his sister, and his parents were nearly destroyed."

Years later David would compare notes with others who'd lost a brother or sister through violence and grow to understand that what he experienced was truly fairly universal. "What I felt was a profound sense of isolation," he said. "Siblings are often the ones forgotten in these cases. There's an orphan experience a lot of us go through. We don't just lose our sibling, but our parents for a time, because they're grieving."

Perhaps more than anything else, Bob and Gay prayed that the person responsible would be found and held accountable. Early on there was hope. That day at the Smither house, the one when they learned their daughter was dead, Chief Stout assured them that he'd find the person responsible. "Now you'll see me turn into the hunter," he told the Smithers.

There were suspects. Within days of Laura's disappearance, law enforcement singled out one man in particular, one with a violent past: William Lewis Reece.

In October 1996, five months before Laura's abduction, Reece paroled out of an Oklahoma prison after serving ten years of a fifteen-year sentence for kidnapping, forced oral sodomy, and rape. On that fateful April day Laura disappeared, he was in the Smithers' neighborhood, working as a bulldozer operator in the subdivision under development adjacent to their home.

Around nine that morning, when Laura walked outside and the light drizzle began, Reece's boss assessed the weather and opted to release his crew. Moments later, Laura jogged away from her home, presumably on the route she often took with her father down Moore Road. About the same time, Reece drove away from the construction site, turning onto that very same road.

At least on the surface, Reece appeared to be cooperating. He'd given permission for the FBI to search his house and trucks. He'd even agreed to multiple polygraphs, yet they'd been inconclusive, perhaps, authorities said, because he'd fidgeted and coughed during the pivotal questions.

While Reece had caught the attention of law enforcement, there were other suspects in Laura's death. One was a man who lived in the area who'd made sexual remarks to another young girl. Then there was the tantalizing confession of a man who claimed to have been on the scene when a friend forced Laura into his truck and murdered her. Yet when the trailer where it was supposed to have happened was searched, not one piece of evidence was found. Finally, there was the Harris County Jail inmate who'd been found with a photograph of a young girl resembling Laura in his wallet. None of the other leads panned out, and before long all except the possible connection to Bill Reece were abandoned.

When he talked to the Smithers, Chief Stout gave them the impression that he believed Reece was Laura's killer, but prosecutors argued that they lacked enough evidence to charge him with the crime. Frustration grew.

What was clear in the aftermath of the search for Laura Smither was that something remarkable had happened in Friendswood, Texas. The death of every victim is unique, yet what stood out about Laura Smither was how she inspired thousands to set aside their own lives to fight for a common goal.

Early on, it became evident to Gay and Bob that their community's response had been extraordinary. Even while the search for Laura continued, a father of a missing daughter came to them begging for help. "He saw what was happening on television, how so many volunteers helped us. He wanted to know how to organize his own volunteers to look for his daughter," said Bob. "We helped him as much as we could." In the end, the man's daughter's body was found by volunteers on the same day as Laura's.

Based on that experience, in the months following their daughter's death, Bob and Gay talked with Chief Stout. Looking at the situation, the chief agreed that what had happened in Friendswood was an anomaly, a rare triangle of trust, a coming-together of the family, the community and law enforcement. Perhaps to make some sense out of the tragedy, not long after Laura's memorial service, Bob began pulling together all the notes he'd made about who did what during the search for Laura. The result was a manual of sorts that described how to look for a missing person.

Then something happened that would focus the Smithers' work, an event that would redirect their lives, giving them a cause for years to come. That August, four months after Laura's death, a truck was found on I-45, one that belonged to the C. H. Cain family, who lived on an appendage off the causeway bridge between the mainland and Galveston called Tiki Island. Seventeen-year-old Jessica Cain had been on her way home from a night out with friends when she simply vanished. Her truck was found abandoned, with her purse inside, on the shoulder of I-45. Within hours of the mysterious disappearance, the Smithers' doorbell rang. "It was one of the Cains' neighbors," said Bob. "They were coming to us for help. They wanted to know how to organize the search."

"Here we were, these damaged human beings, and someone was coming to us for help. Something was very wrong if they needed us," Gay said. Yet she and Bob couldn't turn the Cains or any relative of a missing loved one away. They had unwillingly become part of a painful union.

"The hell of not knowing is every parent's nightmare," said Bob. "Until you've walked that road, you have no idea of the darkness."

# Chapter 16

## A Daring Escape and Pieces of the Puzzle

**Webster, Texas**
**May 1997**

Detective turned private investigator Sue Dietrich, taken in 2012.
*(Courtesy of Kathryn Casey)*

"**N**inety-seven was a tough year," said Sue Dietrich, as we huddled together in a small Italian restaurant, planted flush against the southbound Interstate 45 feeder road. Later, Dietrich, a retired cop turned private investigator, lingered in front where I snapped her photo with cars whizzing behind her. The background, of course, seemed fitting, since I-45 anchored the bloodshed we'd come together to discuss.

Inside the restaurant, Dietrich and I toyed with salads and whispered about the summer of 1997, when young women were repeatedly abducted in Harris and Galveston counties. First twelve-year-old Laura Smither, her slain body found in a retention pond. Then in May, Dietrich consulted on the case of Sandra Sapaugh, a woman kidnapped from a parking lot. In August, the missing girl's name was Jessica Cain, her abandoned pickup found on I-45's shoulder.

As we talked, the sadness from Dietrich's many years in law enforcement hung on her like a weighty shroud. Throughout our time together, the aging investigator brought the conversation back to the man she believed responsible for the carnage and accompanying misery. "He's a monster," she said, lips pursed.

At the tables surrounding us, couples and families gathered over steaming plates of pasta, many laughing and smiling. I nodded, signaling that I understood, and I thought Dietrich looked tired. Years in law enforcement had etched deep lines around her eyes.

We'd met for the first time in the midnineties in Alvin, Texas, the same small town where Colette Wilson, the dentist's daughter, had disappeared decades earlier. Back in the day, I paid my bills writing magazine articles, and Dietrich was a feisty blond detective in high heels and manicured nails, one who'd cracked a big case.

Two-year-old Renee Goode, a sweet child with light brown curls, died during a court-ordered overnight stay with her father, Shane. The police quickly wrote off the cause of the child's demise as some unidentified, unexplained illness. But Renee's mom and grandmother believed Shane Goode murdered his little girl to exact revenge against his ex-wife and avoid child support. Repeatedly rebuffed by the police and the county's medical examiner, the two women found no help until they met Dietrich. Unlike many others, she listened and assessed the evidence, deciding those who loved Renee had ample reason to be suspicious. It was Dietrich who interviewed Goode, obtaining a statement that later, along with a second autopsy, led to his conviction for murder.

If any doubt remained, Shane Goode ultimately wrote a confession letter from inside prison walls.

Three years after little Renee's death, in 1997, it was another talent that brought Dietrich center stage in the investigations into the I-45 killings. Along with her duties as an investigator, Sue Dietrich was a certified forensic hypnotist. The lead she ultimately constructed from the clues made all the difference. "If it hadn't been for Sue Dietrich, we might never have seen the big picture," a grateful prosecutor confided. "She pieced the puzzle together."

That spring, Sandra Sapaugh's life was in turmoil.

The mother of two young girls, the nineteen-year-old had dropped out of school in the ninth grade. A striking beauty with long brown hair and a voluptuous figure, Sapaugh did what she could, dancing in topless clubs, to support her children. Her night wasn't going well in the early hours of Saturday, May 17, when she pulled into the lot of a Webster, Texas, convenience store. On this particular evening, she dropped her kids off with their grandparents and drove her red Dodge Astro minivan back to an apartment that until recently she'd shared with her husband, her mission to collect her clothing and her children's things and move out. She left hours later with the minivan loaded and $200 her soon-to-be-ex spotted her to tide her over until she and the children resettled.

Sometime around one, Sapaugh pulled into a Stop & Go on West Nasa Road I, a major thoroughfare that runs east off I-45 toward the Johnson Space Center. Across the street, a Motel 6 where she planned to stay was booked solid, and Sapaugh decided to call a friend. Still years before cell phones became the norm, she parked in front of the pay phone on the outside of the store. As she exited the truck, she noticed a man dressed in jeans, a white, short-sleeved T-shirt, and a black cowboy hat standing beside an oversized white pickup, a dually with four wheels on the rear axle, parked near the store Dumpster. Something about the guy made her uneasy. Quickly, she shuffled inside for change. When she walked out, the man waited, watching her.

"I don't like the way this guy's looking at me," she told her friend on the pay phone. The call ended, Sapaugh shrugged off her apprehension, ignored the stranger, and left. Her plan was to drive across the street to a Waffle House, a small, boxy establishment open all night, where her friend would meet her. She pulled out of the store's lot, glanced in her rearview mirror and saw that the white dually followed directly behind her. Then, as she steered into the restaurant's lot, Sapaugh realized something was wrong with her minivan.

In a parking space near the road, she came to a stop. Moments later, she lowered her window as the man from the convenience store approached. "I noticed that your tire is flat at the Stop & Go," he said with a slow smile. "Why don't I help you?"

Wary but grateful, Sapaugh climbed out of the van to look at her misshapen front driver's-side tire, flat to the rim. Had she run over something? A bad night had just become worse. "I'll see if I have a jack," he said. Sapaugh thought little of it when the man, instead of going to the large aluminum toolbox anchored to the pickup's bed, walked toward the front of the truck and opened the hood.

The young mother had bigger problems; she wasn't even sure that she had a spare. She popped the van's back open to look inside. The man made her uncomfortable, but she'd never changed a tire and needed the help.

"Would you get the rag out of my truck for me?" he called out to her.

In response, Sapaugh strode over to the truck's open driver's-side door and glanced inside. "I don't see it," she shouted back.

"Look again," he said. "It's on the passenger side."

Following his instructions, Sapaugh leaned into the truck, scanning the floor and seat for the rag. It was then that she felt the man at her back. Her mind registered the touch of a knife blade to her throat. Reacting quickly, Sapaugh grabbed for the knife, but the man overpowered her and hastily pushed her inside.

"Get in, and don't yell!" he ordered, clambering in behind her.

Inside the truck, Sapaugh sprawled out on the passenger seat. She flipped over, but her legs were caught, spreading awkwardly across the man's lap. The entire inside of the truck was in darkness, all the lights turned off, but in his hand, she saw the glint of the knife as he growled, "Stay down, bitch!"

Her pulse quickening, she watched helplessly as he threw the truck into drive and pulled out of the restaurant parking lot. "Where are you taking me?" she asked.

"Dallas," he said.

Instead he drove to the Motel 6, the one where earlier Sapaugh had hoped to book a room. If the hotel had a vacancy, she would have been inside sleeping instead of trembling with fear in the stranger's pickup. But this wasn't the time to think about that. Instead, she tried to talk the man into going into the motel office and getting them a room. "We don't have to drive anywhere," she said, hoping to put him at ease. "We can stay here. I'll stay with you." If he went inside to try to register, she might be able to escape. Her fear grew as he put his hand down her blouse and fondled her breast.

The man wasn't interested in a hotel room. That wasn't what he had in mind. Moments later, he'd moved the truck again, this time into the back parking lot of a U-Haul rental agency a short distance away. She shivered with fear as he put the truck in park, then turned toward her and grabbed her blouse, tearing it open. She felt sickened as he put his mouth on her breast. "Take your pants off," he ordered.

"No," she balked. She thought she saw him put the knife

between his legs, as he continued to suck and fondle her breast.

"Take your pants off!" he insisted. Although terrified, she refused.

It was then that he threw the truck into drive and headed west on Nasa I toward I-45. He appeared anxious, eager to get what he wanted. In the van, the man roared orders at Sapaugh. "I said take your damn pants off!"

Out the window, Sapaugh watched stores whiz by and headlights shining, as inside the dark truck she struggled, not sure what to do. When he shouted at her again, she stalled for time, asking, "Can I take my shoes off first?"

"No!" he shouted, but when she argued that she needed to remove her shoes before slipping out of her blue jeans, he reluctantly gave in. By then the truck was barreling northbound on I-45, Webster's lights and civilization fading behind them. In the darkness, the interstate was nearly deserted.

Employing the excuse of removing her shoes, a pair of sandals, Sapaugh pulled her legs off the man's lap. In the passenger seat, she acted as if she were attempting to follow his directions and slowly took off her shoes. As she fumbled with her jeans, she looked about her, searching for a way to escape. It was then that she noticed that the passenger-side door was unlocked. In a single motion, she grabbed the opportunity, seized the handle and swung the door open. Instantly, the man slammed his foot on the brake and snatched the back of her shirt. Not giving in, Sapaugh struggled. Below her bare feet, the interstate's coarse cement surface dashed by. They battled, the truck slowed but still moving, until her shirt finally gave way and tore. He lost his grip, and she fell.

Tumbling from the moving truck, Sapaugh hit the cement hard then rolled across the harsh pavement, skinning the concrete, hitting stones and debris. Once she stopped, every joint ached and her knee throbbed, but she had no time to give in to her injuries. Instead, to her horror, she heard the

truck stop ahead of her. Then she heard him shift into reverse.

He was coming back for her.

On her way home from her sister's bachelorette party, Minerva Torres drove her black Dodge Charger north on I-45
sometime after 1:00 A.M., when a barefoot woman startled
her by running out of the darkness, staggering in the middle
of the freeway, limping and waving her arms. In the backseat, Torres's young nephew yelled, "That lady is hurt. We
have to help her! Stop!"

Torres did, pulling the car to the shoulder and parking it,
then running to the woman.

"Help me!" the woman screamed. "Please, help me! I
jumped from a truck."

"You jumped?" Torres repeated.

"Yes, I jumped from that truck, there!" Sapaugh shouted.

Torres scanned the highway and spotted a white dually
pickup pulled off to the side, its headlights turned off but
the backup lights lit, as if it were coming toward them in reverse. Quickly, Torres guided the injured woman to the car.
The stranger's clothes were torn, and she was bleeding. As
Torres lowered the injured woman into the passenger seat,
Torres's frightened nephew cried.

"Is that your boyfriend?" Torres asked the injured woman.

"No. I don't know him," Sapaugh said. "He had a knife."

Torres eyed the truck that lurked ominously just ahead.
"We need to get out of here."

Hurriedly, Torres threw her car into gear and sped up. Sapaugh saw the dually pull out onto the freeway and take off
down the interstate. The man had given up. He was leaving.

At the next exit, Torres pulled off the interstate onto the
service road. Her intention was to take the injured woman
directly to the hospital. But once they were in the car, Sapaugh pleaded with Torres to take her instead to the Waffle
House, where her friend would be waiting. Complying,
Torres looped around and drove south to Webster. Once

there, she ran from the car into the restaurant. Inside, she shouted at the woman behind the counter to call an ambulance and the police. Back at the car, Torres searched for something to stem the injured woman's bleeding. She found a shirt she pushed against Sapaugh's chest. When the ambulance pulled up, Sapaugh was in the passenger seat, the door open, her feet on the parking lot's surface, dazed, blood streaming down her face and body from gashes and scrapes. Every movement brought excruciating pain.

To the first officer on the scene, Sapaugh described the horror that night had brought and the man responsible. He was white, approximately five-nine, about two hundred pounds, with dirty blond hair and a mustache. And something she'd noticed was that he had bags under his eyes, which she described as "loose facial skin." Although stunned from all she'd been through, she was as precise with the description of the truck, an older model white Ford or Chevy dually pickup with an extended cab, an aluminum toolbox on the bed, and a black stripe along the side. From the sound of the engine, she thought it might have been a diesel.

Torres, who'd grown up working on her brother's cars, gave a nearly identical description of the truck she'd seen on the highway, speculating it was a Ford.

Brought into St. John Hospital in nearby Clear Lake on a backboard, Sapaugh appeared calm as doctors assessed her wounds. She had a gash on her scalp that needed to be stitched quickly to stop the bleeding, a cut above her eye, and abrasions on her left breast. Her hands too painful to move, she couldn't sign a consent form. In her bloodied and torn clothing, angry red lacerations and swollen painful bruises covered her from her face to her feet. Fearing internal bleeding or a concussion, the attending physician checked her into the hospital, wanting to monitor her condition. Three days after she jumped from the truck, her body black-and-blue and sore to move, Sapaugh, still traumatized, left the hospital and checked into a shelter for abused women.

Soon after, she made her first trip to the Webster Police Department to assist officers investigating her case. Once there, she described the man for an officer at a computer, one using Identi-Kit, a program designed to construct composites of suspects. The result was a sketch of a man with baggy eyes, a mustache, stubble on his chin and cheeks, and slicked-back hair. Later that day, the drawing was released in a bulletin to agencies across Texas along with written descriptions of the man and his truck.

The face of Sandra Sapaugh's kidnapper. *(Courtesy of the Harris County Sheriff's Office)*

Throughout the afternoon at the police station, Sapaugh had been on edge, uncomfortable. As precise as she was about the man and the truck, she'd given the police little to work with, since white dually trucks weren't uncommon work vehicles in southeast Texas. There was one piece of information police had hoped for more than any other, one that Sapaugh had been unable to supply: a license-plate number.

The following day, Sue Dietrich's phone rang in her office. "It was a detective in Webster. He asked me to drive to their office to hypnotize a victim and a witness," said Dietrich. "The hope was that under hypnosis, the women might remember more."

Six days after her abduction, Sandra Sapaugh sat in a darkened office with Dietrich and a Webster detective. As a video camera recorded the session, Dietrich asked Sapaugh to describe what had happened to her and everything she could remember about the man and his truck. Dietrich then attempted to relax the woman and put her under hypnosis. Although she'd only used hypnosis on witnesses a few times before, all initially went well. But as Dietrich asked questions, Sapaugh felt drawn back to the inside of the white truck, to that night when she'd feared for her life. In a matter of moments, the young woman became intensely frightened. Thrust back into the truck barreling down the interstate in the darkness, Sapaugh relived the terror, fearing she either had to jump from the moving truck onto the interstate or die at the hands of a killer. "It was hard on her," said Dietrich. "We tried, but she couldn't come up with any more than she'd told us before the session. No license number. She was so upset, we had to cut the questioning short."

Although disappointed, Webster police had one more possibility. The night of the attack, the police found a second witness, a clerk at the Stop & Go who'd just happened to walk out to the Dumpster with a bag of garbage while Sapaugh was inside getting change. The clerk gave a nearly identical account of the man she'd seen standing next to his truck, except for one point, describing his cowboy hat as tan not black.

As with Sapaugh, Dietrich first had the woman describe what she remembered, then put her under hypnosis. This time an additional detail did emerge, that the man wore a gold-nugget pinkie ring. While interesting, that clue gave little more to go on.

In June, a month after her abduction, the Sapaugh kidnapping case was classified as inactive with no leads.

Two months later on August 17, seventeen-year-old Jessica Cain stood onstage at the Harbor Playhouse in Dickinson, seven miles from the Waffle House restaurant where Sapaugh had been abducted. The recent high-school graduate from Galveston's O'Connell High School had moved to Tiki Island, an affluent community on a thumb-shaped appendage underneath the Galveston Causeway, four years earlier. The family had lived on a farm on acreage in East Texas, but moved because her parents heard of drug running in the area. "We thought it would be safer," said Jessica's dad, C. H. Cain.

Jessica Cain, looking over her shoulder.
*(Courtesy of C.H. and Suzy Cain)*

A hard worker, Jessica had amassed enough college credits in high school so that in the fall she'd enter Sam Houston State University in Huntsville as a sophomore. It would seem ironic later that her planned major was criminology.

That night at the theater, with Jessica's parents in the audience, the opening was a resounding success, earning the cast a standing ovation. In a fifties musical revival, Jessica played a breathless Marilyn Monroe onstage. Caught up in the exhilaration of the evening, at one point Jessica urged her father from the audience to do an unrehearsed jitterbug in the aisle. "That was the way she was, impromptu," he'd say proudly. "Jessica was bubbly, and she stood out. She attracted attention." Flushed with excitement, wanting to celebrate with her friends, after the performance Jessica asked her parents if she could attend a cast party at a nearby Bennigan's restaurant. C. H. and his wife, Suzy, gave permission. Most nights Jessica's curfew was midnight, but this was a special occasion, and Suzy instructed their daughter to be home by one thirty. The last thing Jessica said to C. H. was, "I love you, Daddy."

From the restaurant that evening, the cast left for the apartment of one of the members. It was after 1:00 A.M. when Jessica told a friend she was tired, not feeling well, and she wanted to go home. Jessica had left her ride, her father's 1992 Ford pickup, at the Bennigan's. At five-foot-four and 140 pounds, Jessica had a fair complexion, a heart-shaped face, medium brown, chin-length hair, and blue eyes. In the restaurant parking lot, the friends who dropped her off saw her get in her truck and pull out onto the road, then drive toward her home.

At the house, Jessica's dad had gone to bed, while her mother intended to stay up and wait for their daughter. At some point, however, Suzy dozed off. When she awoke about two thirty and Jessica wasn't home, Suzy woke up C. H. It wasn't like Jessica, a good kid who followed directions, to be so late. "I immediately panicked," he said.

The first thing C. H., a program manager for Exxon, did was to drive the area, circling back to the theater, the Bennigan's, the places he thought his daughter might be. When he didn't find her, he kept looking. It was about four that morning when he spotted the pickup truck about four miles from the house, on the shoulder of I-45's southbound feeder lane, where the interstate ran through the small town of La Marque, pointed south as if Jessica had been on her way home. When he pulled over, C. H. Cain found the pickup locked, Jessica's wallet, keys, and driver's license on the seat. There were no signs of a robbery.

An odd coincidence was that the Cain family's truck wasn't far from the spot—across the highway—where eleven years earlier Shelley Sikes's blue Ford Pinto had been found mired in the mud. That was the only connection, however, since Sikes's kidnappers, Gerald Pieter Zwarst and John Robert King, couldn't be suspects. Both remained in Texas prisons serving life sentences for aggravated kidnapping.

On this night, police responded fairly quickly, and C. H. explained that Jessica was a responsible young woman, one who knew that the roads could be dangerous. "She drove with the doors locked," he said. With the police, C. H. stressed that his daughter wouldn't have stopped for just anyone. "She had a mobile phone, but not with her that night."

In the days that followed, Jessica's parents reeled from the knowledge that their daughter was missing. "We were in shock, disbelief," said C. H. "We didn't see how it was possible." Ironically, earlier that summer, the Cains had watched the extensive news coverage of the search for Laura Smither, and when Laura's body was found, C. H. cried, wondering how anyone could abduct a child. "We never thought it could happen to us," he said.

On the news the following days, Jessica Cain's parents pleaded with her captor and begged their daughter not to give up. But there were no signs of Jessica. As they had for so many others, thousands of those who lived in the small towns around I-45 banded together, mounting searches. Among them were familiar names and faces from other area tragedies. Bob and Gay Smither counseled the Cains, shoring up their own pain to give them support, and Shelley Sikes's dad, Eddie, and Laura Miller's dad, Tim, helped with the search. Years later, Tim Miller would recall thinking at the time that the whole world must have gone crazy for so many girls to be taken from their families.

Leads were followed, but to no avail, and after approximately two weeks, the searches thinned out, then eventually stopped.

In the bulletins circulated to media about the case, police mentioned two vehicles seen that night, ones that might be connected with the abduction. One was a red Isuzu Amigo, the other a full-sized, light-colored truck with a toolbox on the back bed and lights across the top.

The nineties were turning into another bloody decade in the far southern reaches of Houston. Perhaps few understood how bloody until an article ran in the *Houston Chronicle* on Sunday, September 21, 1997, the month after Jessica Cain's disappearance. Entitled "Elusive Answers," it said the Smither and Cain cases were reminders that many young girls had disappeared and been murdered in the area in the previous decades, dating all the way back to the eleven girls who'd died in and around Galveston in the 1970s. When asked for a comment, Krystal Baker's mom, Jeanie, said, "This could happen to anyone's child."

Accompanying it, the *Chronicle* published the first "Mysteries along I-45" chart, with photos of the girls and details from their abductions. It wasn't that in other parts of the city and across the nation girls, boys, women, and men didn't disappear. It was that this particular chunk of the Gulf Coast appeared to have more than its share of such tragedies, and too many of the cases remained unsolved.

Why? "Get murdered in Dallas, Chicago, inside Houston, and you're dealing with cops who know how to work murders. In these small towns, they see them so rarely, they're over their heads," a seasoned prosecutor said with a frown one afternoon, shaking his head in regret. "These are small agencies, some of the cops have big egos, and the cases cross jurisdictions. It's not unusual for an investigator to guard his cases and not cooperate with other cops from other agencies. That means the folks investigating don't always talk. And that hurts the effort. It can be fatal to an investigation."

In hindsight, it was a cop who did make the effort, one who got in her car and drove to another small town to compare notes, who made a difference.

As the horror unfolded in 1997, Sue Dietrich left her slot as a detective at Alvin P.D. to sign on as police chief of Jessica Cain's hometown, Tiki Island. It was in that capacity on October 3, that Dietrich drove to Friendswood P.D. to chat with her counterpart there, Jared Stout. It was a friendly call, just checking in with the chief of a nearby jurisdiction. Afterward, something interesting happened. "We were talking, and the Smither case came up. He told me about this guy, his prime suspect. Chief Stout was frustrated that they hadn't made an arrest. We talked for a while, and I left. I honestly didn't think a lot more about it. But then I woke up in the middle of the night. I literally sat up in bed and thought, *I wonder if that's the guy?* I thought about the physical description Stout had given me of his suspect and the guy's pickup, and suddenly I remembered that May, and what Sandra Sapaugh told me about the man who had abducted her. The descriptions were so similar, that I picked up the phone and called Friendswood and told a detective that maybe they should compare notes with Webster P.D."

A 1997 photo taken in Houston of William Lewis Reece. *(Trial exhibit)*

The man Stout described to Sue Dietrich was an ex-con, a paroled sex offender from Oklahoma, William Lewis "Bill" Reece, the prime suspect in the Smither case. On the morning of Laura Smither's disappearance, Reece was on his second day on the job as a bulldozer operator at the subdivision under construction just down the road from the Smithers' home. He'd only paroled out of an Oklahoma jail six months earlier after serving time for forcible oral sodomy, abduction, and rape. At about the time Laura set off on her run that morning, Reece drove down the same road after being released from work because of the impending rain.

Within days of Laura's disappearance, Reece had been

questioned, but no solid evidence emerged to peg him as her killer. What spurred Dietrich's memory and led her to recall the Sapaugh case was Reece's appearance, his height close to the man Sapaugh described, protruding bags under his eyes, a mustache, and a receding hairline. And then there was Reece's truck. It matched Sapaugh's description: a white Ford dually diesel with an aluminum toolbox on the back and a black pinstripe down the side. It also resembled the description of the truck seen on the night Jessica Cain disappeared, including the amber running lights across the top.

As Dietrich thought about the similarities, she wondered, if it was Reece who pulled Cain over that night, could the amber running lights have tricked the teenager into thinking she was being stopped by a police officer? "Her parents were adamant that she wouldn't pull over for just anyone," said Dietrich. "I may never know for sure, but I could picture how it could have happened."

A mug shot of William Reece and an evidence photo of the truck he drove. *(Courtesy of the Harris County Sheriff's Office and a trial exhibit)*

By the time Reece was brought in for questioning in Webster that fall, he had an attorney at his side. His mustache had been shaved off, and rather than an aluminum toolbox on the pickup's bed, he'd installed a cowboy camper.

The reason he'd been contacted, the officers explained,

was to see if he'd be willing to cooperate by participating in a lineup. Reece and his lawyer declined, but the possibility didn't appear to bother the ex-con, as he laughed and joked with the officers, as if the prospect of standing in a lineup wasn't troubling. Not dissuaded, the next day the officers brought a photo lineup to Sandra Sapaugh that included Bill Reece's picture. "That's him," she said, pointing at Reece's photo. "That's the man."

Rough around the edges with a slow country drawl, Reece had grown up on a farm in Yukon, Oklahoma. He'd dropped out of high school in the ninth grade and made money driving trucks, working construction and on rodeos and ranches as a farrier, shoeing horses. He'd married a decade earlier, but that ended in divorce after he'd spent much of the marriage in an Oklahoma prison. Looking at Reece's record, there were similarities between his prior offenses and Sapaugh's abduction. He'd held one of the Oklahoma victims at knifepoint, and one of the women had been abducted along the side of a highway. Her car had broken down, and Reece, just like the assailant in the Sapaugh case, acted as if he were a Good Samaritan, stopping to render aid.

In the early-morning hours of October 16, 1997, police surrounded William Reece's run-down apartment on Fauna Street not far from Hobby Airport south of downtown Houston. They had a warrant signed by a judge for his arrest and search warrants for his home and truck. Reece came quietly. Inside the apartment, officers photographed a black cowboy hat like the one Sapaugh described on her assailant the first time she saw him, at the convenience store. Later, when the truck was inspected, they entered into evidence two knives, including a switchblade-type knife discovered in the pocket of the driver's-side door.

Once Reece was under arrest, he was transported to Houston P.D.'s Southeast Command Center. Sandra Sapaugh waited. In a small room behind one-way glass, accompanied by Reece's attorney, a representative from the Harris County

District Attorney's Office, and an officer from Webster P.D., Sapaugh watched through a one-way mirror as five men filed into the adjacent viewing room. The officer would later say that Sapaugh's eyes locked onto Reece the moment he entered. All the men were instructed to repeat a phrase the kidnapper had uttered, "Stay down, bitch!"

"Number four," Sapaugh said, identifying Reece as the man she'd risked her life to escape that night. "That's him."

As soon as Reece's name hit the newspapers, tips came into Webster and Friendswood P.D., from women who'd encountered him in Houston. Many talked of the way Reece looked at them, how uncomfortable it made them feel. One call was from the Diamond B. Ranch in Friendswood, not far from the Smither house, where Reece shoed horses. The ranch's owner said he had to watch Reece carefully because young women who boarded their horses there complained the farrier gave them unwanted attention.

Something else came up when the caller relayed Reece's reputation at the ranch; four days after Jessica Cain disappeared, Bill Reece did something very strange. Without being asked to, he used his bulldozer to move a large manure pile on the ranch. That spurred investigators to bring in cadaver dogs and equipment to search the pile. Fighting rain, they worked for two days, finding nothing but not abating suspicions that somehow the manure pile was involved in Jessica's disappearance.

The same day as the search at the ranch, Chief Stout in Friendswood went public with his suspicions, announcing that his main suspect in the Smither case was under arrest in Harris County for aggravated kidnapping. Before long, reporters matched up the information, and the news hit the front page of papers across Texas: Stout had a person of interest in the Smither case, and his name was William Lewis Reece.

Not one to shy away from the publicity, Reece granted his own interviews from jail, telling the press that he wasn't the man. "It's a crock," he said, in his slow Oklahoma drawl. "They need someone. They don't have anyone. I know it's not me. They have nothing. They know they have nothing . . . I'm not the kind of person to kill. I would never hurt kids . . . The real killer is still out there."

Yet there was some fascinating evidence uncovered during the searches of Bill Reece's apartment and truck. The state lab analyzed fibers taken from an afghan throw found on the back of his couch and from the truck's floor mats. In both cases, the samples were consistent with fibers recovered from the only clothing still on her body the day Laura's remains were found, her tan socks.

Longtime prosecutors Ted Wilson and Donna Goode Cameron. *(Courtesy of Kathryn Casey)*

"If we'd had the evidence to go after Bill Reece for Laura Smither's murder, we would have done it," retired prosecutor Ted Wilson said. It had been fifteen years since Reece's trial, but Wilson bristled at any suggestion that he could have charged Reece with Smither's murder. He was in the office of his second chair on the case, Donna Goode Cameron, who had also left Harris County but landed in Galveston, where she was the district attorney's second-in-command, the office's first assistant. Both Cameron and Wilson were affable, and they talked candidly about William Reece's 1998 trial for the kidnapping of Sandra Sapaugh. Like two tested warriors who've fought the hard battles, they looked back on those days with pride and a sense of what was accomplished, along with perhaps a sadness about what remained undone. "The Smithers believe that Bill Reece murdered Laura, and they think we should have tried him for that, but that wasn't our best case," said Wilson. "It never seemed to get any better for us than that he was in the area."

"We never got to the point where we thought we could prove it beyond a reasonable doubt," agreed Cameron.

Wilson looked at Cameron and frowned, as if revisiting a painful decision. "We had witnesses in the kidnapping case. We had to live with the evidence we had."

Under the best of circumstances, charging Reece with Laura Smither's murder admittedly wasn't the tightest of cases. After all, no one saw Reece with the girl; not a single witness came forward. Those fibers, the ones from Reece's truck floor mat and afghan that matched strands found on Laura Smither's socks? Well, Ted Wilson said it wasn't enough to be conclusive. "We had somebody run the numbers," said Wilson. "We couldn't prove that those fibers could only have come from William Reece's truck. That wasn't possible."

That didn't mean that Wilson and Cameron didn't try. There were bruises documented on Laura's body, and that resulted in speculation that they could have been bite marks. William Reece had distinctive teeth. The front ones splayed out, gaping in the front. A court order secured a dental impression of his teeth for comparison. The results didn't offer any insight. In fact, the experts later doubted that the bruises were even bite marks.

"Could William Reece have murdered Laura Smither? Yes. He was capable of it," said Wilson. "But the waters got muddied for a lot of reasons."

In the spring of 1998, the public became aware of how muddied the Smither case had become. There'd been an error, the kind that can fatally wound an investigation, permanently relegating it to a cold-case file. The scene was the Harris County Morgue. There, Laura's sad remains were improperly handled. The result: hairs were inadvertently transferred to Laura's corpse from another body autopsied in the morgue, another murder victim. Complicating the matter further, the assistant medical examiner who did the autopsy refused to conclusively attribute the hairs to contamination.

At the time the morgue's mistake hit news outlets, reports of the disappointing turn in the Smither case rocked Houston. After such an effort to find Laura, with so many identifying with the family and all they'd suffered, the criticism of the ME's Office from politicians, law enforcement, even folks on the street was scathing. If Wilson pursued Reece for Laura's murder, the ineptitude of the morgue's staff gifted any good defense attorney assigned to the case with a plateful of reasonable doubt to serve potential jurors.

Yet the Sapaugh case wasn't a slam-dunk either. There were potential complications. The first one, said Cameron, was "would anyone care?"

The problems were multiple. Her profession, a topless dancer, invited scrutiny, and the prosecutors worried about how Sapaugh would hold up on the stand. Cameron wondered if some jurors might secretly hold her job against Sapaugh. Wilson was less worried than Cameron. "I didn't care if she danced topless, and I didn't think a jury would either," he said. "If you're kidnapped at knifepoint and have to roll out of a car on I-45, we're in your corner."

As the trial approached, Wilson and Cameron reached out to Reece's two victims in Oklahoma, the women he'd been convicted of sexually assaulting. The prosecutors believed they should be able to present the cases to the jury, based on the similarities to the Sapaugh kidnapping. "Neither one would come. They refused. They were still deathly afraid of Bill Reece," said Cameron.

Preparing for trial, Reece's defense attorney brought motions before the judge for multiple reasons, one of which was a request to bar Gay and Bob Smither from the courtroom. They, understandably, wanted to be there, to look in the eye the man they suspected murdered their daughter, to hear the evidence, and perhaps to hear him be convicted and sentenced by a jury. Anthony Osso, a highly regarded Houston attorney who'd been assigned to represent Reece, however, insisted that some jurors might recognize Laura's parents, and that by their presence, they could taint the trial with suspicion of Reece's involvement in Laura's murder. The judge ruled that the courtroom was open to the public, and the Smithers wouldn't be kept out.

At the same time, Jessica Cain's parents had no plans to attend. On a Geraldo show that aired while Reece awaited trial, they said they didn't believe he was Jessica's abductor. They believed their daughter had been taken and was still alive and was being held captive. On the program, they pleaded with whoever kidnapped her. "I pray that she'll return home, because her daddy and I still want her . . . we want her back home," Suzy Cain said. When asked what they would tell their daughter, she said, "Never give up."

"**A**n abduction is every woman's worst nightmare," Ted Wilson said in his opening statement on April 29, 1998, day one of the Reece trial. ". . . It's more than a nightmare" to Sandra Sapaugh. "Because it wasn't a dream . . . The nightmare . . . became a reality for her . . . She had to make a decision whether to risk her life to save it."

In the audience, the Smithers watched along with a packed courtroom filled with reporters and curious onlookers. The first witness on the stand was the initial officer on the scene that night at the Waffle House, who testified that

Sapaugh was injured "head to toe" and in shock. From the beginning, the man said, the victim had been consistent in her description of her attacker and his truck, even offering such small details as that the truck had manual cranks for the windows and a mounted cell phone. But some of the details, Osso pointed out, didn't match Reece's dually truck. For instance, it had an automatic transmission not a manual one, as Sapaugh described, and the interior seats were blue, not black. Would the jurors find the discrepancies troublesome?

When Donna Cameron questioned Minerva Torres, the twenty-six-year-old described in detail the night her nephew cried as she rescued a bruised and barefoot woman on I-45. How many passersby would have stopped in the darkness? How many would have instead trounced on the accelerator and driven off? If she had, what would have happened to Sapaugh? Torres had seen the backup lights on the white dually. Was the man intending to pursue and reclaim his victim?

On the witness stand, Sandra Sapaugh appeared vulnerable and ill at ease. She wasn't used to such questioning. When she described her family, she mentioned that she now had three children, including a three-month-old infant. At the time of her abduction, the night she jumped out of the truck, Sapaugh didn't yet know it, but she was pregnant.

The questions Donna Cameron worried about had to be asked. What did Sapaugh do for a living? Then and since, she worked as a topless dancer. "Have you ever been arrested for anything?" Ted Wilson asked.

"No," Sapaugh answered. When asked if she saw the man who kidnapped her in the courtroom, she pointed at Reece, wearing a blue suit in his seat beside Osso. "Yes. That's him."

"May the record reflect that William Reece has been identified by the witness," Wilson said. Turning to Sapaugh, he asked, "Were you scared?"

"Yes," she answered.

As the trial progressed, Osso was vigilant, objecting when Sapaugh pointed out things inside the truck she remembered from her abduction, like a notepad with a cord hanging from it. And he hammered on any inconsistencies, questioning if Reece had a mounted cell phone in his truck at the time of the abduction. The truck didn't have manual window handles in the front, as Sapaugh had said. Couldn't that mean she'd been wrong about the truck and man she'd identified? Wilson pointed out with Sapaugh on the stand that Reece's truck had power windows in the front but cranks in the backseat, suggesting that may have been what Sapaugh saw in the darkness.

Much of the testimony centered on the composite, which became state's exhibit number 66. Did Sapaugh tell the officer who drew it that the man had a beard? She answered that she hadn't, and that the darkness around the cheeks and chin were an indication of stubble. In her testimony, she described her abductor's front teeth as crooked, but was that what she'd said earlier? Osso suggested it wasn't, but Sapaugh disagreed. She insisted she'd had a good look at the man, and he was Bill Reece. Osso proposed that perhaps she'd been maneuvered into her testimony by overzealous officers who'd led her to pick Reece from the lineup. Sapaugh denied that it was true, and swore that it was Reece's face she remembered glaring at her that night in the truck.

Why did she decide to jump? Wilson inquired.

"If he was going to kill me, I would just kill myself," Sapaugh testified. Osso stood up to object.

Sandra Sapaugh remained on the stand for much of the next day. Repeatedly, the questions came back to her first statements and what she remembered, how it all compared with the evidence, especially the photos taken of William Reece's truck. Next to his attorney, Reece sat quietly, often his face a blank but at times appearing to jeer at Sapaugh. Osso wanted to know if Sapaugh's judgment could have been influenced. Had she been drinking that night? She denied that she'd had any alcohol, and a doctor later testified that the reading of .007 on her medical records was low enough that it could have resulted from the use of an alcohol swab when her blood was drawn.

Throughout the trial, as he fought for his client, Anthony Osso's attack was two-pronged: pointing out what he referred to as inconsistencies in Sapaugh's statements and the evidence, and secondly what he labeled as a rush to judgment spurred on by suspicions his client was guilty of another crime, Laura Smither's murder.

While there'd been much attention paid to keeping the Smither case out of the courtroom, Osso brought it in, arguing that it had poisoned the trial. The suspicion surrounding Reece regarding Laura Smither's murder became an explanation for why the ex-con was targeted in the Sapaugh abduction. Police couldn't gather enough evidence to charge Reece for Laura's death, so they set him up on the kidnapping charge. Sandra Sapaugh, Osso suggested, had been manipulated into naming Reece as her attacker.

With three talented attorneys in the courtroom, the battle was fierce. Bench conferences abounded as they fought over what would and wouldn't be allowed into evidence, which witnesses could and could not testify.

"My client doesn't have loose skin, does he?" Osso asked, repeating the description Sapaugh gave to police the night of the attack.

But Reece was in the courtroom, sitting within the jurors' view with his saggy eyes. "Yes, he does," Sapaugh countered.

The Stop & Go clerk pointed to Reece, and she, too, identified him as the man with the white dually in the parking lot that night. She noticed the gold-nugget pinkie ring, one the prosecutors had pictures of on Reece's finger.

Back and forth the attorneys argued. Osso pointing out that Reece had a cowboy camper not a shiny aluminum toolbox on the back of his truck, to which Wilson produced a witness who testified that Reece had repeatedly changed the truck, and that at various times it had just such a toolbox.

Sue Dietrich didn't take the stand until the trial's second week, and after Wilson led her through her testimony, Osso attacked her credentials, suggesting that perhaps she led Sapaugh and used her to entrap his client. Wasn't Dietrich simply trying to help Chief Stout in Friendswood make a case against Reece for Laura Smither's murder? "You and Chief Stout needed to find a way," said Osso. Dietrich denied that was true, contending that Sapaugh's description of the man remained the same before the hypnosis and after.

When Osso took over the courtroom, he presented forensic experts who testified that no hair or fibers from Sapaugh were found in Reece's truck, nor any of her fingerprints. The reverse was also true, that no fibers from Reece's truck had been found on the clothing Sapaugh wore that night. But Wilson recounted all that had happened to the victim, from rolling on the pavement, getting in and out of Torres's car, the ambulance, onto the gurney at the hospital, suggesting evidence could have been lost. When it came to those two knives, the state's expert hadn't been able to prove that either had been used to puncture the tire on Sapaugh's minivan. "That doesn't mean that they weren't used," the man insisted.

Finally, Sapaugh had testified that her attacker came at her from behind with the knife on his left hand, but Bill Reece's sister took the stand and testified that her brother was right-handed. On and on the arguments raged, while in the audience Bob and Gay Smither watched, wondering if the man seated in the courtroom with them had murdered their daughter.

Donna Cameron began closing arguments asking, "Does a topless dancer deserve to be picked up off the street at knifepoint and be automatically disbelieved and her testimony discarded?" Rather, Sapaugh was a nineteen-year-old single mother, one who'd dropped out of school to raise her children and was making her living the only way she knew how. But what about Bill Reece? Cameron pointed out that he fit the description, that he looked like the composite, and that his truck was a nearly identical match to the accounts given by all three eyewitnesses: Sapaugh, Torres, and the convenience-store clerk. Reece carried knives with him, and he had a history of sexual assault.

"Inconsistencies are significant," Anthony Osso countered, maintaining the identification of Reece was flawed. "He's the wrong guy!" There wasn't "one iota" of physical evidence tying Reece to the case, and "misidentification is a major problem." It all boiled down to a lack of evidence, in Osso's argument, and the state hadn't proven its case beyond a reasonable doubt.

Ironically it was Ted Wilson who tried to remove the shadow of Laura Smither from the courtroom, when he pointed out in his closing statement that the Smither case wasn't the one the jury was charged to decide. All they had to consider, he said, was whether the three eyewitnesses were telling the truth. That night in the Waffle House parking lot, William Reece had no way of knowing what Sandra Sapaugh did for a living, Wilson maintained. What Reece saw was a woman with children's clothing in her van, a young mother. And he abducted her at knifepoint. If Sapaugh hadn't gotten everything right, it was amazing how much detail she'd remembered.

"If someone holds a knife to you for six to ten minutes, and you thought he was going to kill you, you would never forget him," Wilson argued. "Somebody has got to stop this guy!"

Six hours later, the jurors returned with a conviction. Bill Reece was guilty of aggravated kidnapping.

Although fear kept them from testifying earlier, now that they knew the man who'd attacked them was going to prison, the two women Reece had been convicted of assaulting in Oklahoma summoned their courage to take the stand during the sentencing phase.

The first was a young wife who in April 1986 had been

a nineteen-year-old college student whose Ford Mustang broke down along a highway in a driving rain. Bill Reece pulled over in his eighteen-wheeler, smiled at her, and offered her a ride. She made the unfortunate decision of accepting and climbed into the truck.

The daughter of a police officer described how the saggy-eyed truck driver pulled a knife on her in the truck's cab while they were parked in a grocery-store lot. "I knew he was going to kill me," she said.

When she asked him why he was "doing this," he answered, "I'm crazy."

Inexplicably, Reece duct taped the girl's hands, then pledged his love, saying that he wanted to marry her. "I had to get out of there somehow," she said. And so she played along, claiming she returned his affection. Yet he wasn't about to give her any freedom. In response, Reece forced her into a sleeping bag, zipping it around her like a cocoon. They ended up in a distribution-center parking lot. He had her in the truck's sleeper compartment, where he first tried to undress her. She fought, and he ended up forcing her to perform oral sex. "I thought he was going to rape me. I thought he was going to kill me. I thought he was sick," the woman said on the stand.

She cajoled him into believing that she would marry him and be with him, and he finally released her. Reece was arrested that same afternoon.

"Had you ever been that scared before in your life?" Donna Cameron asked.

"Never," the woman answered.

The second woman testified that Reece was so out of control in Oklahoma that year that one month later, while under suspicion in the first case, he climbed in through the window and raped her, while her babysitter and child slept in the next room. She insisted that she didn't know Bill Reece and had never seen him before that night. She woke up thinking her husband had come home, but it was Reece straddling her, naked, ripping her clothes off, putting his hand to her throat and pushing her down on the bed, while he kneed her between the legs. When she tried to scream, he started to choke her. "If you wake up anyone, I'll kill you," he threatened.

In his closing, Anthony Osso attempted to distance the Sapaugh case from what the jurors had just heard by arguing that the two Oklahoma women had nothing in common with Sandra Sapaugh. Again, he brought up the inconsistencies in the description of the truck, attempting to plant a seed of doubt regarding his client's guilt. And he reminded the jurors that they weren't to consider the Smither case, in which Reece had never been charged.

Once Osso sat down, Ted Wilson rose to address the jury.

"Life isn't always fair," he said, referring to the two women Reece victimized in Oklahoma. They'd done nothing wrong, yet had suffered and would always bear the scars from the attacks. They didn't deserve what had happened to them. In those cases, Reece served sentences that kept him in prison for a decade, but the women "had gotten life."

After his release, Reece left prison and Oklahoma, moving to Houston. Sandra Sapaugh didn't deserve what had happened to her either. "Back at it again, he gets caught again," said Wilson. "And he stands before you asking for mercy . . . This man has shown what he's made of. This man has shown that he's driven to kidnapping and abusing women . . . He is a predator . . . William Lewis Reece needs to be stopped, and you can stop him."

Ted Wilson asked the jury to put William Reece away for life. Instead, they came back with a sixty-year sentence, one that would make him first eligible for parole in 2027, at the age of sixty-eight. "We were happy with that," said Wilson.

After the trial, Bill Reece was shuttled off to a Texas prison while Gay and Bob Smither struggled to find closure.

The following year, in 1999, the Smithers filed a wrongful death suit against Reece for their daughter's death. They were awarded $110 million in a default judgment, when Reece didn't defend himself. "We knew we'd never see a penny. It wasn't about money," said Gay. "But it was all we could do to make him accountable for Laura's murder."

Finally, five years after Laura died, Gay and Bob decided they had no choice. "We had to go on with our lives, if not for ourselves, for our son." The first step was to clean out Laura's bedroom. The process went on over a period of days, as they donated many of Laura's possessions and gifted others to her friends. But there were things Gay didn't know what to do with, including items from the recovery-site memorial and Laura's more intimate clothing. "We decided we'd have a sacramental fire," said Gay.

The blaze was lit in the backyard, and over a day they slowly deposited Laura's things into it, precious items that they were in a sense offering up to the heavens. Their son, David, helped, and so did friends. One after another, they freed Laura's spirit, releasing it in small clouds of gray smoke. It wasn't that it didn't hurt but that it had to be done. Then, when they were finished, in the living room Bob and Gay took down Laura's picture and hung a framed statuette of a ballerina, placing figurines of angels beneath it. They would never forget their daughter, but they had to find a way to endure. And for David, it would mean that he

The memorial to Laura in the Smithers' home. *(Courtesy of Kathryn Casey)*

wouldn't be confronted with the loss every time he walked through the front door.

In time, they began to heal.

In the year that followed, drawn by all they'd suffered, knowing the pain of other families in their situation, the Smithers officially founded the Laura Recovery Center, a nonprofit dedicated to helping communities search for the missing. They used the notes they made during the search for Laura to draw up a handbook, detailing how to harness a community to help law enforcement. It was something they felt called to do. Since then, the Center has assisted in thousands of searches. "We do this in Laura's memory," said Gay. "We do this because it's something we can do."

Yet that day in their living room as we talked about their lost daughter, Gay and Bob Smither made it clear that there was something more they wanted, the one thing they viewed as perhaps having the power to bring some justice. "We still want to see Bill Reece prosecuted for Laura's murder," said Bob, his jaw stern and his gaze rock hard. "We will never know until there's a trial. We want our day in court."

# Chapter 17

## "I Am Not a Serial Killer"
## William Lewis Reece

**The Ellis Unit**
**Huntsville, Texas**

William Lewis Reece.
*(Courtesy of the Texas
Department of
Criminal Justice)*

It was a breezy, blue-sky mid-March day, picture-perfect, yet I fought a nagging unease on the drive to Huntsville, Texas, ninety minutes north of Houston. My destination was the Texas Department of Criminal Justice's Ellis Unit, where I had a 1:00 P.M. interview scheduled with William Lewis Reece, a man many suspected was a serial killer.

In the time I'd been working on this book, I frequently heard Reece's name; everyone from Sue Dietrich to an FBI profiler, Bob and Gay Smither, the police officers I interviewed and a seasoned prosecutor told me they considered Reece the primary suspect in Laura Smither's murder. There was also speculation that his white Ford dually could have been the vehicle seen on the night Jessica Cain disappeared, her pickup truck found on the I-45 feeder road after she left a theater-cast party.

Yet some investigators, primarily in the Cain case, while not ruling out Reece, saw other possibilities.

For instance, before his death in 2001, private investigator Willie Payne, hired by Jessica's parents, expressed interest in a League City mechanic named Jonathan David Drew, serving a life sentence in a Texas prison for the November 1998 murder of a Houston waitress. What caught Payne's attention and suggested Drew might be involved in the Cain case was that Drew was known to have been in the area at the time. He also had a red Amigo, matching the description of one of the vehicles on the scene the night Jessica disappeared.

Tiffany Dobry Johnston's mother considered Bill Reece a friend.
*(Courtesy of Kathy Dobry)*

Still, Reece remained not only a viable suspect in the Laura Smither and Jessica Cain cases, but also in at least one Oklahoma murder: that of Tiffany Dobry Johnston, abducted from the Sunshine Car Wash in Bethany, Oklahoma. At the time, Tiffany was a nineteen-year-old newlywed, one who worked two jobs to help pay the bills and planned to attend Oklahoma State University in the fall. The date of her disappearance was July 26, 1997, a little more than three months after Laura Smither's murder and three weeks before Jessica Cain vanished.

What was particularly interesting in the Johnston case was that Bill Reece had a link to the victim. "I knew Billy," said Kathy Dobry, Tiffany's mother. "I knew his family."

Dobry had her ironing done by Reece's mother, who ran a small laundry service out of her home. While Dobry knew Reece had been in prison, she said that at the time she didn't know why. "His mom never said, but I had the impression it was drugs or something. I didn't know it was sex crimes."

Did Tiffany know Reece?

Kathy wasn't sure. Her older daughter accompanied her to drop off ironing at the Reece house on occasion, and Bill Reece had been home at the time. But Kathy hadn't taken Tiffany, her younger daughter, there. Yet Kathy wondered if Reece could have seen her with Tiffany, maybe in a store or just around town. During the time Kathy knew him, she thought of Bill Reece as a friend. She even introduced him to her grandchildren and asked him to deliver something to her older daughter's house. "If I'd known he was a sex offender, I wouldn't have done that," Kathy insists.

On the day Tiffany vanished, her car sat abandoned at the car wash for hours before it was noticed. Like the Jessica Cain case, Tiffany's car was found with her wallet and money inside. In the Johnston case, the body was found quickly, the next day, discarded along the side of a road. Like Laura Smither, Tiffany was strangled.

Early on, police in Oklahoma focused on Reece as a prime suspect. That suspicion never faded.

Although she heard he was a suspect, Kathy Dobry doubted the accusations against Bill Reece. She couldn't fathom that someone she considered a friend would be coldhearted enough to murder her daughter. Then there were the assurances Reece's mom gave her. "She told me Billy wasn't even in Oklahoma at the time. He was in Houston."

In fact, just days after Tiffany's murder, Reece's mother called Kathy Dobry offering condolences. During that call, Mrs. Reece claimed that police were unfairly targeting her son. Bill was so upset by the unfair accusations, the old woman said that he'd be calling Dobry to talk to her. Not long after, the phone rang again. This time Bill Reece personally told Kathy that he wasn't in Oklahoma but in

Houston on the day Tiffany was abducted. "I didn't kill your daughter," he insisted.

Despite all the conjecture about what William Lewis Reece might or might not have been guilty of, the man I was scheduled to talk to, TDCJ inmate number 00831080, had never been charged with or convicted of a murder. He was serving time in Texas on two counts. The first was theft. One of the investigators on the Smither case wondered how an ex-con recently out of prison bought a bulldozer, an expensive piece of equipment. It turned out that Reece hadn't. The bulldozer Reece used as a contract construction worker was stolen. The second, of course, was the sixty years a jury handed down for aggravated kidnapping in Sandra Sapaugh's abduction.

Was Reece one of the killers who'd made the I-45 area their hunting ground? That was an unanswered question.

My apprehension subsided by the time I sat across from Reece. He appeared thinner than in the prison photo I'd been given, looking a bit drawn. I didn't know if it was true, but I heard that he'd been ill. Clean-shaven, his once-shaggy mop of dark blond hair had thinned. Cut short, he had it skinned back. His complexion had faded as well, a prison pale that looked vaguely unhealthy. His eyes were a washed-out blue. I doubted that those who'd known him fifteen years earlier, at the time of his arrest, would have recognized him. But then, prison and time tended to do that to inmates. It had been my experience that they rarely aged well. The only features that reminded me of the preprison Reece I'd seen on television interviews were his splayed-out, remarkably crooked front teeth, the prominent bags under his eyes, and his continual smirk. Although I'd said nothing that could be at all considered amusing, Reece appeared entertained by my visit.

"How much, uh . . . do I get anything out of this?" he asked. That wasn't an unusual question, but rarely had I heard it so quickly in an interview.

"I don't pay for interviews. I don't pay sources," I said. "What you get is that you get to tell your side of the story. I'm here to listen to anything you'd like to tell me."

At first, it appeared that wasn't enough. "I can't help then," he said, his lips curling into a jeer. He pointed at a group of large envelopes he had on the desk in front of him. "See, I've got everything right here. I've got the Innocence Project working on this. The FBI done cleared me."

"Did you kill Laura Smither?" I asked.

"No."

"What about Jessica Cain?"

He turned away, shaking his head, looking at me warily out of the corners of his eyes. "Who's that?"

As we talked, he claimed he'd never heard of Jessica although investigators I interviewed said they'd made it known to him that he was a suspect in the case. Pam Mitchell, the lead detective on the Cain case, made repeated requests to interview him.

"If they had what they said they'd had . . ." he said, not finishing his sentence. "You see they lied to the public . . . If they had evidence against me, wouldn't they have charged me?"

"There are people who say you're a serial killer, Bill," I said.

"I am not a serial killer," he maintained. "The people who say that, they'll say anything. And I didn't kill that little girl."

"Why do you think so many people think you murdered Laura Smither?"

"I don't care," he said. "There's not a damn thing that links me to anything." When I asked about the fiber evidence—the floor mat and afghan fibers on Laura's socks that reportedly matched samples from his truck and house—he brushed it off, as if it was impossible and not to be considered.

Although early on he'd made motions as if he were going to leave when I refused to pay him, Reece leaned forward in his chair and opened his envelopes, producing copies of search warrants the Friendswood police issued at the time of

Laura's murder. They were warrants tied to other suspects. "They lied when they said I was the prime suspect," Reece said. "There were others."

What Reece didn't mention, but I had been told was that the warrants he held in his hand had been executed, and no evidence was found suggesting the other suspects were involved. The men he was referring to had all been cleared.

"And it's in here, too," he said, holding up a copy of Laura's autopsy. "It said I didn't do it either."

All the investigators I'd talked with about the Smither case, none of them had suggested anything in the medical examiner's report excluded Reece as a suspect. "Show me what you're talking about," I suggested.

Instead, Reece slipped the autopsy report back in its envelope and changed the subject. I brought it back to Laura Smither. "Do you remember what you did that day?" I asked. "The day Laura was abducted?"

"I sure do," he said. Reece then calmly recounted what he said he'd done on April 3, 1997, arriving at work at the construction site early that morning, only to leave when it began to rain. He then drove down Moore Road sometime around nine, approximately the same time Laura left the Smither house to presumably jog down that same country road.

"Did you see Laura?" I asked.

"Nope," he said.

The way Reece told it, all the evidence against him, from the fibers to a knife that was found in his truck, was all manufactured. "That knife was in my apartment on the entertainment center. Now how'd it get in my truck?" he challenged, implying it had been planted by police. "They all know I didn't do it, that nothing at all links me to that girl's murder."

"So what do you think happened here?" I asked.

"I don't care," he said, chin jutting out, defiant. "I had enough from people out there. They all know that I didn't do it."

Behind the prison partition, Reece shifted in his chair

when I asked about his recollection of the day Bob and Gay Smither confronted him in a jail visiting room, wanting to know if he'd murdered their daughter. "I told them the same thing I told you, that I didn't do it," he said, shaking his head.

He'd been an easy target, Reece said, an ex-con just out of prison on sex-crime convictions, one who'd been nearby at the time Laura disappeared. Why was so much attention focused on him? "You don't know your ass from a hole in the ground, what would you do? You got people hounding you. You got a guy who just got out of prison. Let's pin it on him," he said with a fixed, angry grin, explaining why he'd been fingered. "It's all a crock."

"Those charges in Oklahoma?"

"If you look at those, you'll see they've been reversed," he insisted. "I was acquitted of the charges."

But that, too, wasn't true. The abduction case had been returned to the court for a second trial, but it wasn't because of a lack of evidence. It was on what could be termed a technicality, the way the charge against Reece had been written. Certainly nothing that would have exonerated him. Instead, to avoid a retrial, Reece was released for time served.

"One of the girls I knew really good," he said about the women he'd been convicted of attacking in Oklahoma. In that case, he claimed rather than rape it had been consensual sex. The young mother had testified at Reece's Houston trial, however, and under oath said she and Reece weren't friends and that he'd entered her bedroom through the window while she slept.

The second case? Reece maintained he was just being a good guy, that out of concern for the young woman's welfare, he'd given her a ride when her car broke down. He'd never held her captive and forced her to have oral sex, he said, although that's what she said and what he'd been convicted of. As he talked, he often grinned and shook his head, as if it were all too much to even consider. So many were against him, and he'd been abused by the system.

At each opportunity, I brought our discussion back to Texas. "So you never saw Laura jogging down that road?"

"No," he said again.

Again I asked, "What about Jessica Cain?"

Earlier Reece had denied he even knew who Jessica was, but this time he answered differently. "I remember them asking me about that, but I thought they had someone on that . . . Some boyfriend, I don't know." When I said that there had never been an arrest and that he was the one whose name kept surfacing as a suspect, he again shook his head.

"You had a white pickup truck then, a dually with lights on the top?"

"A dually, yeah. A four-door," he confirmed. There was a light-colored truck seen that night, the one Jessica Cain vanished. When I asked if he was there, he answered, "It wasn't mine."

"You've spent nearly half of your life in prison," I commented. That wasn't an exaggeration. Between the two prison stays, the fifty-three-year-old had served twenty-five years behind bars.

"Yeah," he said. "I don't like to think about that."

While he served his time, Reece complained that the world had gone on without him. His father died in 2001 and his mother in 2005. "That's why I'm so angry. I'm in here, and I didn't do any of it."

The Smither and Cain cases weren't the ones that put Reece behind bars, but that was what I was most interested in, so I kept working the conversation back to that evidence, asking again, "What about the fibers on Laura's socks, the ones that matched your blanket?"

"I don't think they have that. I think they're making it up to say they have something," Reece contended. As for the knife that was found in his truck, he again claimed it was planted.

Why did he move the horse ranch's manure pile not long after Jessica Cain disappeared? The way Reece told it, he was just trying to be helpful. Although the owner of the ranch told police that he'd never asked to have the hill of manure moved, Reece insisted that "it was too far out in the road," blocking cars coming for a wedding at the ranch.

In Oklahoma, Reece was already charged with the forced oral sodomy of the college student he abducted off the side of the highway. It seemed particularly brazen to just six weeks later commit the second crime, where he entered through the window and raped the second woman. "He was really cool about it," the arresting officer in the first case told me. "He didn't look the least bit worried."

In Texas, it seemed to be a similar situation; Reece was already under suspicion on the Smither case when Sandra Sapaugh was abducted and, if he was involved, when Jessica Cain disappeared off the I-45 shoulder.

There was one more thing that echoed what he'd done in Oklahoma, something Reece described doing on the day Laura Smither disappeared. In Oklahoma, after he abducted the university student, Reece drove her in the eighteen-wheeler to public places, ending up at a distribution center where he was scheduled to pick up a load, acting as if he had nothing to hide. In Friendswood, shortly after leaving that morning, Reece circled back and drove past the construction site. Why? Did he want someone to see him and believe that he was alone? Was he attempting to enlist an eyewitness to tell police he didn't have a twelve-year-old girl in his truck? "My boss saw me, and I was alone in the truck," Reece told a reporter.

Of course that begged the question: Would anyone have seen Laura if she'd been bound and gagged and forced onto the backseat floor or enclosed in the toolbox on the truck bed?

Our interview continued, and again I asked Reece to describe everything he'd done that day, after he left the construction site. He responded that at the time the FBI asked if he could prove where he'd been. With a sneer, he said, "I done wrote it down for them."

Patiently, I asked him to repeat it for me.

"There were three girls I was seeing at the same time . . . Two of them's married. I went to see this one that I was seeing. She wasn't home, so I went up to Telephone Road and took a ride, went all the way near Hobby Airport to my apartment. I wasn't feeling good. Something I ate that day? I don't know; I was feeling sick. Anyway, I started washing clothes. The steering was hard to turn on my truck . . . My ex-wife called me, and I talked to her on the phone in the morning. Then I left and went to Telephone Road and 518, and this guy put a belt on my truck . . . I had a little old cow dog, an Australian shepherd with me. I stood there while he worked on my truck. Then I went back to the apartment and laid down."

According to Reece, he knew nothing about the Smither case until the next morning, when one of his three girlfriends told him about the kidnapping. "I wasn't worried about the Smither case. I knew I didn't do it." When police contacted him about the Sapaugh case, Reece said he "figured they were up to no good."

Screwing his mouth into a sarcastic frown, he scoffed at the accusations against him. "If I was their prime suspect, there'd be something," he said. "After all this time? All the tests they done and everything . . . They cut my seats up in my truck, my carpet, everything. There's nothing there."

He then talked about his truck, and that he modified it, taking off the toolbox and installing a cowboy sleeper on the pickup's bed, a compartment the size of a small mattress he could lock, large enough to camp out in on the road, or, some of those who pegged Reece as a killer pointed out, to confine a victim. A boxed-in bed with a door, and a toolbox above it. "I added that," he said defiantly.

In prison, Reece worked indoor in the factory that made pants for the guards. His job was to supervise and keep the workers' lines flowing. "I'm not in a cell. I'm in a dorm. Like a stall. It's mine. It's not bad," he boasted. "The food here is all right."

My time drawing to a close, before I left I asked again

why so many saw him as the chief suspect in the Smither and Cain cases. "Easy out for them. They don't know who done it or what happened. They fucked up so much, it's unreal," he said. Referring to Laura Smither, he contended, "I don't do little kids. I've never been convicted of anything to do with a child."

"What kind of guy would do something like that? Kill a young girl like Laura?" I asked.

At first, he simply leaned back in the chair and stared at me. "He'd have to be someone who's throwed off," Reece finally assessed. When I looked perplexed by the term, he explained. "He'd have to be not all there."

That brought to mind the Sapaugh trial, the punishment phase, when the first of his Oklahoma victims testified. When she asked him why he'd abducted her, why he was tying her up and forcing himself on her, what she said he replied was, "I'm crazy."

As proof of his great success with women, Reece then again brought up his ex-wife and the three women he claimed to be seeing during the summer of 1997. "I had four girls I was with. I didn't have time," regarding murdering Laura Smither, abducting Jessica Cain, and kidnapping Sandra Sapaugh. For emphasis, he said it again: "I didn't have *no* time, man. I was too busy."

"Did you carry a knife?" I asked again.

Earlier Reece had claimed that the knife had been planted, but now he said that he did carry knives for work, two, a small one on him and a second knife, one in his horseshoeing box, that he kept in his truck toolbox. On the ranches, he used it to cut back cuticles on the horses' hooves.

The guard walked past and shot me a look that said my time had lapsed. I had to leave. As I collected my belongings, I asked, "Bill, do you feel sorry for the Smithers?"

"Yeah, I do, because the police fucked it up . . ." he told me, his face a model of concern. "The person could be out running around. They should have gotten the man who done it."

In the more than a year that followed, I repeatedly asked for a follow-up interview with Bill Reece. Each time he turned down my requests. While he never agreed to see me again, Reece and I corresponded. His letters, a scrawl of half-printed, half-cursive writing across unlined paper, were often angry. Off and on, he made demands. The biggest one was that he refused to agree to another prison visit until I told him what I'd decided about his case. From the tone, it was evident that he wanted me to tell him that I believed he was an innocent man. Only then would he cooperate.

As much as I wanted to interview him in person at least one more time, to have a second opportunity to talk and see where it might lead us, I couldn't tell him that. It wasn't true.

I had reached a standstill with the Smither case. Although I believed Reece to be the probable killer, I feared that no one could ever be certain. Based on our encounters, our one interview and the letters, I doubted, if he was guilty, that he'd ever admit murdering Laura. Consistently, he'd owned up to nothing, still denying that he'd assaulted the two women in Oklahoma.

One of the final things Bill Reece said to me was, "I never killed no girls." Was he being unjustly accused? Or was Reece lying? Could he be the monster so many believed? As in so many of these cases, it felt as if I stood on quicksand, suspecting yet unsure.

Then a remarkable series of events fell into place. In late summer 2014, as I put the finishing touches on this book, Kathy Dobry, the mother of Tiffany Dobry Johnston, the newlywed Reece was suspected of murdering in Oklahoma in July 1997, called me. She had news. The investigation into her daughter's death had been reopened. When the evidence was reexamined and swabs taken at the time of Tiffany's autopsy were resubmitted to a lab, a partial DNA profile had been developed from genetic material found inside Tiffany's vagina. Although further analysis and review might be done to confirm the findings, the test results thus far indicated that the partial DNA profile was consistent with a sample taken from William Lewis Reece.

Not long after, I talked with a reliable source who confirmed what Kathy had told me. As he described it, although it was a partial not a complete profile and therefore not a conclusive match, the numbers were such that it was unlikely that the source of the DNA was anyone other than Bill Reece. The same investigator also verified that authorities now had witness statements placing Reece not in Houston, as he'd told Dobry, but in Oklahoma on the day Tiffany was murdered.

In addition, records showed that a long-distance calling card tied to Reece was used at a pay phone outside a Denny's restaurant seven miles from the car wash where Tiffany Johnston was last seen on the morning of her abduction.

For so many years, Dobry hadn't considered that Reece could have been responsible. To her, he'd always been a friend. But when she heard what investigators had uncovered, that changed. Based on this new evidence, she told me: "I think that he could have done it. I think Bill Reece murdered my daughter."

Meanwhile, I heard that with the Oklahoma news, the investigations into Laura Smither's and Jessica Cain's cases were both being reopened. Seventeen years after Laura was strangled and Jessica disappeared, there was a renewed push to find answers.

As I put this book to bed, there was the expectation that before the end of 2014 the Johnston case would be taken to a district attorney and, if the DNA evidence held up and prosecutors agreed that the case was strong, William Reece could be charged with murder. In the coming years, it seemed possible that he could again find himself in a courtroom, this time charged with murder.

Would the jury believe him if he told them what he told me? "I never killed no girls."

# Epilogue

## Why Here?

I began this book in the fall of 2011, and it would take three years to complete. Early on, six months into the research, I realized that it was changing me. I watched more carefully, assessed strangers with a jaundiced eye, wondered what hid below the surface. And I became fearful. Not for myself—I've lived much of my life—but for others, the children and teenagers, young men and women I saw on the street. Especially those walking alone, as Krystal Baker had been in March 1996, but even those in cars late at night, like Shelley Sikes on that tragic Memorial Day weekend in 1986.

The pressure built. In late 2012, I spent a day driving to places police call dump sites, the fields where more than forty years earlier Debbie Ackerman's, Maria Johnson's, Sharon Shaw's and Renee Johnson's bodies had been found. I wrapped up for the day by walking through the grass at the Killing Field on Calder Drive, looking at Tim Miller's sad, weather-beaten wooden cross. Around four that afternoon, I was tired and disheartened, troubled. It was difficult not to imagine what it must have been like for each of the girls, how they suffered.

Before heading home, I stopped to buy a drink at the Wendy's on Main Street in League City, a short drive from the Killing Field, a block west of I-45. I stood at the cash register paying when I noticed a teenage girl enter, perhaps thirteen or fourteen. Her long brown hair was tied in a tight ponytail, and although it was cool outside, she wore a scant T-shirt and short shorts, white tennis shoes.

Seated at a table, I rested and checked e-mail on my phone, but my eyes trailed back to the girl. She wasn't attracting attention, merely buying a hamburger and a Coke, taking the tray to a table and eating. She appeared content, unconcerned. I needed to go. If I waited much later, I'd hit Houston's crushing rush-hour traffic. But I stayed. I stayed and watched. As the girl finished her food, she grabbed her purse and left. I stood up. I felt anxious, ill at ease, as I walked out the restaurant door. She cut through the parking lot to the corner, then crossed Hobbs, the side street, before seizing on a break in the traffic to rush across Main to a gas-station convenience store.

I didn't realize at first that I'd followed her to the intersection. When I did, I stopped.

The gas station looked familiar. It was then that I recognized that it was the same convenience store where in 1983 and 1984, Heide Fye and Laura Miller were last seen alive. Until that moment, I hadn't made the connection.

The sun glared off the cars and pickup trucks. A busy street dotted with fast-food restaurants and businesses. A girl alone. The same gas station. I took a deep breath.

"Calm down," I muttered.

Logically, I understood that every day in League City, in Texas, across the nation and the world, teenage girls walk country roads and city streets. They jog like Laura Smither on the morning she disappeared. Like Jessica Cain, they drive home after a night out with friends. The vast majority arrive home safely. I knew my concern was unwarranted, but I couldn't quiet my mind. "This is crazy."

For moments, I thought about returning to my car, but I couldn't make myself. I needed to be sure that the girl was safe. I fleetingly considered running across the street and confronting her, warning her of the dangers, chastising her for going out without a friend, telling her what occurred twice at that very same location three decades earlier. *Didn't she know the dangers?* The teenager, unaware of my interest or my irrational intentions, leaned nonchalantly against the gas-station wall.

"Maybe she's waiting for someone," I whispered. "She probably is."

Moments later a car drove onto the gas-station parking lot, and the girl waved. It stopped next to her, and she disappeared inside. When the driver cut across Main Street and drove past me, I saw the teenager in the passenger seat and the profile of a middle-aged woman behind the wheel, happily chatting.

While I focused on the cases off the I-45 Mysteries Chart that occurred between 1970 and 2000 for this book, the tragedies haven't stopped. In this new millennium, five more photos and names have been added to the list. The first was Tot Harriman, a fifty-seven-year-old woman who disappeared on July 12, 2001, after leaving her son's League City home. Tot lived in Florida but wanted to buy property in the area, to be closer to family. She drove away and was never seen again. Exactly a year later to the day, twenty-three-year-old Sarah Trusty took a bike ride and didn't return home. Two weeks later, her body was found in a Texas City dike.

Terressa Vanegas was only sixteen on the night in 2006 when she walked home from a Halloween party. A man on a motorcycle discovered her body days later on the edge of a Dickinson High School practice field. That same month, the body of Amanda Nicole Kellum, twenty-seven, was found by fishermen near the beach community of Omega Bay, beaten and stabbed.

Taking a few days off from her job in a Beaumont law firm, Bridgette Gearen, a twenty-eight-year-old mother of a toddler daughter, rented a beach house with friends. Waiting for the others to dress to go out, Bridgette walked out onto the sand at dusk in July 2007. Perhaps she wanted to watch the waves or feel the salt breezes. When her friends looked for her, Bridgette was gone. The next morning, her body was found near the shoreline. She'd been beaten, strangled, and raped.

The logical question: Why here?

Galveston County Lieutenant Tommy Hansen had contemplated that question for decades. As a younger man, he investigated many of the cases in this book, and he was one of the two officers who questioned John Robert King and Gerald Pieter Zwarst regarding their involvements in the abduction of Shelley Sikes. In 2013, he helped pull together the case against Clyde Hedrick for the killing of Ellen Beason.

"We have a very distinct group of factors here," said Hansen, his hands arched before him, in thought. "With the beaches, Galveston County is a playground for the fourth largest city in the country. People flood here during the summers. People pass through, and we have no record of their ever being here. They stay on the beach, rent houses or condos, come and they're gone. These are small towns, but during the summer and on holidays, the population swells."

Geographic characteristics, he speculated, added into the equation, including seventy miles of beachfront, a multitude of bayous, and vast undeveloped tracts of land, many with water running through them, offering possibilities for the disposal of a body and evidence.

In addition along with the tourism, the area was highly industrial, workers migrating in for jobs in processing seafood, chemical plants, oil refineries, or for slots on the cruise ships that circulated in and out of the port. "Galveston is a beautiful place, but we have an extremely transient population," said Hansen. As an example of the problems that brought to a criminal investigation, he mentioned 2007's Bridgette Gearen case, one where leads had been plentiful and he hoped to eventually make an arrest. "Bridgette didn't live in Galveston. She was here for the weekend. Neither did any of the suspects or the witnesses," he explained. "It makes the investigation that much more complicated."

Perhaps more frightening was what retired FBI profiler
Mark Young contended over sushi in a Houston restaurant
one evening. Young, a tall, dark-haired man with a ruddy
complexion, wasn't so sure that what was happening along
the Texas coastline wasn't transpiring in other parts of the
United States, and the world. While some of the cases on
the chart appeared to be single murders, crimes of opportunity like the abduction of Shelley Sikes, when it came to at
least Galveston in the seventies and the Killing Field, the assumption remained that the persons responsible were serial
killers. "At any one time, there are about six hundred serial
killers in the U.S.," Young said. "Of those, maybe half are
active. The others have aged and stopped killing, or they've
stopped for other reasons, like sickness, or they're in prison
for other crimes."

Young's bottom line: "Things like this happen all over
the world. This isn't a new phenomenon. These guys have
always been with us."

Events that unfolded while I worked on this book backed
Young's contention that serial predators aren't headquar-
tered in any particular location. In the fall of 2011, police
announced that they believed ten bodies found in beach
communities on Long Island, New York, were all victims of
the same killer, active over a period of fifteen years. Then
on May 6, 2013, Amanda Berry miraculously gathered the
courage to escape from Ariel Castro's house of horrors in
Cleveland, after a decade in captivity. With her came her
daughter fathered by Castro and fellow victims Gina DeJe-
sus and Michelle Knight.

Despite the headlines they make, perhaps it's good to
remind ourselves that such crimes are rare. The vast majority of murders are committed by family members and
friends, acquaintances. Stranger murder is scarce, and the
FBI estimates that those by serial killers account for less
than one percent of the killings in the U.S.

Still, they exist. Young helped facilitate the entering of
the I-45 cases into VICAP, and he spent his career chroni-

cling such crimes and going into the prisons to interview serial killers. Asked for his best advice, the retired FBI agent didn't hesitate. "Don't get in the car. Never let anyone transport you anywhere unless you're sure you know the person and where you're going . . . All the killers I interviewed told me the same thing: When the victims got in the cars, they knew they had them. From that point on, it was all over."

Retired FBI profiler Mark Young spent his career hunting killers. *(Courtesy of Kathryn Casey)*

When asked about the girls on the chart, Young acknowledged that anecdotally it appeared that the I-45 area in question had more than its share of unsolved cases. Why the cases weren't resolved was also something that Young considered. One factor, perhaps, was that eleven different law-enforcement agencies covered the area. "They all think of it as their case, and that keeps information from being shared," he said.

I saw that in person one afternoon while interviewing two of the officers involved in the cases. I'd just brought this same subject up. Back in 1992, I'd circulated through this part of Texas writing a book on a serial rapist named James Bergstrom. In *Evil Beside Her,* I documented how Bergstrom jumped jurisdictions to avoid being identified, and how law enforcement in the various communities failed to know what was going on just across their borders. "Is it still like that?" I asked.

The officers said it wasn't although one admitted that in the past, her agency hadn't "played well with others."

When I brought up whether or not there was movement in any of the cases, the woman officer said that she thought there might be a new effort on one, based on what had recently taken place; someone from the Galveston County Sheriff's Office dropped in their offices requesting copies of records.

"Did you give them what they wanted?" the detective asked.

"Not everything," she said, then laughed.

My impression, then, was that perhaps the same old problems plagued the area with its multiple jurisdictions, and that as Young described territorialism helped condemn the investigations to failure.

In the first years after Jessica Cain's disappearance, her father, C. H., attempted to tackle that issue. He lobbied the Texas state legislature for the formation of a new group of officers employed by the Department of Public Safety, the government branch that in-

Jessica Cain in 1997.
*(Courtesy of C. H. and Suzy Cain)*

cludes the State Troopers and Texas Rangers. This newly formed force would have been composed of specially trained officers designated to strictly investigate abduction cases. In his plan, the team—equipped with helicopters, tracking dogs, all the latest search devices—would move in immediately when there was a kidnapping, to help local law enforcement. That way, experienced investigators would be in charge from the beginning, not small-town police departments that rarely if ever saw such cases.

Unfortunately, C. H. Cain was unable to convince legislators to back the idea.

After working on this book, I have to agree that C. H.'s approach makes sense. Nearly all the victims' families I interviewed voiced frustration with inexperienced police departments. Precious time was often lost and leads too often ignored or mishandled. It wasn't that local police weren't good people who wanted to solve the crimes, but that they had no or limited experience with such cases. "They were basically learning on the job, on my daughter's case," said one father. "They just didn't know what to do."

As my work on this book draws to a close, I consider how far I've come. The I-45 Mysteries/Texas Killing Field chart remains taped on my wall. The girls' faces look out at me, and I hope that, while I haven't brought any of their killers into a courtroom, I have provided insight.

Did I cover every case? No. One of the girls, I found, didn't belong on the chart. Allison Craven's mother returned to the family apartment after running errands in 1971 and found that her daughter was gone. The teenager's remains turned up in a field the following year. Allison has been on multiple versions of the Unsolved Mysteries chart since its inception. She shouldn't have been. Shortly after her death, a neighbor, Henry Doyle Shuflin, Jr., admitted abducting Allison from the complex's laundry room. He pleaded guilty in 1973 and was sentenced to twenty-five years.

In other cases, although I tried to track down family

members and records, I was unable to uncover enough information to include them in the book.

There were also suspects whom I decided to forgo, for the most part because I discovered no evidence linking them to the murders. That doesn't mean something—perhaps DNA—won't come to light in the future, but at this time there was nothing to report. One was a dead drifter named Bobby Jack Fowler who has been linked to at least one murder in Canada, that of sixteen-year-old hitchhiker Colleen MacMillen. There is, at the time of this writing, speculation that Fowler may be responsible for more killings in the Pacific Northwest and Canada. Fowler lived on Bolivar Peninsula, just north of Galveston, from the mideighties through the midnineties, leading to speculation that he claimed victims in Texas as well.

There are also theories that Anthony Allen Shore, already on Texas's death row for one murder and suspected of three others in the Houston area, might be involved in some of these killings. Shore went to high school in the Clear Lake area and preyed on young girls. Thus far there's nothing beyond speculation suggesting he might be involved in the murders of any of the girls on the I-45 chart.

I also certainly don't mean to suggest that these were the only murders in Houston during this time period or the most important, or that only girls and young women fall victim to such homicides.

In fact, coinciding with the time period during which the Galveston Island killings took place, in the seventies, one of the largest and most brutal serial cases in American history unfolded in the Houston area, and nearly all the victims were teenage boys.

On August 8, 1973, Elmer Wayne Henley, Jr. called police to report that he'd just killed a man named Dean Corll. When questioned by police, Henley told a terrifying account of helping Corll abduct, rape, and torture teenage boys. For months after, bodies were pulled from under Corll's home and his boathouse. The press labeled him the

Pied Piper and the Candyman. In the end, authorities theorized that Corll committed at least twenty-eight brutal murders, making him the most prolific killer up to that time in U.S. history. Five years later, in Chicago, a man named John Wayne Gacy surpassed Corll's record by murdering at least thirty-three boys.

For the most part, I now look at the I-45 chart with new eyes. I'm grateful that the Cain, Smither, and Johnston cases are all being investigated. As for the others, the folks I interviewed insisted that there's no evidence left from most of the murders, but I wonder if some might still exist in dusty evidence boxes on forgotten shelves. I've repeatedly asked authorities to look and, if anything is found, to send it out for testing. I hope that happens at some point. Consider the difference Sherry Willcox, the evidence officer, made in the Krystal Baker case. She cared, persisted, and she solved the crime.

Mark Stallings said he left Janet Doe's clothes on when he dumped her body in the Killing Field in 1991. Perhaps those clothes wait in a box somewhere. Perhaps they could be sent to the lab. If DNA was found, that could either confirm or rule out Stallings as the killer. It matters on more than one level. Yes, it could help answer painful questions. But based on what Stallings might be able to tell authorities, it could also identify a victim, give Janet back her name. It's possible that her family still grieves for her, wondering if she's alive or dead.

Through my interview with Stallings, if he's telling the truth, we now know that the description of Janet law enforcement has worked with since her discovery in 1991 may be wrong. For the past twenty-two years, Janet's been labeled as in her mid-twenties or older. If Stallings told the truth, the woman he murdered was a teenager.

Do I have disappointments? Sure. For instance, I requested prison interviews with John Robert King and Gerald Pieter

Zwarst, the two men convicted of abducting Shelley Sikes. I undoubtedly naively hoped to convince them to divulge the location of her remains. It's time. This case needs closure, and Shelley's parents deserve to be able to bury their daughter. King and Zwarst refused to meet with me.

The truth is that despite my best efforts, there are cases in this book that will continue to haunt me, especially that of Laura Kate Smither. I will forever see her face, that endearing smile. Did Bill Reece murder her? Did he abduct Jessica Cain? I hope we know answers to both questions someday soon.

The most frightening thing about these cases? The killers all appeared so ordinary.

If Kevin Edison Smith stood at my door and had a good excuse for being there, I may have let him in. He didn't, after all, look like a killer. But then, what does a killer look like?

What of these men? What shaped them? Why does anyone commit such heinous acts?

A 2005 study published by the FBI listed a set of factors when the perpetrator is a serial killer. One is a genetic tendency, something in a person's psychological makeup that's described as predisposition. The second is an early linkage between sex and violence. Certainly the histories Ed Bell and Mark Stallings recounted during my interviews fit that mold. I don't mean to suggest that their upbringings excuse their crimes, but isn't it important to consider how they were formed? Is there any other way to hope to comprehend why such criminals exist? Perhaps if we understand what fashions them, one day we may find a way to intervene.

It has often been said that evil flourishes within shadow. In the end, if nothing else, I hope this book serves as light into the darkness.

*Kathryn Casey*
*February 2015*

# Acknowledgments

This has been a long road, but I haven't walked it alone. Off and on, I've been assisted along the way. Thank you to:

- Jane Farrell and Sandy Sheehy for reading and commenting on the manuscript.
- Carey Smith, who helped me weed through decades of newspaper articles, pasting and clipping and never complaining, and who covered a day in court when I had to be elsewhere.
- The folks in the Texas Department of Criminal Justice media office who processed my many requests and arranged my prison interviews.
- Retired Harris County prosecutor Edward Porter, always a good friend, pulled old records to determine the resolution of a case.
- Suzanne Lowe Birdwell for the great map at the beginning of the book.
- Lysa Nistico for clipping photos out of a PDF. I had no idea how to do it.
- Mary Anderson tracked down obscure newspaper articles.
- Private investigator Gina Frenzel sought out contact information for sources.

- Elizabeth Peacock, M.D. and Vladimir Parungao, M.D., who patiently explained medical evidence. If any confusion or mistakes remain, it is on my part, not theirs.

- Dale Lee, Galveston County court reporter, who helped with the evidence on the Hedrick case.

- My editor, Emily Krump, and all the great folks at HarperCollins.

- All those who let me bend their ears and bounce off theories, and those who gave guidance on how things worked and where to look for answers.


Finally, I am deeply grateful to everyone who agreed to be interviewed, especially the victims' loved ones. I thank you for telling me about your daughters, sisters, and friends. I will never forget them.